MEMORIES OF A SECRET AGENT

MEMORIES OF A SECRET AGENT

PAUL KRAMER

Published by: Theresa Kramer.

Library of Congress Control Number:		2005911143
ISBN 10:	Hardcover	1-4257-0574-X
	Softcover	1-4257-0573-1
ISBN 13:	Hardcover	978-1-4257-0574-9
	Softcover	978-1-4257-0573-2

This book was printed in the United States of America.

To order additional copies of this book, contact:
Xlibris Corporation
1-888-795-4274
www.Xlibris.com
Orders@Xlibris.com
32644

For Theresa

PREFACE

It is essential for the reader to remember that this is a memoir; in other words, a record of events based on the author's experiences and feelings. Because of the secrecy restrictions at the time these events occurred, and in some cases for many years thereafter, the author kept no diary, notes, or record and wrote no letters describing his work. Furthermore, almost without exception, all the people with whom and for whom he worked are now dead. Consequently, in writing this book, the author has been entirely dependent on his memory. At the age of ninety-one, this memory may have at times been defective or twisted. However, there can be no doubt the story is true. Careful research of the archives of the Office of the Coordinator of Inter-American Affairs, the U.S. Navy, and the CIA should substantiate this. But even here, there will be difficulties due to secrecy and the "deindexing" of the FBI's Latin American files by its then-director rather than turn them over to the hated CIA. Moreover, the author's foolish refusal to accede to the request of his commanding officer to write the history of the naval operation Road's End immediately after its conclusion and for which he had received a commendation has erased forever the details of that historic event. Finally, the tragic suicide of the CIA's director of operations subsequent to the Kim Philby espionage scandal diminished the possibility of a proper analysis of events surrounding it in Washington . . .

INTRODUCTION

When reading this book, it is essential to keep in mind a fundamental tenet of intelligence, namely that all agents are on a need-to-know basis. In other words, only that aspect of an intelligence operation absolutely necessary for the efficient conduct of a mission is revealed to the agent. The rest is deliberately withheld.

There is a very good reason for this. First of all, this methodology is designed to protect the intelligence apparatus from indiscretions on the part of the agent, either deliberate or inadvertent. Secondly, it is adhered to in order to prevent an agent from revealing secrets to the enemy should he be captured and/or tortured. For he cannot reveal that which he does not know. Also, sometimes in the interest of security, the need-to-know rule is carried one step further and a secret agent is deliberately misled as to the sources of information that form the basis of his work.

To the outsider, this may seem ludicrous, but it is not; the wisdom of it can best be explained by what happened to me soon after I was initiated into intelligence work in August 1940, as a special assistant to Nelson Rockefeller, who had just been appointed coordinator of inter-American affairs. At this time, Mr. Rockefeller and, via him, I, as well as the FBI with whom I sometimes worked, were deliberately misled by British Intelligence into supposing that the information we received from the British came from intercepts of airmail between Latin America and Europe that had been secretly opened, read, and resealed in Bermuda and Trinidad and then sent on its way. But this was only partly true. Some of the material that concerned my secret work depended on the fact that the British had broken the German code. But this was then such a deep secret that only two people, aside from President Roosevelt, knew the facts. The rest of us were deliberately deluded, and with good reason. Any sort of leak to Germany that their code had been broken would have caused the Nazis to change not only their code but also their method of encipherment, with disastrous results to Great Britain.

All this secrecy can sometimes complicate an agent's life and work, as it did in my case and as the reader will discover. Furthermore, secrecy can be carried one step beyond the foregoing and can thus create totally absurd situations, one of which I describe here so the reader may understand the complications involved.

At one point, I was loaned to the State Department for a week to do some work for President Roosevelt under the supervision of then-undersecretary of state Sumner Welles. Thus, when I was ordered to report for duty to the State Department, I was told to take with me enough clothes and toiletries to last a week because, for security reasons, I was to be locked in a room at the State Department until the coming event, with which I had to be familiarized in order to do the work, had become public knowledge. Upon my arrival, complete with my neatly packed suitcase, the official who greeted me burst out laughing. Although my superior in Rockefeller's office and I both thought him in the dark, he knew that I had a "top secret/eyes only" security clearance, and my presumed State Department incarceration would thus be totally unnecessary. This incident has always seemed to me a perfect example of the wheels within wheels of the life of a secret agent.

It is also true that all this hugger-muggery had an impact on my personal life. Marriage, for example, was unthinkable. No marriage could survive stealing out of bed at 3:00 AM to slip into our offices unnoticed in order to nick typewriters and then being unable to explain why to a loving wife. This is to say nothing of having to move into a YMCA for a while, going to the office during the day as if nothing was going on at night, or spending Christmas at work. Even as a single man, my relationship with a woman was always clouded with the suspicion on my part that the sex involved had developed out of the partner's desire to find out what I really did, which, of course, I could not reveal. Also, how could I maintain a structured relationship with a woman when I had to cancel rendezvous at the last minute for inexplicable reasons?

The hugger-muggery also impacted on my working life since I always had an overt job designed to conceal my covert work; or alternatively, a covert job structured to conceal my deep covert work. This sometimes aroused jealousies and nasty intra-office gossip and hostility. My overt or covert associates could never understand why I had access to the top brass, to say nothing of my access to all three presidents under whom I served. In the latter case, however, we were able to conceal it since I never set foot in the White House and always dealt with the presidents via an intermediary. Here there was only one slipup since I had arrived late for work so that my immediate boss found out about it. Fortunately, he was a friend and bore me no ill will for this transgression of the layers of the intelligence bureaucracy.

But surely, the reader will say, all this confusion due to out of channel secrecy must have vanished when you became a navy officer. Quite the contrary. When I was interviewed by the chief of naval intelligence for my navy job, he made a couple of comments about things that would happen to me once I was overseas, the implications of which I simply didn't understand. These comments, I supposed, were designed to warn me of things to come. They didn't. I had to experience them, and just how they evolved is described in this book.

Some of those who read this will no doubt ask: "Wasn't your life dangerous?" The answer to this is, no, not particularly. I was shot only once, and the wound was insignificant. Also, if the work was considered risky, my superiors always instituted certain precautions. Although this was comforting, it could also be annoying so that the added protection I was given seemed, at the time, just as unpleasant as the degree of danger it was designed to circumvent.

Visualize this scene: I am a lowly navy lieutenant, junior grade, spending the weekend at a Red Cross hostel at a beach resort near Brisbane, Australia. I am emerging from the surf in swimming trunks, refreshed and happy. Standing at the water's edge is a large man, an ex-navy champion boxer and chief petty officer in full uniform, armed with a .45. His eyes remained glued on me while I was in the water, and whenever I disappeared beneath the waves, his face assumed an anxious frown. There is a towel draped over his free arm. When I am finally up on the beach, away from the ocean's roar, I overhear a sunbather ask her companion, "What do you think he is, some sort of prisoner? He doesn't look like a Nip."

The truth, of course, was somewhat different and far more convoluted. I was by no means a prisoner. The chief petty officer was my bodyguard, assigned to protect me from the enemy. But the enemy was not the Japanese with whom we were at war. Quite the contrary. He had been ordered to protect me from Soviet agents who presumably were our allies. Keep in mind that the Cold War had not yet begun. There were rumblings that had come my way, but nothing more.

Because of all this, my work gave me a sort of fatalistic attitude toward life. *So what?* I would say to myself. *If things go wrong, or become annoying, there is nothing you can do about it. You're single; you have only a brother and a mother, both of whom have their own lives to live. Also, they haven't even a glimmer of what you really do. If anything happens, so be it. That's life, or fate, or God's will, or whatever you care to call it. Anyway, it all stems from the life you have deliberately chosen to live. When it all started, you could have refused to lead it. But you didn't. If the truth be known, you were somewhat exhilarated at the prospect, although it is true that you had no real idea of what was going to happen to you. So just relax and bend with the wind like bamboo. Simply do your duty, live day by day, and let fate handle the rest. And above all, at all times and wherever you are and whatever happens to you, enjoy the life you are leading.*

This attitude failed me only once. I was a patient in an army hospital, recovering from a severe case of a tropical fever. I had just discovered I had no clothes. According to my nurse, upon my arrival, on a stretcher and in a coma, everything I had on had been burned as a precaution against the spread of infection. As for my gear, I had none. It was found later that day in a locker reserved for the effects of the deceased, awaiting shipment to a U.S. depot for the remains of the soldiers of the armed forces. All this plunged me into an unaccustomed fit of depression. But when the doctor was summoned, he thought nothing of it. "Lie back in your bed, relax, and try to enjoy it," he said. "What you have is perfectly normal—a post-dengue fever depression."

Perhaps, therefore, I've made a mistake. Maybe this book should not be titled *Memories of a Secret Agent*. On the contrary, and especially today when self-improvement has become so popular, it should be called *How to Live Day by Day and be Happy*, even though my work contributed to the imprisonment, execution, murder, defection, disappearance, and suicide of more people than I now care to count.

PART I

The Coordinator of Inter-American Affairs

1

My modern European history studies at Trinity College, Cambridge University, England, were completed by June of 1938. Given an M. Litt. degree, I returned to the United States in the midst of the Munich Crisis. G. P. Gooch, the professor of modern European history in 1936-37, (H. W. V. Temperly, the regular professor, was then on leave) had instilled in me his own contempt for both Stalin and Hitler. A man of considerable distinction, a prolific writer, and a former Member of Parliament, Gooch was an old-fashioned Gladstone Liberal and a devotee of the great Victorian historian, Lord Acton, who had coined the aphorism "Power tends to corrupt; absolute power corrupts absolutely." Gooch also felt that extreme imperialism did the same thing and had given me specific examples of British men so corrupted. Before I returned to the United States, he had told me he wished to help me toward a career and I should feel free to call on him for help at any time.

By July 1940, with the war going on in Europe and after having resolved a number of family problems, I was ready to take a full-time job. I thus went to see a high official in the Justice Department who had been a Rhodes Scholar. When he learned that I studied modern European history at Cambridge under Gooch, had written a thesis on Latin America, and, as an extracurricular activity, had written for and acted in the annual Footlights shows, he said quietly, "Go no farther. I am almost positive there will be an interesting job for you in a new agency to be created sometime in August. Wait for it and let me know at all times where you can be reached."

This somewhat mysterious remark produced the following results:

August 2, 1940

Upway Corner,
Chalfont St. Peter
Buckinghamshire, England

My dear Kramer:

We have taken refuge here from Kensington and are quite comfortable. There is a garden.

Yesterday, an old friend with British government connections came here to ask if I could recommend you for a confidential U.S. government post that would require a knowledge of Latin America, foreign language skills, acting ability, and some graduate experience with modern European history. I recommended you highly.

Sincerely,
G. P. Gouch

Western Union Telegram

August 17, 1940

Paul Kramer, Hotel Ponshewaing, Alanson, Michigan

Report to work with Coordinator of Commercial and Cultural Relations between the American Republics on August 19, State Department Building.

Signed: Asst. Coordinator Karl B. Spaeth

At that time within the U.S. government, after the fall of France in 1940, there was a unanimous opinion that something had to be done about Latin America where traditional trade routes were in disarray and there was a general political instability due to the war in Europe.

The special treatment that the area had been receiving since 1933 when President Roosevelt first inaugurated his Good Neighbor Policy had contributed to his great personal popularity in the area. Furthermore, U.S. isolationists and noninterventionists—"America Firsters" and Fortress Americans—who opposed favoritism for a beleaguered Britain in the European war and insisted on neutrality, could only support Roosevelt's friendship with Latin America. Most Americans believed that the United States should fight if any part of North or South America was attacked.

Meanwhile, Nazi agents in Latin America were not only buying precious war materiel for their European war machine, but they were also seeking to establish a solid racial nucleus of German Aryans for the purpose of raising the German nation to a dominating position.

Faced with this situation, the Roosevelt administration enjoyed a free hand in Latin America, which it did not enjoy elsewhere vis-à-vis the war in Europe.

Meanwhile, Britain was continuing to expand its worldwide intelligence network and was secretly opening all airmail between Latin America and Europe in Trinidad and Bermuda. These intercepts revealed that many agents of U.S. commercial firms in Latin America were either pro-Nazi or secret Nazi agents. This material was fed to the British Security Coordination (BSC), as it was called; in fact, it was a branch of British Intelligence located in the Rockefeller Center in New York City. Stephenson, its director, had worked out an arrangement with the White House whereby this data would be turned over to the FBI, which would sanitize it from the standpoint of source and forward it to the newly established Coordinator of Commercial and Cultural Relations between the American Republics, which was to be headed by a young Nelson Rockefeller.

Acting on this secretly acquired information, Rockefeller was not only to engage in preclusive buying of war materiel such as cotton linters, abaca, and industrial diamonds, but also to develop a voluntary blacklist of pro-Nazi commercial representatives and agents in Latin America. At this time it had to be voluntary since, because of U.S. neutrality, there was no law or order prohibiting trade with Nazi Germany or Fascist Italy. However, the persuasive power of Nelson Rockefeller and his family, who were fully supportive of his work, plus that of all the other powerful people he recruited to help him, was not inconsiderable.

It was this organization to which I was assigned by the White House on August 19, exactly two days after the office was officially founded, which was the same day I had received the telegram summoning me to work. In accordance with the telegraphed instructions, I found Karl B. Spaeth, who was obviously very busy and harassed. He told me several things. He had been a Rhodes Scholar. He had gone to Dartmouth with Nelson Rockefeller, the coordinator whom I would meet presently. Spaeth and with his wife Sheila were living with Nelson at his newly acquired house called the Baker Place just off Foxhall Road. In the office, I was to find Arthur Jones, a Rockefeller family employee from New York, who would swear me in and arrange for me to be paid. Nothing was said about what I was supposed to do, and nothing was said about some sort of British connection. He simply called me Paul, told me to call him Karl, and explained that everyone was on a first-name basis.

Arthur Jones turned out to be a jolly man with a loud voice and a mustache, unusual in those days. He had me sign a bunch of papers, swear some sort of loyalty and secrecy oath, and then explained, to my total astonishment, that I was now on the White House payroll. He pointed out that this had two advantages. The White House would cash checks for me so I didn't need to bother with a local bank, and its motor pool was available for my use at all times. He did not, however, explain why I had been put on the White House payroll, and I asked no questions. He took me to meet another Rhodes Scholar named Andrew Corry, who would later become ambassador to a clutch of countries, and then found a desk for me in an office that I shared with a secretary; Will Clayton, the president of Anderson, Clayton & Co.; and Joe Rovensky, the executive vice president of the Chase Bank and a Rockefeller family confidante.

These two men, Will Clayton and Joe Rovensky, were two of the most remarkable men I ever encountered in my working life. Clayton was a Texan and the principal owner of Anderson, Clayton & Co., a worldwide business devoted to the purchase and distribution of cotton, which was listed on the New York Stock Exchange. Handsome, tall, with graying hair, and very soft-spoken, he was an assistant coordinator and a dollar-a-year man at President Roosevelt's request. Since Nelson Rockefeller was a Republican and young, the president had insisted that a more mature ranking Democrat be made an assistant coordinator. Clayton had a difficult wife who loved Texas and hated Washington. As a result, he did not socialize with other top Rockefeller associates and employees. His work habits were unusual for such a rich and powerful man. He would arrive at his desk at 7:00 AM and go through his "incoming" basket. Since he knew shorthand, he would answer the letters that needed his immediate response and compose the necessary memos for his secretary to transcribe during the day for him to sign before leaving the office. For this reason, he was never under pressure and could relax and attend meetings in a leisurely manner.

Joe Rovensky was of a totally different mold. More intense, he was the son of a Czech Lutheran coal miner who had grown up in West Jeanette, a small mining town in Pennsylvania. Totally self-made, he had gone to Wall Street as a young man, made a fortune, and come to the attention of Nelson Rockefeller's father. It was he to whom the father had turned for help in guiding his sons, who needed someone to put them in touch with the rough-and-tumble of the real world. Thus, it was Joe who had showed the boys the fleshpots of Paris and the life of men in the coal mines of Pennsylvania. Joe had his favorite among the Rockefeller boys. It was not Nelson but his brother Winthrop who, Joe once told me, was the most human of all of them. Since Joe and his wife had no children, he took a special interest in young men like me who were just starting out. Characteristically, when Joe died, he did not leave his money to a wealthy niece who was married to a very rich man but to the town in which he had grown up. One of his favorite sayings, which he often repeated to me, was "Never worry about the money. Do the job, and the money will take care of itself."

During the few days I was in their office, I often heard the two of them discuss the problem of preclusive buying of industrial diamonds, abaca, cotton linters, and platinum. Since I hadn't the remotest idea what preclusive buying meant, I asked Andrew Corry one day at lunch. He explained succinctly that it meant buying up something so that someone else, who you presumably didn't like, couldn't get to it, and then he changed the subject.

After a few days of not doing anything, Nelson Rockefeller sent for me, welcomed me aboard, and subjected me to a five-minute monologue on why he had accepted the job of coordinator. Because of holdings in Creole Petroleum, the family was drawing, out of Venezuela alone, x millions of dollars a year. He gave me the precise figure, which I have since forgotten. Because of this, Nelson said he felt bound to put some of it back into Latin America. This was why he was on the job and why I had been hired to work for him.

Subsequently, I was to find that although everything he had told me was true, it was totally misleading. Nelson had a low draft number and wished to avoid being drafted. He turned to Anna Rosenberg, a labor consultant to the Rockefeller family who was close to the labor leaders of the period, and Harry Hopkins, the presidential confidante. At this particular juncture, someone with Rockefeller's particular talents and connections was needed, and with Anna's maneuvering for him, he got the job, the true covert nature of which I shall explain later as it affected me personally.

My first impression of Rockefeller, who was thirty-two years old at that time, was of someone with robust, good health and possessing considerable physical power. He had broad shoulders, fairly powerful arms, and a broad and deep chest, but this was somewhat misleading. He suffered from debilitating insomnia and required and received in his office massage by a highly regarded specialist three to five times a week. He could also be easily angered if he felt that part of his work had passed out of his control. He tended to be highly impatient. But he was a superb salesman, and this characteristic, combined with the Rockefeller family's interests, enabled him to staff his office with a totally remarkable collection of talents. His upper echelon staff included at one time or another, Jock Whitney, back from Hollywood after financing and guiding the making of the movie *Gone With the Wind*; Don Francisco and Bill Benton of advertising fame (the former had coined the phrase "Sunkist Orange"); Wallace Harrison, one of the architects of Rockefeller Center in New York; Berent Friele, the largest coffee buyer in America for the leading grocery chain A&P; Percy Douglas of Otis Elevator Company, and many others. If Nelson felt there were gaps in his staff, prominent consultants were brought in.

Like so many successful salesmen, Nelson simply couldn't cope with nor would he discuss an abstract idea or principle. He was, I think, genuinely happy in his job as coordinator, despite a number of reversals, some of which were his own doing. I say this because years later Mary "Todd" Rockefeller, his wife at that time, confided that the happiest days of their married life were those spent in Washington while Nelson was coordinator.[1]

I must have come back from my interview with Rockefeller looking sadly perplexed over the fact that although I was sure that the office had some sort of British connection, it hadn't been mentioned; instead, there had been the lengthy description of Nelson's acceptance of his position, complete with figures of the Rockefeller income from Creole Petroleum.

Joe Rovensky gave me a sharp look. It was as though he was fully aware of my confusion just by looking at me.

"Paul," he said, "if you've got a date for tomorrow night, break it. I want you at my place promptly at eight o'clock for a penny ante poker game."

That night I found myself with five dollar-a-year men from the office including Nelson, Jock Whitney, and Joe Rovensky. The only stranger was Percy Foxworth from the FBI's New York office. At the time, I was

---

[1.] Nelson also affected a public, outward simplicity of living that was false. Nothing could have been more baronial than the family's style of living at their secluded estate in the Pocantico Hills, north of New York City where distinguished guests could be met by a coach-and-four for a tour of the grounds. This outward simplicity could be carried on to irritating proportions. Around the time of Pearl Harbor, he bought a little yellow mini auto called a Crosley in which he liked to careen about as a gesture to necessary conservation, although there were as yet no shortages. This very uncomfortable vehicle resembled in size and discomfort the American Austin with which it competed. The Austin is best described by the following:

> There once was a man from Boston,
>> Who bought an American Austin.
> He had room for his ass,
>> And a gallon of gas.
> But his balls hung out,
>> And he lost 'em.

Nelson was also adept at soft-soaping people. If a senior of his staff became ill, flowers were sent to his bedside and a solicitous phone inquiry on his medical progress. While engaged in this, however, he would be winking and smirking at the others in the room to the effect of "Boy, I'm really stroking him, and he loves it."

utterly bewildered as to why such a young (I was twenty-five) and totally junior staff member had been included in a poker game where all the others were big shots. However, there seemed nothing I could do about it except apply myself to the game and play as best I could. I hoped someone would later bother to explain to me what was expected of me, job wise. The game broke up promptly at 10:00 PM and Foxworth said he would drive me home.

We didn't go directly to my place on Nineteenth Street just below Dupont Circle but detoured instead alongside the Mayflower Hotel.

"You see that second entrance?" He pointed it out to me. "Tomorrow morning, at seven thirty, go in there and take the elevator to the third floor. When you step off, you'll be recognized and shown to a leased apartment. I want you to have breakfast with me."

"You're a good poker player," he continued. "I liked the way you sized the game up. Those multimillionaires are competitive as hell, and it was important to them that they beat me because I'm an FBI man. They didn't care about you. You got wise to the set-up and bet accordingly. I liked that."

At one time, my mother visited Washington and discovered, to her horror, that I didn't own an auto she could borrow. So she went out and bought herself a new Cadillac. She left it behind for a week until her driver could come east and pick it up. One day, I drove it by Nelson, who was standing at the curb with an associate. "There goes Paul Kramer," he said, "driving a new Cadillac. I wish I could afford one!" He was driving his Crosley at the time.

Nelson had three secretaries. One had the duty of recording on three-by-five-inch file cards the names of visitors, the purpose of their visit, the weather at the time, and any item of dress, like a vivid tie or a well-cut suit or an unusual shirt. Should they ever meet again, Nelson would open the conversation with "Hey, remember the weather the last time I saw you? It was raining cats and dogs," or, "What happened to that tie you were wearing? It was a knockout!"

He tried his best to ingratiate himself with President Roosevelt, but it didn't work. He was always sending him little gifts and always got a polite thank-you note back, but no invitations to Hyde Park or to the White House. The best he got was an invitation to a movie shown in the little White House movie theatre, and he got this one because the film had a Latin American theme and was part of Jock Whitney's motion picture program by which Hollywood was successfully persuaded to produce movies and create stars glorifying Latin America, and thus the Good Neighbor Policy. It worked, and we got stars like Carmen Miranda and Dolores Del Rio, plus a Disney cartoon film. The public loved it all, and, of course, had no idea why it happened.

I said nothing. What could I say? Foxworth apparently felt it necessary to instill in me some self-confidence. Otherwise, why bother about the $5.23 I'd won from Rockefeller and Whitney?

That night, alone in the bedroom of the apartment I shared with Floyd McCaffree, who did research for the Republican National Committee and who would later become its chief of research, I should, I suppose, have tossed and turned while speculating on what was in store for me the next morning at the Mayflower. Nothing of the sort happened; I simply collapsed into a deep sleep until my alarm woke me at 6:15 AM. All speculations as to what I had become involved in had totally vanished the moment I hit the sack.

This ability to sink into a deep sleep at will was, I learned, a valuable asset to a secret agent. No matter how trying the circumstances or how dangerous my life became, I was always able to cut it all off at will and thus could avoid the nerves and jitters, and even the alcoholism and insanity other coworkers developed.

Percy Foxworth was already eating when I was ushered in, and he motioned for me to sit down opposite him and wait until he finished chewing his bacon.

The pause gave me time to look at him carefully. Foxworth, who, I soon discovered, hated his first name and insisted he be called Sam, was unlike any other FBI agent I had previously met. Thirty-three years old at the time I met him, he was warm and outgoing and friendly and had a marked Southern accent. He was, he later told me, a history buff, and since he had served for four years as an administrative assistant to the director of the FBI, he had an unusually deep knowledge of the bureau's inner workings prior to becoming the assistant director in charge of the New York City's Field Division. He was also considered at the time to be the bureau's expert on foreign agent subversion. He had two outstanding outward features: very large, full lips and a warm voice, the timbre of which was compelling.

"I'm going to have to talk to you for about fifteen to twenty minutes nonstop," he explained. "Frankly, I've rehearsed it in my mind already, simply because I've never been involved in anything quite like this before. Heretofore, I could let a man get involved in an undercover operation gradually as he was being trained. But in your case, there is no alternative. When you leave this room, you'll be on your own."

"What I'm about to tell you can best be described as top secret, and, knowing the British, it will probably remain so for thirty-five to fifty years. For reasons that you will be able to deduce for yourself once you have the full picture, it is of particular importance to Mr. Hoover that it remains secret. Everything has been done to keep your role a secret, and you will be expected to do the same. For example, all records that you were first hired by the White House and then immediately assigned to Rockefeller will eventually be erased. However, in the interest of your future career, the director, at my insistence, will arrange for you to be transferred to the Rockefeller payroll within six months to a year. Your employment, if anyone wants to know where you worked when you apply for a future job, will start from then, not before. If at any future time you feel the work you are doing is about to be revealed, report this to me immediately."

I said nothing, simply finished my orange juice, and very carefully and silently placed my empty glass beside the plate in front of me while I looked directly into Foxworth's eyes.

This produced a burst of friendly enthusiasm. Foxworth got up from the table and began to pace up and down.

"By God!" he exclaimed, "the Brits were right. You are a superb actor. You didn't say a word, but your body language with that glass and that trusting kid's look in your eyes; it said it all, all I needed to know. You're in, Paul. You're in."

Foxworth's enthusiasm for my acting ability struck me as odd. True, my Cambridge Footlights work had led to an appearance on a BBC Empire broadcast and then a job offer, which Professor Gooch had insisted I turn down. If I remained silent about the need for secrecy, it was simply because I was in awe of the whole thing. But if I was "in," as Foxworth put it, just exactly what was I in?

He let the phone ring exactly four times before answering.

"Foxworth . . . What does he look like? He is short, five foot five maybe, has blond hair and blue #3 eyes, has a slim build, looks something like a jockey . . . his outstanding features? He has two. A face that makes him look like a high school kid. I've never seen anything quite like it. He's twenty-five but looks nineteen. Can he act? He's got the body language of a miniature John Wayne. If people don't trust him, they belong in a booby hatch. We made the right decision, you can depend on it."

Foxworth smiled when he put down the phone. "As you can guess, that was the director. It's as if he needs reassurance that BSC recommended the right man. That's the second time he's asked me about you, and this time he couldn't wait. I'm scheduled to see him at lunch in four or five hours. But he just couldn't wait.

"Well, as I said before the director called, you're in, Paul, you're in, and what you're in is a three-way operation between Rockefeller, the FBI, and the British Security Coordination, or, if you like, the British Intelligence in New York. You had a famous professor named Gooch who admired you. He recommended you to London. They in turn told Stephenson, the head of British Intelligence in New York. The three of us, Rockefeller, the FBI, and the BSC, needed a point man in the Rockefeller office. The director wanted that man to be an FBI man.

Rockefeller and the Brits said no, they wanted someone with your qualifications. Someone young and physically active, a good linguist trained in diplomatic history with proven acting ability. Frankly, we had no one who came anywhere near those qualifications, so you got the job. And since I saw you at poker last night, I'm damn glad you did.

"This evening Percy Douglas from the Rockefeller office and I are leaving for Latin America to set up a network of men from the FBI and the Rockefeller office to determine who among the US commercial representatives in Latin America, are Axis-oriented. At the present time, we are totally dependent on British Intelligence for this information. The British are secretly opening all airmail between Latin America and Europe in Bermuda and Trinidad. The one exception is mail that goes out of Brazil via an Italian airline. In this way, we discover Axis-oriented people. They turn over this information to us, we sanitize it from the standpoint of source, and forward it to the Rockefeller office where it will be used to compile a blacklist of those Axis-oriented commercial representatives. You, by the way, along with Nelson and Joe Rovensky, are the only one who knows where this information really comes from. America, of course, is still neutral regarding the war in Europe, so there is no law prohibiting Axis friends from being on American or American-associated payrolls. But between Rockefeller, his family, and the other dollar-a-year men Nelson has recruited, your Office for Coordination of Commercial and Cultural Relations between the American Republics, as it is now called, can be damn persuasive.

"Soon a newly appointed press chief will be sworn in as an assistant coordinator. You will work for him in a totally overt capacity. He plans a large press division. Basically, the plan is to start up a Spanish and Portuguese language press wire service that will propagandize the Good Neighbor Policy and explain to the Latinos why, although we are neutral in so far as the war in Europe is concerned, we are rearming.

"That's the background, and here's where you come in. We know from certain intercepts that information about this plan has leaked. We also know, via British intercepts, that the Axis—and that means Germany, Russia, and Japan, who are now allies—plan to lay down informants on the Rockefeller payroll, which is being set up so hurriedly that there has been no time to properly check antecedents. On a signal from the FBI, you are to cultivate the friendship of these informants to see if they will lead you to any confederates. Also, you are to look at all Form 57s of people hired by the Press Division and let me know of anything suspicious. You will also be asked to file identifying scars on the type of their typewriters or, if they write longhand, to insert invisible magnetic threads in their envelopes. We can then signal the British to be alert to their correspondence to Europe. I usually come to Washington every Thursday evening, stay here, and meet with the director on Friday. You will have access to Rockefeller and Rovensky at all times.[2] Finally, you must remember to be a loyal employee of Jamieson, the new press chief. That may be difficult for you, as we understand he is likely to resent anyone in his shop who goes over his head, especially someone he didn't personally hire. You'll just have to work that out. Jamieson, however, must never know what you are really up to and why you were hired.

[2.]   What precisely the Rockefeller office was up to and determined to subvert in these early pre-Pearl Harbor time was spelled out in a press release on 8 January 1941. (There was of course no mention of the BSC-FBI connection as the principal source of information for this subversion and the use of the words *nazi* or *fascist* was studiously avoided.):

1. U.S. business is frequently represented in Central and South America by firms and individuals now known to support objectives contrary to the best interests of the American republics.
2. These representatives often use advertising appropriations of U.S. business firms to force newspapers, and in some instances, radio stations, to adopt anti-American editorial policies.
3. Many employees of U.S. companies or of their affiliates in Central and South America are known members of local anti-American organizations.
4. Many anti-American firms, which formerly sold only European products, have now succeeded in obtaining agencies for U.S. business. These new connections are keeping them alive and enabling them to maintain their trade contacts.
5. In many cases, they openly declare they will return to their former lines at the expiration of the war.
6. Many of these agents who now represent U.S. firms are obtaining through this medium confidential trade information, which was made available to anti-American powers.
7. Profits thus derived from representation of U.S. firms are being used to finance operations of propaganda agencies in Central and South America.
8. Many of the firms representing U.S. companies also serve as centers for distribution of anti-American propaganda and literature.
9. Many of the large anti-American firms have established their own purchasing agents in the U.S., and with the goods obtained in the market, remain in business.
10. Officers and employees of a number of firms representing the U.S. businesses are officials of anti-American powers.

"The Rockefeller office's budget calls for the setting up of a small secret fund, which can be used to finance operational projects of a secret nature in Latin America. You may be asked to handle such projects either directly or indirectly from time to time. Because of your high-security clearance, you will be one of the few persons in the office qualified to do this.

"Now, are there any questions?"

"No sir, none at all. I hope I'll remember everything you've just told me. Besides, I have the impression that the whole thing is on a need-to-know basis."

"You catch on fast, Kramer, real fast. I like that."

"Well, I guess I better be going. I hope you and the other Percy, Percy Douglas, I mean, have a good trip."

"By the way, never call me Percy. Call me Sam, and remember, if there's any trouble, call me. Hopefully, I'll be in the New York office. If not, you have to fend for yourself. If, by chance, a real emergency arises and I'm in Latin America and won't be back soon, go to Stephenson in British Intelligence or BSC, as we like to call it. Rovensky knows his office number; it's in the same building as the Rockefeller family's offices.

"There's one final thing, and it will, I know, make you real happy. Joe Rovensky is outraged over your niggardly salary. I'm to have the White House up it three notches at monthly intervals. Then, when you get transferred to Nelson's payroll, they can up you some more notches without civil service howling. The reason for all this is that you'll probably have certain out-of-pocket expenses, and there's no way to reimburse you."

I stood up and sought to shake Foxworth's hand in a combined gesture of good-bye and compliance with the secrecy imperative, but Foxworth would have none of it. Instead, he put his arm around my shoulder while he guided me toward the door. When we reached it, he held me while he applied some pressure to my arm using his left hand.

"Before you leave here," Foxworth explained, "I want to give you some fatherly advice. It's going to be as personal as an older man can give a youngster, and I hope you will understand. I'm going to give it to you because I trust you.

"The work you're getting into is as isolating as hell. You'll find yourself working six or seven days a week, cut off from all genuine, trusting human relationships. Take it from me, and I don't really know why, but you'll find you'll want to fuck even more than normal. It's the only way you can get relief from the intrigue, the only real way you can forget, even if it's just for a moment, the pressure and the duplicity. So do it often, even if you have to pay for it. And for Christ's sake, be careful. In this work, you never know who your enemies really are."

I met with Foxworth in person only once again. From then on, I dealt with him only by phone or through the FBI agents he had selected to come see me in my office in Washington. Foxworth was killed in 1943 in a plane crash in Dutch Guiana while en route to Casablanca in North Africa to prepare for a meeting between President Roosevelt and Winston Churchill.

It was just a ten-minute walk from the Mayflower to my office in the old State, War, and Navy Building, and I found I was glad I was alone. There would be time to think. But what was there to think about? Somehow or other, I had been maneuvered deep into the secret world of intelligence, a world that in 1940 hardly existed in the United States, whose military attaché in Moscow was, for example, a veterinarian. War or no war, I felt sure there would be no way out of it for me for a long, long time.

Fortunately, I was not a total novice to the ins and outs of international relations; it had been part of my history studies with Professor Gooch. J. Edgar Hoover's political constituency, his support in Congress and from the nation at large, came from the isolationists and the America Firsters and Fortress Americans who would be the first to howl if they found out that the FBI was playing footsie with the Brits at the expense of Germany while America was neutral. The best way to ensure my silence would be to keep me in intelligence work forever. The same would be true of a Republican, like Rockefeller, who had political ambitions in mind. The only thing for me to do was take it in stride and do my best.

As I climbed the granite steps of the old State, War, and Navy Building, then occupied by State, with a few offices allotted to Rockefeller, I recalled Foxworth's warning about knowing who your real enemies were. At this juncture, I doubted I had any. But in the future, there were two things I could do for protection: I could go to a gym two or three times a week to keep in shape. And like the steps I was now climbing, I could start to encase myself in a granite shell so that emotionally, as well as physically, I could be prepared for whatever would come. Let what Foxworth had called my "trusting kid's look" be a camouflage for the granite shell beneath.

When I reached the topmost step, I felt my body give a sudden involuntary jerk, and I couldn't help but laugh inwardly at myself. All those fancy thoughts about Hoover and the isolationists, about keeping fit and the need for a granite inner self were OK, but they hadn't the remotest connection with what my real need was at the moment: a willing, pliant, encompassing woman who would drain the fire that erupted within me and get me to relax again. If there was still nothing for me to do at the office, I would go out and find one. Foxworth had been right about the sex angle.

2

My first sally into counterespionage a few months after I had established my overt self as a special assistant to Frank Jamieson, head of the Press Division, did not evolve out of information supplied by the British Security Coordination in New York. On the contrary, it was the other way around; it developed from detailed study on my part.

In accordance with Foxworth's instructions, I carefully inspected the Form 57s of all newly hired employees of the Press Division. One Walker G. Matheson, according to his job résumé, had worked for the *Japan Advertiser* in Tokyo for several years as a reporter and rewrite man, his employment ending in late 1940. There were two troubling things about these dates. The *Japan Advertiser*, a privately owned paper belonging to an American citizen, had been seized by the Japanese military in 1938, and its owner and staff immediately left for the United States. Why had Matheson stayed on the payroll? Also, what had Matheson done during the interval between leaving the *Advertiser* and being hired by the Rockefeller office?

I called Foxworth in New York. "We've got a new employee named Matheson. There's a gap in his employment record. He's taken a room in a low-rent area here, so I assume he's not the prosperous type who can afford to goof off. Ought you check with the British Security to see if they have anything on him? Also FBI files. He could of course have been ill. He doesn't look healthy. Premature gray hair, thin, a pasty complexion. He might be a heroin addict, especially since he never rolls up his shirt sleeves."

"It doesn't sound like much, but I'll check."

"Well, I've got something else which either you or I should follow up."

"What's that?"

"His previous employer on his '57 was the *Japan Advertiser*. That was a very influential English-language daily in Tokyo. It was seized by the Japanese military

28

in 1938, but Matheson's Form 57 indicates he stayed on for a year after it was seized and converted into a propaganda weapon. The owner, who was American, returned immediately to the United States, but Matheson stayed on. It would be nice to know why. I don't like to ask him and thus start raising suspicions around the shop."

"What was the name of the owner?"

"Wilfred Fleisher, of Philadelphia. Fleisher's a prominent family there. They're connected in some way with music publishing."

"Maybe you've got something, maybe you don't. Meanwhile, check to see if he uses his office typewriter for personal correspondence, and let me know before Thursday. If he does, I'll send you wires for the envelopes, and meanwhile, you can nick the lowercase *e* and the capital *T*. I doubt we'll get anything, but it's worth checking."

Oddly enough, Foxworth's somewhat casual response to my suspicions didn't discourage me. On the contrary, I felt a sudden surge of physical warmth pour through me. For the first time in my life, I realized I had been endowed with real power. It was almost as if I had a pistol in my hand aimed directly at Matheson's head with the choice of shooting him dead, taking him captive, or letting him go free. The final decision was not to be mine. I realized that and was happy it was in other hands. But I also realized I now had real power, and it was stimulating.

The only other time I'd felt a similar charge had been derived from a victory at a steeplechase. I'd been riding since I was five years old at the family's farm in northern Kentucky. At Princeton, because of my small size and light weight (I'd graduated at nineteen and was not even fully-grown upon entering college), competitive field sports were out as far as I was concerned. The only thing I was good at was mounting a horse and riding and jumping it. Thus, I used to go to an indoor riding rink and exercise horses that were too thoroughbred and high-strung for their owners to ride. I became especially attached to a mare named Popover that belonged to a kindly and very rich man who was too heavy to ride it. I schooled it five days a week. One night the rink's owners organized an elaborate show, and I entered a bareback steeplechase contest. Almost all my competitors were grooms. I won the contest hands down. Most of the others fell off their horses before the race was over.

"Well, if you are actually going to check," I told Foxworth, "also look for a Matheson Walker as well as a Walker Matheson. The Japs reverse name orders in their lingo."

My suspicions had been correct. British Security located a record of an incoming letter, pre-Pearl Harbor, from Tokyo to M. Walker, recommending him for employment by a magazine called the *Living Age*. This once-popular magazine had been secretly bought by the Japanese military and converted into a U.S. propaganda vehicle that subtly explained Japan's invasion of Manchuria and other parts of China as pacification measures designed to bring peace and suppress banditry. Further investigation revealed that Matheson had gone to work for the Rockefeller office direct from employment by the *Living Age*, and before that, the *Japan Advertiser*. Also, it was found that upon arrival in the United States, he had applied at the State Department for the necessary forms with which to register as an agent of a foreign government but had never completed the forms or filed them with State. According to Foxworth, they now had enough evidence to follow Matheson's every move, but it was the British who uncovered genuine incriminating evidence in the form of a letter from Matheson. It was mailed in a covering envelope and addressed to an outwardly innocuous address in a residential area in neutral Madrid, Spain, which was, in fact, an Abwehr address. From Spain, it was forwarded to Tokyo. Foxworth never revealed to me the contents of this letter; all he said was that they now had enough to arrest and convict him of espionage, and he told me to inform Rockefeller that the FBI would come to the office to arrest him at 10:30 AM the following Thursday.

I deliberately delayed my arrival at the office until 9:45 AM on the day of Matheson's scheduled arrest. Instinctively, I felt it would precipitate trouble with Jamieson. "Whatever happens," I said to myself, "don't lose it. Stay cool."

The moment I walked into the outer office, Vonette, Frank's secretary, told me he wanted to see me immediately. He was alone. He had his heavy thick glasses off and was massaging his eyelids. He didn't ask me to sit down.

"You're late," he commented. His voice was soft, but there was acid in it.

"Yeah. Mary Lou and I worked late last night answering some letters for Nelson's signature. Do you want to see them?" I asked.

"Mary Lou got here on time," he said, ignoring my question. "But when I asked her to take some dictation, she refused."

"Not surprising. I told her last night not to get involved with anything that would tie her up past ten thirty when I'd need her urgently to take some dictation and write up a memo I had in mind."

"A memo. On the Matheson dismissal?"

"Yes, that's right."

"Look. I want to make something clear. You work for me. Anything you or she has to do comes later. Got that?"

"OK, I'll send her in. I can type up the memo myself."

"Anything you write for Nelson on the subject of Matheson's arrest comes to me first. I decide if it goes forward or not," he added.

I could have argued about this but decided against it. There was a way around it. I would simply go to Nelson's secretary and ask her to tell Nelson at the first opportunity that Jamieson had fired Matheson before he was arrested and let it go at that. Then, if Nelson asked me to write up a memo on the details of the case, it could include the classified information about the FBI and the BSC, and I could write it at home, and Jamieson would never see it. The truth was I had slipped up by planning to do it at the office, but my idea had been to get it to him fifteen minutes after the event, before any news of it spread around the office.

All this thinking made me totally unprepared for what came next.

"By the way, Paul," Frank said as he put his glasses back on. "I want you here in the office with me when I fire Matheson, and that's an order."

"Do you think that would be wise?"

"What do you mean?"

"This place is a beehive of gossip, and I don't want the boys in the pressroom to know I had any connection with Matheson's dismissal and arrest."

"I've already discussed it with Harry Frantz who, as you know, is in charge of the pressroom. Anyway, there's not a man there who doesn't already know you have access to Rovensky and Nelson, to say nothing of anybody else of importance in the shop. They are all newsmen. They can figure things out for themselves. You know that."

"OK," I said as I looked at my watch. "Look, Frank, it's now 10:05. Hadn't you better send for Matheson?"

"Tell Vonette to send for him. I'll be here when he arrives. Just be damn sure you'll be here too."

I left immediately and told Vonette. Then I went out into the corridor.

The FBI was already there. They had commandeered one of the elevators, dismissed the operator, and held the door open and ready to receive a dismissed Matheson who presumably would be accompanied by several FBI agents. They had also cleared the corridor once Matheson had responded to Jamieson's request that he come to his office immediately. Since Frank, against my better judgment, had insisted that I be present at his dismissal, I followed Matheson into Frank's office and stood with my back to the door through which he had entered so that he would then be forced to leave via the door that opened into the corridor where FBI agents were now waiting.

Jamieson surprised me. After motioning Matheson to a chair in front of his desk, he sat back and picked up Matheson's Form 57, which I had placed on his desk blotter. Jamieson's hand was shaking, and it suddenly struck me that he was physically afraid. But what could he be afraid of? Certainly not Matheson—a wisp of a man and probably a heroin addict.

Jamieson spoke in such a low voice; it was hard to hear him. He began by praising Matheson's work, which he termed excellent. I realized at once that this was Jamieson's way of stroking his own ego. As a Pulitzer price winner, he hadn't hired a dud; on the contrary, he had recognized and hired a skilled and able newsman. That would no doubt be his defense if Rockefeller ever chided him on his ineptitude.

Matheson remained totally silent and stared fixedly at Jamieson. When Frank came to his failure to record his previous employment by the *Living Age*, Matheson slumped forward slightly and lowered his head so that he was no longer looking directly at Jamieson but at the edge of his desk. The moment Jamieson dismissed him, Matheson stood up. Jamieson tried to shake his hand, but he waved him aside. He sought to leave via the same door through which he had entered, but when he saw me blocking it, he stared at me for a moment. There was no hatred in his eyes. Although he could not have known my role in his dismissal, he was certainly shrewd enough to know that there must be a reason for me to block the way and gesture toward the door to the corridor. He walked out in total silence. A moment later, there was the audible click of handcuffs.

Jamieson sank back into his chair. He was still trembling. I left him without a word, went to my desk, and called Foxworth in New York. "The deed is done," I said. "It went without a hitch." Then, after a pause, "That was my first. Do you think there will be more?"

"Who knows," Foxworth commented and hung up. After calling Foxworth, I went immediately to Nelson's outer office and asked his secretary to tell him that Matheson had been arrested by the FBI at 10:28 AM, just after Jamieson had dismissed him. It had gone without a hitch.

"Paul," Imogene Spencer, Nelson's secretary, said as she looked up at me from her typewriter and smiled. She was so damn beautiful I couldn't help but feast my eyes on her. Her dark eyes glowed, their natural warmth enhanced by a frame of dark hair, and her lips bore the trace of a smile. "It's not like you. Shouldn't you put it all in a memo? You know better than I how meticulous Nelson is. He keeps a special locked safe in his own office, and your file is in it. What's the matter, is it Jamieson?" The trace of a smile had broadened after she mentioned Frank's name, and her eyes sparked with amusement.

I had often considered asking Imogene for a date but had thought better of it. She was in Nelson's territory. He'd already given her an auto so she wouldn't have to go home alone on a bus late at night. This was, I realized, step one in his seduction of her. The next would be a breakdown of his own car so could she drive him home? He had also given her so many salary raises that civil service had sent an investigator to look into it. Then something unexpected happened to forestall Nelson. The young investigator fell for Imogene, hook, line, and sinker, and she for him.

Normally, in such a situation I would have reached in my pocket for a pack of cigarettes before answering the question. Instead, I totally ignored her query. All I did was mutter "God, you're beautiful" just loud enough for her to hear, and then turned on my heel and walked out of her office. I'd resolved from the beginning that I would never ever say anything that was in any way critical of Jamieson to anyone in the shop. He was my problem and no one else's. I'd solve it somehow. Curiously, I found that Matheson's arrest and the conviction as an enemy agent I assumed had followed had become totally abstract in my mind. I might just as well have read about it in the newspaper rather than have been a part of it. What stuck in my mind, what Foxworth had not prepared me for, was the hostility that both Rockefeller and Jamieson had felt toward me.

When I had first gone to Nelson to tell him the FBI was coming at ten thirty the next morning to arrest Matheson and charge him with being a Japanese agent, Nelson had stiffened perceptibly, then given me a hostile look, then glanced down at the papers on his desk and barked out an order: "Get him off the payroll. I don't want a Jap agent on my payroll when he's arrested."

It was this order that I took to Jamieson. Another hostile look. Admittedly, people can become irritated at the bearer of bad news, but there was no recognition of the teamwork or the brainwork involved in catching Matheson, or in uncovering the secret Abwehr address in Spain; nor was there any apparent pleasure taken in the fact that an enemy agent had been weeded out of the office and brought to justice.

Instead, Frank Jamieson fought the whole thing. "But I haven't any grounds for dismissing him. His work is excellent," he argued.

"Yes you do," I had pointed out. "He failed to mention his employment by the *Living Age*. That's all you have to say. He'll get the point. It's owned by the Nips."

"But how do you know that?"

"I do, that's all. Take it from me; just mention it to him. I guarantee he'll understand. If you want me to, I'll be glad to read to you article after article, explaining that all that the Nips are doing on the mainland of Asia is suppressing banditry and bringing in law and order."

"All right. Now leave me. I've got serious work to do."

Early the following morning I ran into Joe Rovensky in the corridor. He stopped me to ask that I show up a few minutes early at his apartment for the poker game that night. Noting the surprised look on my face, he explained that I had never met his wife and she wanted to meet me.

"Thanks, Joe," I said. "I'll be there."

"Good," he said. "Mrs. Rovensky thinks you're a real hero."

"Why in the world does she think that?"

"Well, I told her how you caught a Nip agent single-handed."

"But that's not true. It was a real case of teamwork between me, the FBI, and the BSC."

"That's not what Stephenson told me," Joe snapped and then bustled down the corridor.

Both Joe and his wife gave me a great welcome, and when I turned down the drink he offered, he asked me why.

"Well, frankly, I sort of lost track of the time at the gym I go to for a workout, and before I knew it, there wasn't time to eat if I was to get here early as you asked me to."

"You mean you haven't eaten. Then let me order something. This place is sort of a hotel, and they can send something up for you."

"Thanks, but I'd rather not. Your game always breaks up early, and I'll eat when I get home."

At this point, Mrs. Rovensky, a short, dumpy woman, reappeared with a box of Ritz crackers. "Well," she said, "if you won't eat, you can munch on these with a drink. Just ask Joe to make it light."

"My wife is real proud of you, Paul," Joe put in as he gave me a weakened Scotch and water.

"Oh, I am!" she exclaimed. "I am, and Joe told me how no one else at the office is allowed to know what you really do. That must make it awfully hard for you. No wonder you keep so thin. But you shouldn't go skipping meals like you've done."

With that, Mrs. Rovensky disappeared again, and Joe motioned me toward an easy chair at the other end of the room away from the poker table.

"Paul," Joe asked, "how much are you earning?"

"Four thousand, six hundred dollars a year."

"And a little over a year ago, you started with what?"

"Two thousand, six hundred dollars."

"And next month when you are to be shifted to our payroll from the White House's, what have you been promised?"

"Five thousand, two hundred dollars."

"And I understand Arthur Jones has already told you that you are to get another raise. It just goes to show what I always tell young people. Do the job and the money will take care of itself."

"That's true, but the only problem is I really have two jobs, and my one boss doesn't know about the other. He suspects something, but he can't figure it out."

"I'm aware of the problem, but it's nothing compared with the row going on between Hoover and Bill Donovan, whom President Roosevelt has decided to put in charge of a master spy agency."

"I know a bit about it from some of the agents I work with. But as they put it, "Possession is nine-tenths of the law, and we already got Latin America.""

"Let's hope for your sake it stays that way. But be careful. One of the things that worries me is that Jamieson has hired a number of left-wingers and, according to Stephenson, the Communist Party line is to make as much trouble as possible for the intelligence people and exploit the hostility between Donovan and Hoover."

I've always thought that if Nelson and the other players hadn't arrived at this moment, I might have followed up on Joe's statement and pulled out some specific details. But this, of course, became impossible, and I immediately shifted my mental gears into a poker motif and thought no more of it.

The game turned out to be a lot of fun for me. Joe Rovensky was determined that I win that particular night and supported my game in such a way that I won a few large pots. The two new financial types down for the Italian airline project both lost to me, as did the A&P coffee man. I must have won $5 or $7, no big deal; but then those men, as Foxworth had pointed out to me, were ferociously competitive, even for pennies.

Since it was a balmy spring night, I decided to walk back to my place. But at the last moment I got sidetracked. Instead of going right up to my apartment and fixing myself a little supper, I stopped in a bar for a real drink. With the drink in my hand, I phoned the Hopkins Institute of Facial Massage, a classy brothel I sometimes patronized, which operated in an apartment house on Connecticut Avenue opposite the Wardman Park Hotel. I didn't get home until two o' clock, and supper or no supper, I slept until ten o'clock in the morning.

3

At this point, and in the interest of clarity, now that the reader has witnessed the beginnings of my work as a secret agent, it is perhaps best to digress and answer some questions that will inevitably arise. Did my background or my parents have any influence on my work or my presumed skills at it? Certainly not directly, by the accident of indirection, yes, they did.

An important point here is that when I was a child and growing toward adulthood, I felt no genuine affection toward either of them. My mother had the Victorian habit of fainting when confronted with anything she didn't like. Thus, as a child, I quickly learned that there was no sense going to her for help or solace if there was any blood from an accident. I'd have to go to my dad, and he, in turn, regarded the necessary bandaging and disinfection of a scratch or cut an unwelcome intrusion on his occupation of the moment.

Furthermore, at the dinner table, a formalized occasion with the servants substituting a variety of plates and silverware for this and that, Dad was a total autocrat. Gossip was not permitted. He insisted that talk be limited to science, politics, literature, and finance. Meanwhile, he clearly liked to sauté me in the frying pan of his biting wit. Thus I was subjected to remarks like, "The reason I married late in life was so I'd be dead before I could see what damn fools my children would be. Alas, I didn't wait long enough." Or, "A parent is a child's worst enemy. They should be sent off to boarding school at the first opportunity," or, "You have no wit. Careful or you'll become a crashing bore."

I couldn't help but admire his direct and incisive approach to problems, but I couldn't see how his way of doing things could ever apply to me. When consulted, he never wrote a memo or a letter; he simply told people how it was in a biting and often sarcastic way. Thus, for example, his friend Herbert French, the head of Proctor & Gamble, had come back from Germany after a post-World War I visit for a new patent he had bought for an unnamed substance that was to become known as a detergent. French asked Dad for an independent opinion of its merits.

Our large basement laundry was immediately converted into a sort of hydraulic laboratory, and all clothes, curtains, and linens were sent out to a commercial laundry. After a couple of weeks of testing the new invention in everything from rainwater (soft) to well water (hard) to municipal, chlorinated river water, as well as testing its ability to cleanse the clay tubes of a Pasteur filter, Dad called Mr. French. I overheard what he said. "What you've got," he explained, "is a substance that is better than soap in hard water areas but presents no advantages in soft water areas. What you should do is market it first in hard water areas; then the damn fool housewives who live there will rave about its advantages, which the housewives in soft water areas will hear about, and thus they will start using it too, even though it secures for them no useful purpose."

Another incident I recalled is typical of him. He had an associate at the old U.S. Hygienic Laboratory in Washington where Dad spent his winters doing important research on psittacosis, or parrot fever. This associate had caught the disease and died. Dad was determined that his widow, who was penniless, receive a pension via a private bill that he had our congressman from northern Kentucky (where we spent May 1 to October 15 of every year) introduce. A senator from a mining state in the West held up the bill. I overheard the following phone monologue.

"Googh," Dad said, "that damn fool senator of yours is holding up my private bill for a government pension to a widow of a scientist who died because of his work. I want you to tell him to lay off." Googh, I should explain, was Mr. Guggenheim, who owned vast mining properties and smelters in the state.

In fairness to my father, I must admit he saw to it that I mastered what he considered the four manly arts: swimming, riding a horse, shooting a rifle, and sailing a boat. The trouble was he never bothered to give me any instructions. Also, he had a terrible temper, so that I was perpetually afraid I would provoke him into losing it.

At the age of five, I was presented with a pony with bridle and saddle. "Get Joe Zint to teach you how to ride it, groom it, and feed it," he said, referring to one of the farmhands. At twelve, I got a .22 rifle. "Raymond," Dad said, meaning another farmhand, "is a superb shot. That man can drive a flat head nail into a tree with a .22 from twenty feet. He'll teach you." Every Sunday morning Dad would take my brother and me swimming in the Ohio River about ten miles upstream from the farm. Here again he couldn't be bothered to teach us anything. When we were small, he would turn us over to Raymond and tell him to get us to duck underwater and let our breaths out. Meanwhile, he struck out on his own and would think nothing of swimming across the river and back. In northern Michigan where we went in August, Dad kept a sailboat and took me sailing once. "Just watch what I do," he explained, "and then you'll know how to sail." The truth was simply that he didn't like children. They bored him.

At nineteen, when I graduated from Princeton with honors, he announced that I wasn't "yet dry behind the ears." I should go to Europe and grow up. Thus I was sent off to Cambridge University with a letter to his great friend Nuttall, who was a professor of parasitology as well as the Pepys librarian at Magdalene College. Nuttall took care of all the details of my admission and determined that Trinity College would be most suitable for me.

Nuttall was also responsible, although quite accidentally, for my witnessing of one of the most dramatic events of the interwar years—one that left an abiding impression on me, both because of the way it suddenly erupted and because of the totally British and silly way it transpired. Besides me, Nuttall had invited Lord Haldane and some of the men doing interesting work splitting the atom with something called a cyclotron at the university's Cavendish Laboratory. Nuttall lived well, in a large house he had designed himself set in a pleasant garden out on Madingly Road. He sometimes complained about his garden since he wasn't allowed to dig deep in it for fear of disturbing a conduit laid down by the Tudors to feed the fountain in Trinity's Great Court several miles away.

During the meal, a servant brought Nuttall a telegram on a silver salver. He opened it at once, visibly trembled, and paled. "My God," he announced, "they've got Kapitza." In the ensuing hubbub, it was at once agreed that a committee had to be organized immediately to go to the Soviet Union to make sure that Kapitza was not being held against his will "by that scoundrel, Stalin."

Then Nuttall, with an exquisite politeness, held up his hand to silence his guests and patiently explained to me what had happened. It was, as I recall, 1935. Professor Kapitza, a Tsarist exile from the Soviet Union and at the time the greatest expert on heavy water, had been invited to go to Leningrad and lecture at the university on his scientific work. His friends at Cambridge had advised him not to go for fear he would never be allowed to return to Britain and continue his work in the West. Foolishly, he had gone anyway; and now he was not coming back. The committee that was sent to investigate talked with him. No, he insisted, he was not being held against his will; furthermore, he asked that his scientific equipment be shipped to him since it had been given to him personally by Lord Melchett and others and thus belonged to him and not to the university.

This request was turned over to Arnold McNair, the professor of international law at Cambridge who ruled in Kaptiza's favor.

Meanwhile, it should be realized that all this generated considerable attention in the British press, and, since I had been "in" on it at the beginning, this had the effect of making me feel that I had made it with the British Establishment—something I'd never felt at Princeton where the professors were teachers rather than doers. Eventually the whole thing subsided, and the *London* Times published what can only be described as a ridiculous letter from a typical Colonel Blimp, who asked, why all the fuss over Kapitza when everyone knew the situation in the Anglo-Egyptian Sudan was far more serious?

This incident stayed with me and broadened my perspective, just as did my association with fellow students at Trinity. The university had simply refused to recognize my BA degree from Princeton. I had to take undergraduate courses my first year. Thank goodness I did. Thus I was made to examine in detail all the clauses of both the Peace of Vienna of 1815 and those of Versailles after World War I. I also had to read the British diplomatic documents that led up to World War I and attend illuminating lectures by two distinguished historians who explained them. Nothing like this had ever happened at Princeton, where all I got were textbooks. My fellow students were, in fact, being taught how to run a vast and complex empire, and after graduation, they went into the Diplomatic Service, the Colonial Service, or the Indian Civil Service. A number, if they didn't have titles already, acquired them as a result of their work. A few of the oddballs became spooks and showed up later doing weird work in remote places like Yugoslavia, Afghanistan, or China. Some got diplomatic cover. Henry VIII had richly endowed Trinity for just this purpose. The Tudors, who centralized British government, desperately needed civil servants, as we now like to call them. Trinity adhered to this original purpose, had been successful in investing its endowments wisely, and had become very rich. It had also broadened its outlook to include science. When I was there, its master was one of Britain's most distinguished physicists.

My mother was a totally different kettle of fish from my father. In many ways, I think her life was circumscribed by her frustrations. As a young woman, she had gone to college for a year, which was rare in those days. But when she found she was totally unprepared for it by the private girls' school she had attended, she dropped out. She then, as a rich man's daughter, flirted with feminism—something she could afford to do. Thus she became the first woman driver in Cleveland, who liked to charge about town in her Baker Electric, which, judging from a picture I had of her in it, looked very much like a buggy without a horse. She also smoked tiny cigarettes in public and served on the board of numerous charities. Rather characteristically, she became a founder of something called the Martha House. This was a refuge for immigrant servant girls who sought to escape the sexual advances of their masters. Meanwhile, she developed a dislike of her bourgeois existence, married my father, and moved to Cincinnati. Her own father had passed away by then, and she had inherited a comfortable fortune. She promptly had two children and then had to cope with World War I shortages without a husband; he had gone back into the army for the duration. She hated it. The truth was that she loathed anything to do with the mechanics of living. She had only one real skill, and this was outstanding: making money. During her lifetime, she quintupled her father's inheritance despite a couple of reversals due to Prohibition. One of her father's business coups had been the formation of a northern Ohio beer trust, and she owned a considerable amount of stock in it, which became, for all practical purposes, worthless. This didn't deter her; on she went, buying and selling stocks and following the market daily. The 1929 market crash didn't bother her either. She must have seen it coming.

When I turned twenty-one, I came home from England to spend the summer with my parents on the family farm. It was then I discovered that she had made me financially independent. A trust fund she had set up for tax reasons when I was a child had expired along with some sort of life insurance endowment policy.

I got the money along with two ultimatums. I was never in the future to ask her for a *sou*. Indeed, all I ever got from her thereafter was a five-dollar tie for Christmas. Also, since I didn't know anything about handling money, I was to take the stocks, bonds, and money I had received to Lazard Frères, the private bankers in New York who would initiate me into the handling of money. It was all arranged; my account executive had been selected, and I was to stop off there en route to the pier where I would board the ship back to England.

I did this and from then on paid all my bills myself. Meanwhile, Lazard's would call me occasionally and suggest that I sell something for which I would have a nice profit and buy something else. They also did two other things, which at the time struck me as odd. Since I was going back to England and would soon complete my studies there, they insisted that I should meet with Lord Brand, a big wheel in the British Establishment and head of Lazard's London branch, who was married to a relative of Lady Astor's. I didn't know it at the time, but he was also a major figure in British Intelligence. My reception by Lord Brand was chilling. I wasn't sent to his office, but was ushered into an obviously soundproofed room with a heavy door with a peephole in it. Once this was closed, I felt as if I was in the first stage of my eventual incarceration in Wormwood Scrubbs, a notorious British prison. Brand eventually materialized, sat down, and asked me to tell him about my education and training, which I did without interruption. There was no doubt in my mind that I was being sized up for some sort of future employment. When I finished, he rose and simply said, "If you are ever short of money while here in England, just tell us, and we'll advance it to you against your New York account."

The other thing of a personal nature that Lazard's did for me was to somehow track me down at the Fairmount Hotel in San Francisco where I was waiting for a ship to take me to New Guinea and bawl me out. "Hey Lieutenant," one of the partners said on the phone, "don't you know there is a new treasury regulation that freezes all nondiscretionary accounts? This means we can't trade on your behalf once you are overseas. This is designed to protect you in case you are captured by the enemy and held for ransom." Of course I knew nothing whatsoever about such a regulation and sent Lazard's the required telegram issuing them full and complete control of my money and resigning any say whatever over its manipulation. This was a shrewd, if naïve and unplanned, decision. When I finally returned from overseas, I found my holdings with them had doubled. I also found that the French crowd had taken over Lazard's, and my account executive had moved to another firm.

I followed him, and over the years, we became good friends. The point of all this is to show how my mother had made me financially independent. But I should also mention that when she died, she disinherited me "for tax reasons." My share of her estate went into an irrevocable trust for the benefit of my daughter. The truth was she was hard as nails when it came to money and never allowed herself to be guided by sentiment. She wasn't a banker's daughter for nothing. I buried both my parents in Arlington Cemetery with the appropriate military honors in a plot within sight of Dad's uncle's, West Point Class of 1873, and his cousin Robert, also a West Pointer who had been killed while on active duty during the Philippine Insurrection. I felt no real grief at either funeral as I never felt close to or affectionate toward either of them.

Finally, I must advert to my family's lifestyle from May to October. Every year, during this period we were totally transformed from a streetcar, suburban existence in Cincinnati, Ohio, to a totally rural and small-town Southern existence in northern Kentucky. Before the Civil War, downtown Cincinnati or basin life, as it was then called, was very unhealthy. In the summer there was miasma, or malaria as it later came to be called; typhoid, typhus; and cholera. In particular, small children, once they no longer nursed at their mother's breasts, perished by the hundreds. As a result, those who could afford it fled to the Highlands. At this time, my paternal grandfather bought a large tract of land and an uncompleted house—an architectural monstrosity in stone and a mix of a Rhenish castle and a Second French Empire chateau—on a bluff high above the Ohio River, ten miles upstream from Cincinnati. The rural roads were impossible, and the family commuted to its summer home by a river packet. There was even a landing consisting of a big pile of rocks at the water's edge on which the packet's gangway could be conveniently lowered.

The house was absurd by modern standards. There was a huge T-shaped entrance hall with two entrance doors, one on the riverside and another to the carriage drive in the west. This hall led to another large hall and a giant stairway to the second floor; other interior stairways led to the rooms in the two towers and the attics. The living quarters consisted of a library; a drawing room; a stately dining room; a billiard room, which Dad had converted to a laboratory; a family dining room; and a kitchen and pantry. Upstairs there were seven bedrooms, and above these, five tower rooms. There was only one bath, which, along with the kitchen sink and the hot-water heater, got its water from a giant tank that filled one of the tower rooms but was still low enough to catch the rainwater runoff from one of the attic roofs.

After the Civil War, the government decided to move the military post originally created to protect Cincinnati from the Indians to higher land and forced the family to sell most of its land. Only about thirty-five acres remained with the family, and the new Tenth Infantry post totally surrounded the property on two sides. The river ran along the third side and a forest, unused, bordered the fourth. The land that remained to the family consisted of lawns, gardens, a cornfield, an alfalfa field, a pasture for the cows and horses, and a forest.

When my dad married my mother and she saw what was to be her future summer home, she simply refused to live in it. They built a bungalow, the architectural inspiration for which was a house by Frank Lloyd Wright called the Warren Hickox House. It was a failure in every way. Surrounded by huge overhanging eaves and big, roofed porches on the front, side, and back, it was dark and gloomy, and in comparison to the big stone house, was hot in summer and cold in winter. My parents, however, loved it despite the sneers of my dad's sister Stella, who always referred to it as the "bungaloathsome."

When I was twelve, my brother and I were moved to the big stone house. Vic got the blue room next to the bath. I got Great-Uncle Sam's room, which was facing the river, with a thirty-five-mile panorama of the Ohio valley and the rolling hills on the other side of the river. Uncle Sam's enormous black walnut bed had been disassembled and stored elsewhere. In its place, I got an army cot. When I complained, my father said, "Children should not be mollycoddled. They should learn at an early stage to lead a Spartan existence."

In many ways, the farm was frozen in time at about 1853, although my father's father, on his return from serving as an officer in the Union Army during the Civil War, had burned down the slaves' cabins. A town had grown along an interurban streetcar line, originally built to serve the soldiers of the military post and transport them into the city when on leave. Some of the houses were quite large and spacious. These "newcomers" were totally ignored by my parents, who limited their fraternization to the colonel in command of the military post, his wife, and the other old landholding families consisting of the Crawfords, the Brents, and the Spences. The latter two families had intermarried to produce our congressman, Brent Spence, a family friend. When my mother went to the little local bank, which was owned by a new-rich lumberman and definitely a non-U, the teller left his cage, came out to her car, took her check back inside, cashed it, brought her only new bills so she wouldn't soil her hands when she counted them. Bill, the local blacksmith, always dropped whatever he was doing to serve us. The local postmaster had to give me the mail. Our mailbox was too high for me to reach. Also, the counter was high, and only the top of my head showed.

The postmaster would always say, "Who's there? I don't see anyone." I would reach up and slap the counter with my hand.

"It's me," I would say.

"Oh, you mean the Kramer boy. I thought I saw you take your horse and leave it at Bill Uthe's."

"Can I have our mail?"

"Of course, here it is, all wrapped in a bundle with string." He would then shove it, along with a gumdrop, to the end of the counter so I could reach it. "Now," he'd admonish me, "when you cross the street to get your horse, be careful of all them motor cars. They go flying by as fast as fifteen miles an hour."

My playmates on the farm were mostly the children of our many family retainers. There was Freddy, the son of a steeplejack who had fallen to his death, leaving a widow and two boys. His mother worked for us in the kitchen of the stone house, canning and preserving fruits, vegetables, and berries all produced on the farm in huge amounts. Half of this was trucked into our town house for the winter; the other half went to the Cincinnati General Hospital where there was a floor in one of the buildings with private rooms reserved for impoverished gentlefolk. The hospital food was awful, and the presiding nurse maintained a special pantry of foods to liven things up for them. Most of it came from our farm and was one of Mom's charities. Freddy was good at two things: making little tanks out of discarded spools of thread and playing mumblety-peg. To make the tanks, he would notch the outer rims of the spools with his pocketknife, run a rubber band through the central hole, and attach one end to a kitchen match and the other to a broken piece of match. Then he would wind the toy up, put it on a sloping board, and it would climb. We would have massive tank battles with the spools, a la World War I. His other skill, mumblety-peg, was a popular rural children's game in which a pocketknife is flipped into the ground. It meant, of course, much scrabbling around in the dirt and this, I think, added to its appeal. Besides Freddy, there was the local telephone lineman's son who came out to the farm with his father. Since our phone line ran by itself for some distance and was often struck by lightning, their visits were quite regular. Most exotic of all were the Setter kids. The Setter family had taken up residence in an abandoned log cabin at the foot of the hill near the river. Sam Setter didn't work. He had a small pension from the Spanish-American War. He was a good judge of horseflesh, and when we needed a new horse, he was sent out to find one. Sam had seven children and the morals of an alley cat. All the children were gloriously good-looking—blond with azure blue eyes and well-built. But Shelby, my friend, once confided to me, "When Mom has the rag on, Dad and I get to be butt buddies." Shelby was a superb shot. He was also good at mumblety-peg and would sometimes go fishing with me for sun fish on the old steam packet landing. As the Setter children grew up, we automatically drifted apart. Several became prostitutes. Mother took Edith, the nicest and prettiest of the Setter girls, under her wing and got her a real job, working at Putnam's Ice Cream Parlor in Cincinnati. Unfortunately, she caught pneumonia at the age of eighteen and died.

For all practical purposes, the town was run by Chief Cook, who was in fact a deputy sheriff siphoned off from the county seat. We had two—one in Alexandria, in the rural eastern and southern parts of the county, and another in Newport, an industrial town opposite Cincinnati. Cook hailed from the rural part. Because of our status as a landholding family, he always demonstrated suitable deference to us. Thus, he'd come to my dad when his little jail needed painting or to ask permission for a traffic drive against motorists who exceeded the 15 MPH speed limit. "OK," Dad would say, "but don't arrest any of the locals." Dad also had a habit of using the pronoun *they* in a pejorative sense, while the pronoun *we* had attributed to it a sort of royal connotation. Chief Cook came one day to lunch with the ominous news that a black family was interested in buying a house at the other end of town. What should he do about it? Dad's reply was instantaneous. "They," he said, "all ran away to Ohio at the outbreak of the Civil War, and we don't want them back."

At this point, I must have been a freshman in a classical public high school in Cincinnati and had a black friend. "Who's we?" I muttered under my breath and was sent away from the table for gross impertinence.

My attendance at a public high school in Cincinnati represented a personal victory on my part in combination with a concealed elitism on the part of the city. Walnut Hills was a classical high school, which meant you could start with Latin in the seventh grade and Greek in the ninth. This high school had some remarkable teachers, among them Miss Lotze and Mr. Venable, who taught elocution and English, respectively. The school simply didn't tolerate ethnic accents or Negro talk. Any child who showed symptoms of it got especially drilled by Miss Lotze three times a week as to proper pronunciation and the appropriate sounds of vowels and consonants. Our voices were also changing, so we got special exercises in vowels shouted out loud in unison. Mr. Venable was an eccentric and an authority on Shakespeare. He could have taught in any college but claimed it imperative to subject children to Shakespeare if they were to develop any appreciation of it. He was very well-to-do since his father had invented the "Venable notebook," and he still received royalties on the patent. This included a metal spiral that passed through holes in the paper allowing the pages to be easily turned. It's still in use today. Venable made us memorize passage after passage from Shakespeare including "Seven Ages of Man" and Portia's speech on the "quality of mercy." He and Miss Lotze also produced the annual Shakespeare plays that the children put on and were presented with great fanfare in an auditorium downtown. I got parts in them two years running, and it nurtured in me a love of the theatre. At Cambridge I became very active in the Footlights, which put on an annual May

Week show at the Arts Theatre built by John Maynard Keynes and given to King's College in order to keep Keynes' wife, a former ballerina, happy.

At the high school, we also got after-school special instruction to help us with our College Boards in case we were to seek admission to an Ivy League college. To counteract any political fallout from this elitism, the school board gave us for a building the oldest and most dilapidated school building it had. The bathrooms stank, the lunch cafeteria was in a dank basement room, and there were no lockers, schoolyards, and playing fields. Today's educators would throw up their hands over the quality of our surroundings; but this didn't matter. We got a good education and had no difficulty whizzing through our College Boards, especially if we knew Latin and Greek.

The result of this education was that I felt confident I could get into the Ivy League college of my choice, and I dug my heels in and absolutely refused to go east to a prep school. The trouble here was that my parents weren't being honest. I sensed it but didn't understand it. The reason for the prep school was that they wanted to close the house in Cincinnati and spend the winters together in Washington. If I stayed on at Walnut Hills, they couldn't do so. The result was a compromise. Mother would visit Dad as well as her family in Cleveland for a few weeks at a time and leave me alone in the house. I didn't mind. The domestic help functioned perfectly without her. In fact, it made me feel more independent, and I liked it.

These then are the impressions of my childhood and youth that I remember. The reader will have to decide for himself how much influence they had on my fifteen-year career as a covert agent. Certainly, my financial independence enabled me to be more resolute. Also, the Kapitza affair had an influence, as did possibly the Brand interview; but in the latter case, I think it was G. P. Gooch who had the final say regarding my landing a hush-hush job on the White House payroll.

4

To return to my work at the Rockefeller office, it was a Friday, and since I knew that all the assistant coordinators had been summoned to a staff meeting at Nelson's father's house in Colonial Williamsburg, I decided to grab a few hours off and do some shopping. I left my apartment around eleven o'clock and walked leisurely down Connecticut Avenue, window-shopping along the way for two new suits and a pair of shoes. To my annoyance, the office had put me on some sort of White House social list with the result that whenever a Latin American Embassy, and there were twenty of them, gave a large cocktail or dinner, I was invited. I had complained bitterly to Joe about it, arguing that this sort of night work might impinge on my covert duties, but he would hear none of it. "It'll do you good," he argued. "You'll meet lots of people, make some good Latin American contacts that will be helpful to you in the future. Just go out and get yourself some new clothes. You're not much of a dresser, and the way you look is important."

As part of Rovensky's "getting to know" program, I made a date with a woman named Gloriella Solis (not her real name), a Dominican I had met at a Uruguayan diplomatic dinner. We were going to the Philadelphia Symphony concert Saturday night at Constitution Hall. Instinctively, I felt that Gloriella wasn't interested in symphony music. She had other interests, but no need to rush; there was time to explore things.

I didn't see a suit I liked on Connecticut Avenue, but I did notice a plain gold Concord wristwatch, which I decided would go nicely with my English dinner jacket that dated back to my Cambridge days. So I went in and bought it. My mood was definitely buoyant. My happy-go-lucky nature was such that the Matheson arrest and Joe's warning of the previous night were forgotten.

It was a new day.

I continued my stroll by the White House and stopped at Garfinckel's specialty store, bought a suit, and then grabbed a sandwich and coffee before arriving at two o'clock at the office, where totally unexpected trouble hit big. As Foxworth has warned me, "In this game you can never tell who your enemies really are."

The moment I walked into the outer office, which I shared with Jamieson, I felt the hostility. Jamieson's secretary gave me a hostile look and then began to type furiously. My own secretary seemed to be weeping quietly; her eyes were definitely moist, and Wanda, the Native American file clerk who had never previously seemed even capable of a dark thought, looked at me steadily and frowned. My secretary, Mary Lou, followed me into my office.

"Whatever are you going to do?" she asked.

"I don't get it," I said. "Why is everyone in the dumps?"

Mary Lou pointed toward a letter on my desk. It was from Vice President Wallace and addressed to Nelson Rockefeller. It stated in the most emphatic terms that he had been informed by Anna Cecelia Ortiz de Caceres (not her real name), an Argentine woman of distinguished family background, impeccable reputation, and a most reliable source, that one Paul Kramer, a special assistant in the Press Division, was a "dangerous and malevolent Nazi" and should be dismissed at once from the payroll.

Scribbled in pencil at the top of the letter was a penciled note from Nelson Rockefeller's secretary to Jamieson: "FYI, NAR has not yet seen this, having already left for Colonial Williamsburg." At the bottom of the letter was another penciled note, this one from Jamieson: "I shall expect to have a written resignation from you on my return from the weekend staff meeting at Colonial Williamsburg first thing Monday AM."

On reading it, I sank back in my chair, totally surprised at my own feelings. There was absolutely no worry or fear, no distractions over the absurdity of the letter and Jamieson's reaction to it; on the contrary, a sense of total confidence exploded within me. "Oh boy!" I said aloud so Mary Lou could hear me. "If there's going to be a war between me and Vice President Wallace, you can be damn sure I'm going to win it. This letter is rubbish, total rubbish!"

"But what are you going to do?" Mary Lou asked.

"We've got work to do, Mary Lou, quick, hard work. First of all, you call the FBI in New York and see if they can get Sam Foxworth on the phone. If you can't, call Joe Rovensky at Nelson's father's house in Colonial Williamsburg, and see if you can get him for me. Be your usual sweet, tactful, vague self, but be persistent. Meanwhile, I've got things to do in the Translating Section."

In November 1940, before the offices were moved from the State Department building to the Commerce Department building, Nelson Rockefeller had sent for me. I found with him in his office the wife of the then Argentine ambassador to the United States and Miss Anna Cecilia Ortiz de Caceres, a young Argentine woman of striking beauty who stood about five feet and four inches, had light brown hair, china-blue eyes, and a superb figure. Nelson had asked me to find Miss Ortiz a job in the office commensurate within her talents.

I had taken Miss Ortiz to my own office and interviewed her. It was at once apparent to me that she came from a very well-to-do family, had been educated in convent schools, and had "finished" in Paris. I also discovered that she was a superb linguist, spoke perfect English and French as well as her native Spanish, and was, curiously, somewhat fluent in Russian. I also noted that her views on international affairs were pronounced. She felt Argentina must remain neutral in the conflict in Europe, and she had no difficulty in appreciating the wisdom of the existing Nazi-Soviet alliance since the governments of both countries were determined to eradicate unemployment and had the interests of the working people at heart. This had made me wonder if she had formed an understanding with a radical or Communist boyfriend while in finishing school in Paris since nothing in her own background indicated a predisposition for radical views.

After thirty minutes of pleasant conversation, I took Anna Cecilia to the Translating Office and introduced her to Mr. Rivera, its chief. I told him to interview her and, if he found her suitable, to put her on his payroll and take her to personnel to complete the formalities. She went to work in the translating office the following day.

Early in August 1941, after Nazi Germany had invaded its former ally, the Soviet Union, I checked on Miss Ortiz. Rivera reported that her work was excellent and that she seemed content. I then stopped to chat with her and found that her views on international affairs had changed dramatically. Germany was now totally evil, Stalin a noble fighter. Argentina should declare war on the Nazis and side with Britain and the Soviet Union. Winston Churchill, whom she had formerly reviled, was now her hero.

It was with this as background that I went to see Mr. Rivera, who revealed that Anna Cecilia had resigned two weeks previously. He also said that the quality of her work had suddenly collapsed about a week before her resignation and made no sense at all. He then showed me her desk, which was still unoccupied. I inspected it carefully. There was nothing in any of the drawers except, curiously, a few fennel seeds in one, as though they had been accidentally spilled from a bottle before her departure.

I then went immediately to see Miss Mary Winslow, a Rockefeller office employee as well as the U.S. member of the Inter-American Commission of Women, and asked for her help with the Ortiz problem. I told her there was evidence that she might be of unsound mind; if so, would she take over and see that Miss Ortiz was returned to Argentina as soon as possible? Mary Winslow, who was an aristocratic, compassionate middle-aged woman, agreed immediately to take over the problem.

With that done, I returned to my office to find that Mary Lou had indeed been able to locate Rovensky and that Joe would call back in ten minutes without fail. Joe's first words, before I even had a chance to say anything, were "Don't worry, Paul. Disregard Jamieson's appended note. Also, I've talked to Stephenson at BSC by phone, and he will contact Foxworth in Latin America. When he gets back, he'll give you a rundown on Ortiz's background. Carry on."

"Thanks, Joe."

The following Monday, when the office resumed work and all the top executives were back from their meeting in Colonial Williamsburg, the Wallace letter was never mentioned. In view of Jamieson's reticence, I never raised the subject with him.

The only fallout was a visit from Mary Winslow two weeks later. After she had settled in a chair beside my desk, she gave a little sigh as she fingered the pearls around her neck. "Well," she said, "it's over and done with, thank God! She's on the plane from Miami to BA, and when I think that in wartime that poor girl used two seats all because her parents wouldn't permit her to enter a sanitarium here, I despair for Latin America. She traveled with an attendant, all so unnecessary."

"Mary," I said, "I have something to ask you. I understand that your sister has a superb herb garden at your place in Georgetown."

"Well, hardly superb. Because of it we have no flowers, and half the herbs she grows are hideous. What beauty she finds in a basil plant is quite beyond me."

"What are these?" I asked, as I offered her a few of the seeds I had found in Anna Cecilia's desk. Mary Winslow smelled one and then tasted it.

"Fennel, undoubtedly fennel. I hate the stuff."

"What is it used for?"

"It's supposed to allay hunger. But the only thing my sister and I have ever used it for is in preparing fish in a court bouillon. A few seeds in the broth keep the fish solid when you poach it."

"Has it any narcotic properties like nutmeg or cloves?"

Mary Winslow's face brightened. My question had clearly struck a chord of interest. "Curious you should ask that," she commented. "I asked myself the same question this morning when I found some in the bureau Anna Cecilia had used. According to my sister, excessive consumption of fennel can disturb the mind."

"And do you think," I asked, "she chewed them in order to go nuts so we would send her back to Argentina?"

"Entirely possible," Mary Winslow said as she straightened herself, pulled her shoulders back, and placed her beautifully shod feet firmly on the floor. "That girl is totally spineless. And her beauty makes her a menace. She had a lover, you know, a handsome radical. They say he totally dominated her. Then he goes to Moscow for a visit, and her father takes over. Now they tell me the lover is back in Argentina, so she wants to go back to him. But she hadn't the guts to come out and say it. She chews fennel so that, in a disturbed state, we send her back. I only wish I had known about the fennel in the beginning. I'd have given that spineless, dangerous creature a real shaking up."

"So do I," I sighed. I had an impulse to tell Mary Winslow about the vice president's letter but decided against it; she was a bit of a gossip.

"I understand that deluded child has caused you some trouble."

I couldn't help but laugh. Though I had just decided I wouldn't discuss the Wallace letter with her, apparently she already knew. "She has," I admitted. "But what interests me is why. I assume it was not her idea to go to Vice President Wallace but her lover's. But why?"

"Curious," commented Miss Winslow, ignoring the question and altering the direction of our talk. "You know, I've known the vice president and his sister, the one who married the Swiss diplomat, since they were teenagers. He's always been fascinated by the bizarre. I rather think it's because his business was so bizarre. Imagine making a great fortune out of corn seed. A hybrid at that. Anything unlike something else has always been his cup of tea. Poor Paul," she added as she rose from her chair and mussed my hair with her fingertips. "I hope his letter wasn't too devastating."

"Oh, I'll survive," I said as I too rose. "But more importantly, on Nelson's behalf, as well as personally, I want to thank you for your efforts."

"Not at all, not at all. If there is anything I detest, it's injustice; and that letter from Henry was not only unjust, it was ridiculous. To allow himself to be deluded by that spineless child, too absurd!"

Although I had survived the Anna Cecilia incident totally unscathed, it did have an effect on me personally. Foxworth's early warning, "In this game you never know who your enemies really are," proved to have merit. But the incident also made me more resolute. I no longer felt any timidity about my work. With such powerful big shots behind me, why worry? They would come to my rescue even if I were guilty of a grievous blunder.

5

On July 19, 1941, President Roosevelt ended the voluntary blacklist program of anti-U.S. commercial representatives and business firms in Latin America and made it compulsory. A long and detailed list of certain blocked nationals with whom the United States was forbidden to deal in the interest of national defense was issued. Since the Rockefeller office voluntary program thus became official, Nelson's blacklisting activities were transferred to the State Department's newly created Division of World Trade Intelligence, and John Dickey (later to become president of Dartmouth), who had headed the Rockefeller program, was transferred to the State Department although he stayed on the Rockefeller payroll.

As a practical matter this, and another factor unknown to me and which I shall explain later, reduced the contact between the BSC and the Rockefeller office. It also meant a change in intelligence direction since in the same month, the COI,[1] headed by General William L. Donovan, was set up, and Stephenson of BSC much preferred to deal with Donovan than with Hoover.

In an odd sort of way, these shifts in British-U.S. intelligence affected me personally and suggested to me the wisdom of turning down an FBI counterintelligence request.

While all the foregoing intelligence shifts were going on, the Rockefeller office's advertising division went ahead with an elaborate project designed by Don Francisco (the Sunkist Orange man) to manipulate the Latin American press by means of the purchase of advertising space. Less inclined than his office should have been to seek State Department political guidance, U.S. diplomatic missions

---

[1.] The COI Office was the predecessor organization of the Office of Special Services (OSS)

were ignored. This caused friction. Sumner Welles, the under secretary of state, took the problem to the White House and on April 22, 1941, the president wrote Nelson Rockefeller a letter telling him to "take appropriate steps to institute arrangements for assuring that in all instances projects initiated by your office shall be discussed fully with and approved by the Department of State."[2] In other words, "clear things with Sumner."[3]

As a practical matter, Welles had thus killed Don Francisco's advertising project. In the midst of this debacle, an FBI agent, without previous warning from Foxworth who was in Latin America at the time, came to see me to ask that I cultivate Francisco's friendship, nick his typewriter, and search his office for incriminating pro-Axis material.

Instinctively, I recoiled. First off, the request hadn't come from Foxworth. Secondly, it was terribly risky. Francisco was an assistant coordinator. If I was caught and Nelson had to make a choice between Don Francisco and I of whom to sack, I knew it would be me. Finally, it would be very difficult. Francisco had a "secretary" who traveled with him back and forth from New York and stayed

---

[2.] This reversal, when combined with the reversal he suffered during his tenure with Overta Culp Hobby during the Eisenhower administration, had an important effect on Nelson. It convinced him that if he wished to become a really powerful figure in government, he needed something more than ability, energy, and family power. He required an electorate and thus political power. It was this that convinced him he had to become governor of New York. Meanwhile, Frank Jamieson, who had stayed on after the war as his public relations man, had tried to persuade him to run for mayor of New York, but was overruled. In my opinion, Jamieson was right.

Nelson, with his King Charles II's appetite for women and buildings, plus his ethnic and artistic interests, would not only have become very popular in New York City but would have transformed the city's skyline with monumental buildings and cultural projects that would have further contributed to its commercial and artistic supremacy. Instead, he lavished work in these fields on Albany, which, despite them, has remained dull and lifeless.

[3.] In November 1980 Walter Laqueur, editor of the *Journal of Contemporary History*, asked me to write an article for the *Journal* on Nelson Rockefeller and the British Security Coordination. It appeared in January 1981 in Vol. 16, #1, and was later included in the book entitled *The Second World War: Essays in Military and Political History*, published by Sage Publications of London and Beverly Hills, California, in 1982.

Later this article came to the attention of Mary "Todd" Rockefeller, Nelson's wife when he was coordinator of inter-American affairs. She pronounced it the only good article on the coordinator's office ever written and asked the author for five copies for the Rockefeller family's files.

with him at the Hay-Adams Hotel. Besides being pretty and bright, she watched him like a hawk and discouraged him from mixing socially with the other top officials in the office. If I took on the job, I'd have to figure out a way around her, and that wouldn't be easy.

As a result of all this, I simply said to the FBI man, "You know, you guys have to be careful. You don't kill the goose that laid the golden egg."

"I don't get it," he responded.

"What you're asking me to do is extremely risky. Don Francisco is no Matheson. He's a big shot."

"In other words, what you're saying is you don't wish to do it because it's too risky."

"Precisely. But if there is a real espionage crisis involved and Foxworth will explain it to me, I'll reconsider."

To my surprise, the agent accepted my reasoning in good grace, actually smiled, shook my hand, and left; and I breathed a sigh of relief. From that time on, I never heard anyone question Francisco's loyalty, nor did Foxworth ever raise the subject with me. In the back of my mind, of course, had been what Joe Rovensky had reported Stephenson saying about a Communist effort to cause trouble among the various branches of the U.S. intelligence network. I had no grounds whatever for supposing that in this instance the BSC, and in turn, the FBI, had become the dupe of a highly placed Communist agent on the British Intelligence payroll, but having already been a victim of the vice president of the United States being duped by a pretty Argentine girl's Communist lover, I was wary.

Sometime in 1941, I received what seemed to me a curious call from Nelson. "Paul," he said, "in twenty minutes the ex-king of England, now the Duke of Windsor and Governor of the Bahamas, will arrive at the curbside end of the sidewalk leading to the main entrance of our building. He is scheduled to confer with the Bureau of Foreign and Domestic Commerce's expert on the import of fresh tomatoes. I want you to wait for him at the curbside and escort him to the front door of the building and then up to the tomato man's room. Report to me immediately thereafter if he meets with or talks to anyone while en route as well as the nature of their conversation. If he asks who you work for, just tell him you work for me and that you were asked, as a courtesy, to escort him."

"Sure, Nelson. I'll be at the curb waiting. But am I to hang around and escort him back to his car?"

"No, the tomato man will do that."

"I understand."

The whole thing seemed such an odd request, I couldn't help but speculate: "Why me? Is Nelson extending his job as coordinator to the British colonies in the Atlantic? Not likely. Maybe he knows His Royal Highness socially and is just being polite."

This request was ultimately to prove to me the foolishness of someone at my level to speculate when asked to do something odd. "In due time you'll know. Meanwhile, do the job and relax with it." In this case, I later found out that President Roosevelt had asked the FBI to shadow the Duke and note any suspicious or pro-Axis conduct on his part when he was outside the British Embassy and to do it very secretly and discreetly. Apparently my "perfect cover" came into play, and I got the job between the Duke's limo and the tomato man. Also, it is noteworthy that this was the only counterintelligence job that came my way while working for Rockefeller on which he was fully briefed. The reason for this was that Foxworth and Hoover wanted to be sure that Rockefeller didn't sidetrack me with some other request. In all other cases, Nelson was never told the details of this type of covert work. He was simply given the general picture by Hoover and BSC's Stephenson. Wheels within wheels!

6

In January 1942, as a direct result of Pearl Harbor, an inter-American conference was held at Terradentes (tooth puller) Palace in Rio de Janeiro. The U.S. delegation was headed by Sumner Welles. The chief unachieved goal of the conference (Argentina remained neutral) was the unanimous break with the Axis powers by Latin America. Among other promises Welles made at the conference to achieve this was one made to the foreign minister of Bolivia that the United States would contrive to remove from Bolivia two powerful and malevolently pro-Nazi journalists named Quadros and Cespedes.

On his return to Washington, Welles tossed the problem into Nelson Rockefeller's lap and reminded him that he had a secret fund designed for just this purpose. At the first of Joe Rovensky's poker games after Welles' request, Nelson tossed the problem to me with the admonition that I would, of course, work closely with Jock Whitney, who was head of the office's Movie Division; Frank Jamieson, head of the Press Division; and a Bolivian advisor on the payroll. Because of the secrecy of the project, there were to be no files or interoffice memos, and Arthur Jones would release any funds needed for the project on my OK.

This was, of course, what was later to be called by the OSS and the CIA an operational intelligence project. But in these early wartime days, my associates on the project and I called it merely a Secret Fund Project. It never occurred to any of us that there was anything historic about the project from the standpoint of its being the first World War II operational project. It was merely a job to be done.

The day following my assignment to the job, I went to see Whitney's personal assistant who had worked with him on the production of the movie *Gone With the Wind* and suggested that he personally take over the problem of Cespedes. "The guy has worked for some magazines in Argentina as well as for some newspapers in Bolivia. Can you arrange for him to be invited to Hollywood by some movie magazine and then turn on him enough starlets to keep him both content and exhausted during his Hollywood stay? The FBI man in BA with whom I've already checked, reads him as a sort of sex maniac. We'll pay for his travel as well as his salary on the magazine if they won't do it."

"Only for his travel up here. We can get the magazine to do the rest."

"OK, but in fairness to his future employer, maybe you should warn them that the son of a bitch is a fucking Nazi and probably a vicious anti-Semite. That won't go down too well in Hollywood. Arthur Jones will handle the costs, just be sure you've got some chits to substantiate them."

"Consider it done, Paul."

Jamieson was another matter. The moment he learned that Quadros had been assigned to him, he decided the thing to do was place him on the staff of the *New York Times*.

"But Frank," I protested, "intellectually and behavior-wise, the guy belongs in some kooky isolationist rag like one of Father Coughlin's tracts in Detroit."

"Not on your life. This guy will get me an entree to the *Times*. I'll be able to make valuable contacts there through him."

"In other words, Frank, and forgive my bluntness, you plan to use Quadros for your own ends, not in the interest of this particular project."

"Exactly! The guy is no good. Why not make him useful? I'll handle it. All you need to do is see that he gets a plane ticket direct to New York and enough cash to see him through to his first paycheck."

"OK, Frank, but for the record, let me say I see nothing but trouble ahead."

"At times, Paul, you can be a real shit."

A month later, I got a call from Iphigene Ochs Sulzberger, the owner of the *Times*. She explained that she had learned from her man in Washington, Arthur Krock, that I was a thoroughly decent man. He had met and talked with me at a party given by the Hellmans. Quadros, she said, had been a constant source of trouble since he went to work for the *Times*. What should she do?

"Fire him at once," I said, "and tell him to take the train here and come to my office in the Commerce Department building. I'll clean up the mess. Sorry you've had to get mixed up in it. Meanwhile, I'll tell my boss, Jamieson, to call Arthur Krock who can, if he wishes, explain to him what has happened."

That afternoon, Jamieson tried to call Krock. His calls were all refused. Meanwhile, I went to Whitney's office to ask his assistant, Alstock, to send Quadros out to join Cespedes in Hollywood doing similar work. Eighteen months later the two men returned to La Paz, Bolivia. They were no longer pro-Nazi. Hollywood, via Whitney's Francis Alstock, had worked its magic; and Bolivia, the Allies' important source of tin, was no longer afflicted with Nazi journalists advocating Bolivia's neutrality and the sale of its tin to both Axis and the United States, all for the good of the Bolivian workingman.

Meanwhile, another little job had come my way direct from Nelson's office. General Ubico, the dictator of Guatemala, was building a huge and highly decorated new capitol building in Guatemala City. It required elaborate large brass doorknobs and back plates, which could not be made due to rearming shortages. Could I get them for the general? As a matter of foreign policy at that time, the friendship of the general was considered vital. People remembered the Zimmerman telegram during World War I, the German intrigue in Mexico, and Pancho Villa's raids into Texas. History might repeat itself. Accordingly, the United States must have an ally on Mexico's southern border so Mexico could be squeezed simultaneously from both the north and the south if necessary. I was therefore to get in touch with the brass doorknob manufacturers and persuade them to find the necessary metal regardless of shortages.

This wasn't easy. Essentially, after prolonged talks with the brass people, I had to draft a letter from Rockefeller and deliver it personally. Thus, General Ubico got his doorknobs. For some reason I was told not to tell Jamieson what I was doing and had to lie to him to account for the time lost, which included a trip to Connecticut as well as conferences with State and U.S. Army people on the policy behind the need of Ubico to get his doorknobs. The whole thing seemed somewhat silly to me but is an example of the detail behind a secret foreign and military policy decision.

7

The next counterintelligence project, as distinguished from operational intelligence project, in which I became involved, moved at such a slow pace that it took over a year before it was resolved. Operational intelligence involves engaging in secret activities abroad to remove people from the body politic or change attitudes whereas counterintelligence involves the actual catching of spies. The irony of it was that I profited from the friendship I was asked to cultivate. In fact, had it not been for his Nazi affiliations, which, of course, my victim was careful to conceal both in his conduct and conversation, and for the duplicitous conduct on my part, I would have been able to consider Roberto Lanas Vallencia a real friend.

At the time this assignment came my way, I felt neither revulsion in having to exploit my powers of dissimulation nor any fear of being caught out by Lanas. It seemed to me no more than a job to be done.

By this time, the United States had brought the Japanese to a halt at the Battle of Midway, and our victory, I had learned via the grapevine, was due to some sort of intelligence coup. This by comparison made my own little intelligence job more imperative. I'd already taken a swat at the Nips via Matheson; now it was time to take on the Nazis through Lanas.

Furthermore, I liked the idea that no one filled me in on any details about Lanas's Nazi affiliations. All I was told was to go after him. This nebulosity, in my eyes, was total proof of the professionalism in intelligence involved whereby everyone was on a need-to-know basis as a precaution against leaks. Thus the withholding of all details about Lanas confirmed to me the professionalism involved and suggested more heroic efforts on my part.

Foxworth didn't handle this case. He simply told me that Washington had a job for me and that I'd hear from them shortly.

I was in the process of lighting a cigarette when Foxworth told me this: I blew out the match and broke the cigarette in half. "Hey, what gives?" I asked, "I thought you were to be my contact, just as Stephenson is at BSC. What's up?"

"There's a lot up. The whole U.S. intelligence structure has been reorganized, as you know. Also, my supervision of the FBI's Latin American network has been shifted to Washington."

"Well, are you being shifted to D.C.?"

"I don't know yet. But I've told the director that you and I enjoy complete confidence in one another. He is aware of that, and you are to get in touch with me whenever you have a serious problem."

Two days later an FBI agent ambled into my outer office and told Mary Lou he wanted to see me. When he was ushered in and had shown his identification, I listened carefully to his instructions to cultivate Lanas's friendship and to report anything unusual to the FBI.

After the FBI man had gone, I walked into Jamieson's office to discuss some minor matter and found him totally distraught. He had a yellow legal pad in front of him and was holding a pencil. He was clearly trying to write something but couldn't. Instead, he was perspiring and his hand was shaking.

"What's the matter?" I asked, not unkindly.

Jamieson looked at the door to be sure it was closed. "I'm in a bind," he admitted. "Nelson has asked me to write a couple of paragraphs on U.S.-Latino relations for a speech for the president to give next Monday night, and I just can't do it. I'm in trouble."

"No you're not, Frank," I said. "Just relax and let me see if I can do it. If I can't, then you can try again. Nothing's lost. You've got time."

Frank gave me the White House memo asking for the paragraphs, and with the memo in my pocket, I walked out of the building and went to the State Department Library. My history training had come into play. In my eyes, Woodrow Wilson had been the greatest master of the English language in the history of the presidency. What I was looking far was a copy of Wilson's Mobile speech, which, as I recalled, dealt with Latin America. Once found, I used it for inspiration and turn of phrase and dashed off a couple of paragraphs. Back in the office, I edited it, typed it up myself, and gave it to Frank. President Roosevelt ultimately used it without a single change. "Now Paul," Jamieson had said when I had first given him the draft of the speech, "the only thing I ask of you is that you never tell anyone what you have done."

And thus my problems with Frank Jamieson subsided into a respectful working relationship. As Foxworth had originally told me, "You'll have to work out your relations with him your own way." As luck would have it, I finally had been able to do just that.

In my heart, I knew this was a meaningless victory. Jamieson was insecure, ambitious, and jealous by nature. Nothing would cure him of it. My little triumph would make my working life easier. That was to the good. But at the same time, I also realized that I wanted to make people like me because I liked people. And in this sense, the victory was phony. Jamieson, although he now respected me, would never like me. This stemmed from the deceit involved in my work.

However, I also realized that my appreciation of people was an asset. It enabled me to work on an Axis agent even if he was a villain. Punishing him was not my job. That was reserved for others. Mine was to collect supporting evidence that would lead to his conviction or to his confederates. What I found I had to do was simply stow the villainy in the back of my mind, go to work, try to win an agent's confidence, or alternatively, make him believe I was a nice friendly guy but also a fool and his dupe. The British had been right when they considered my acting ability a significant qualification. As the reader will discover, even Commander Hopkinson, my chief in the later stages of the war with Japan, in his typical offhand way, found it a worthwhile qualification.

Before this truce between Jamieson and me was effected, a series of hilarious incidents occurred that are worth describing, if only to elucidate the complications of my position as a secret agent while working for a man from whom my secret work was concealed while, at the same time, working for a Rockefeller.

After a few months, our offices had been moved from the old State, War, and Navy Building alongside the White House to the huge Commerce Department building on Fourteenth Street. Before the move, Nelson had sent down from Wallace Harrison's architectural office in New York another architect to design the new offices. Nelson paid for the cost of this himself.

This architect suddenly appeared unannounced one day at my desk and said that Mr. Inglis, the Rockefeller family historian had told him to interview me about my work. I talked with him in an offhand, bored way and totally avoided mention of my secret work. If the conversation started to veer in that direction and he asked me any questions about the secret fund, I simply told him to go and talk with Arthur Jones about them. Unfortunately, he noticed the trick phone on my desk. This included a complicated little wood-framed box with four red and four green tiny lights plus four miniature levers that allowed me to call anyone in the office direct without going through an outside line. The top executives in the office all had them.

As he closed the interview, the architect announced that it was clear to him that I required a private office. I forgot about the whole thing until moving day when I discovered that, without permission from Jamieson, he had taken one third of Jamieson's new outer office and had built a partition so that I had a long, narrow private office wide enough to accommodate my desk, which was to be placed in such a way that my back would be to one-third of the outer office's window, which had also been portioned off and allotted to me.

But even this insult to Jamieson's prestige, as he regarded it, was not the end of the story. On moving day, it was discovered that my desk was too large to go through the narrow door to my new private office. Special workmen had to be summoned to take the desk apart and reassemble it inside my new office. This took a couple of days while Jamieson showered me with sneers and barbed insults, primarily about my family.

Unfortunately, one of his wife's best friends was a distant cousin of mine. Jamieson had thus met this very rich but hideously eccentric branch of my mother's family. Jamieson, of course, didn't know that I too shared some of his judgments about them since their eccentricities, in which they could indulge because of their wealth, surpassed belief. Mrs. Jamieson's friend's father, for example, after being divorced by a talented wife with good reason, had moved into a room at the Lotus Club along with a life-sized bronze statue of himself in the nude!

But the contretemps didn't stop here. The white walls of my new office were totally bare until I arrived for work one morning and found two paintings fastened to the wall, obviously from Nelson's extensive contemporary art collection. One was a Diego Rivera watercolor and the other a reproduction of a geometric painting by Mondrian. I asked Nelson's secretary why the art. "Oh," she said, "Nelson peeked into your new office the other night to see what it was like. He found the walls too bare for words, so he had the pictures sent down from New York and hung after everyone had gone home."

This seemed to me to be Nelson's way of compensating for Jamieson's fury over the loss of a third of his outer office and a third of its windows. Unfortunately, however, the gesture resulted in driving Jamieson into an even higher state of agitation since he himself had no pictures from Nelson.

The reader should at no time think I was letter-perfect in my work. On the contrary, I was totally indiscreet over one issue. The United States and the Soviet Union were now allies. That was OK by me. Russia's fight with Hitler meant the saving of thousands of American lives. But that didn't mean I had to be pro-Stalin. Jamieson, on the other hand, was a cynic. He wasn't pro-Communist. At the same time, he felt his primary job was to get Nelson a good press even if it meant, because of the influence of Communists and fellow travellers in the Newspaper Guild, hiring a clutch of them in the Press Division. I, on the other hand, although perfectly willing to have the Soviet Union as a wartime ally, was not willing to regard these new employees as any more than our radical elements.

Instead of reading the *Daily Worker* at home in order to note the twists of Communist policy, I read it at the office and often compared it with the captions and articles the Press Division was then turning out. There was a reason for this attitude. Both my mentor at Cambridge, G. P. Gooch, as well as my father were implacable foes of both Communism and Nazism. My dad, for example, had been in Berlin shortly after World War I and had been approached by the then Soviet ambassador to Berlin to go to Leningrad and examine Lenin after he had been shot and wounded. He refused with the biting remark that he had no intention whatever of treating a man "who shoots people simply because they own two pairs of shoes." Dad also read both Hitler and Stalin scientifically. He concluded that both were syphilitic and suffered from softening of the brain. After the war, when he was dead (he died in 1940), I was to find he had been right on both counts.

Jamieson never ticked me off about my radical elements joking, but Joe Rovensky did in a quiet way. Once, in the corridor, he asked me in passing why I was making such a production about the fellow travellers. "It's best to be discreet, Paul. A bunch of them got in to see Nelson and complained that you were a malevolent influence on Jamieson."

This didn't really stop me. I enjoyed the hostility, and in the Commerce Department cafeteria where I sometimes lunched I'd see them eating in a group and give me hostile stares. Foolishly, I relished it. Ultimately, and ironically, I profited from this reputation. My original immediate boss at the CIA turned out to be a former worker in the Rockefeller pressroom. I hadn't known him, but he knew of my reputation. He ultimately became the founder of the neoconservative movement after he became a professor of philosophy at Yale. Due to my reputation, we got along just fine.

8

That Saturday night, before I started cultivating a friendship with Lanas, I picked up Gloriella at her apartment near the Wardman Park Hotel and drove her to Constitution Hall, which was practically the only venue for cultural events in Washington at that time. I had offered to take her to dinner first but she declined. "Too much to do at the embassy," she explained. "I'll just have time to change and grab a bite at home."

The moment we were in the car together and the door was closed, I became conscious of her perfume. Gloriella said it was a Guerlain scent, Shalimar, and she loved it.

"In that case," I quipped, "let us emulate the noble Persians who screwed all day and saved the night for diversions."

"Shalimar Gardens," Gloriella retorted, equally quick on the uptake, "are not in Persia. They are in Lahore in India!"

Not to be squelched, I took her hand and squeezed it. She returned the pressure.

"Where are we sitting? You said over the phone you got these tickets at the last minute, and I know they are hard to get. The Philadelphia Symphony is a sort of big cultural event in small-town Washington."

"Well," I answered, "the White House gave them to me. I haven't even looked at where they are."

"Don't tell me we're in the presidential box. Oh Paul, you should have told me. I would have worn my jewelry."

"You don't need any jewelry, Gloriella. You're a knockout just as you are."

"Well thanks, but I still don't get it. I thought you worked for Rockefeller, not the White House."

"I do. But someone put me on a White House social list. That's how I met you."

"Not quite. I asked to be seated next to you. My friend at the Uruguayan Embassy changed the place cards at the last minute."

"Well, I wouldn't have been at that embassy dinner if it hadn't been for the White House. They put me on the list. Frankly, I hate it. I asked to be taken off, but Nelson said no. So here I am, and as of now I'm damn glad they refused to take me off the list."

"Do you really like symphony music, Paul? Somehow, you seem more the physical type to me. A good baseball game or a boxing match would be more to your taste."

"Do you?" I asked, ignoring Gloriella's question.

"Do you like classical music, I mean?"

"I do in small amounts."

"Well, if you get bored, we can always leave early."

Because it was an exceptionally balmy moonlit evening, we decided to smoke a cigarette during the intermission outside in the fresh air, across the street. In the park adjoining the Ellipse, I found a tree to lean against while we smoked.

"Well, how about it? Do we go back after our cigarettes? Or have you had enough?" I asked.

"But since we're in a box, people might notice and comment if we leave."

"Always the diplomat, Gloriella. Do you really like your work?"

"I love it. So would you if the alternative was living in Ciudad Trujillo."

"Why, is it that bad?"

"Here I can have privacy, total privacy at night. That would be impossible at home."

I looked at her searchingly. I wanted her to know that her comment about privacy suggested something. She returned my look. I tossed my half-finished cigarette to the ground, plucked hers from her fingers, and dropped it. Then I folded her into my arms and pressed her against me as I leaned back against the tree so she could feel how I felt about her. We kissed hungrily.

"Should we go to your place or mine?" I asked.

"Mine."

My car was parked nearby, and soon we were on our way. Gloriella's trust in the privacy of her life in Washington was misplaced, at least in so far as I was concerned.

Unnoticed by both of us, a handsome young man named William Remington, a graduate of Dartmouth and Columbia, an employee of the War Production Board had been sitting alone in the balcony of Constitution Hall. He had kept his eyes fixed on us, and when he saw us leave the Hall during the intermission, he had followed us and concealed himself behind another tree. He just had time to jump into his own car and follow us to Gloriella's apartment. In this way, he found out exactly where she lived. He had already been given my address.

9

Later in life, when some of the security restrictions on my work had been lifted and I could talk about some, but by no means all, of my work, I claimed that the period from November 1, 1942, to January 30, 1943, was the busiest and most nerve-wracking period in my life. As I liked to put it, "I joined the navy in order to get a rest."

Like so many tempests, it began as a gentle breeze. I was in a buoyant mood when I arrived rather late at my office on the first of November. I had stayed with Gloriella, until early that morning and had then gone home to shower and shave before going to work.

On arrival I went directly to Lanas deep in the Translating Section and introduced myself as a special assistant in the Press Division and told him I had a problem.

"Every once in a while," I explained, "I'm asked to supply a paragraph or two for a speech the president is going to give on Latin America. Since it will be a Roosevelt speech, this means it will be translated hastily into Spanish and Portuguese by the various newspapers and wire services in Latin America. You yourselves do it and also send it out in advance to our offices in Latin America.

"But the problem is this. Because of the haste involved, I'd like to avoid, if possible, the use of English words that might be mistranslated and thus have their meanings inadvertently changed. What I wonder is, could you give me a list of English words the use of which I should avoid? No hurry, take your time, but when and if you have a list call me, and then maybe we could have lunch together and discuss it.

Lanas's face combined a look of intense pleasure and puzzlement. Was he pleased that I had sought him out for assistance or pleased, in a more sinister way, that I might inadvertently drop some secrets of value to the enemy? And what was the puzzlement? Did he not understand what I was attempting to get across? In any case, I decided to prolong the discussion. After all, it was a crucial moment in Lanas's life. If he rose to the bait and allowed himself into a working relationship with me, which I in turn could guide into a personal one, he was hastening himself to his doom. I didn't wish to face the possibility that it could go wrong.

"I'll explain to your boss, Rivera, that I've asked you to do a little work for me. He told me, by the way, that you got a Spanish Embassy scholarship to a university in Spain."

"I did," Lanas admitted. "But it hadn't fully recovered from the Civil War. Now, of course, it's different."

"Maybe I should give you a couple of examples of what I have in mind, just to be sure," I interjected. "Take the words *wait* and *hope* in English. They have different meanings in our language, but in Spanish to wait is to hope, and there is little distinction so that the use of these two words in English for rapid Spanish translation is best avoided. Another cruder example would be the word *child*. Spanish insists on distinguishing the gender of a child. We do not; so for translating purposes it's best to avoid the word or a boy child could turn into a girl child or vice versa."

"I've got it," Lanas exclaimed. "You've been totally clear. Perhaps tomorrow or Thursday we might lunch together and discuss the list of words I shall prepare."

With this as a basis, the friendship between the two of us evolved. I found two curious things about him. He was intelligent and disciplined, though clearly underemployed as a translator. I wondered why. Also, he seemed to have plenty of money. He lived alone in a rather high-rent area off Connecticut Avenue near the French Embassy. He drove a good car and wore nothing but tailor-made suits of good worsted material. The patterns were sometimes a bit brash, clearly the work of a Catalan tailor in Medellin or Bogotá, not that of a London tailor, but the suits were well-cut and expensive.

"He's got a checking account at the Riggs Bank," I told the FBI. "It might be worthwhile to run a check on his deposits. He's certainly not living on his salary."

"Meanwhile, my relationship with Gloriella had assumed a routine, but it was she who set aside Thursday as our night. I would pick her up at seven thirty and take her to a good restaurant for supper; then we would return to her place where I would spend the night. During one of these nights, she asked me if I knew a young man named Remington. He was, she claimed, well-educated, but she felt, lacked fire. It was as if he reserved his passions for causes rather than for a woman.

"No, I don't know any Remington. The only thing of this name I know is a typewriter. But how did you meet him?" I asked.

"It's a funny story," she explained. "The other morning my car wouldn't start. I park it on the street, you know. And this man, Remington, came out of the building and asked me if he could help. So he tried, and it still wouldn't start. And then he said, 'You must be late for work already. Why not let me drive you?' Well, he's real cute, sort of clean-cut and fresh, and I said, 'Surely you don't want to drive me all the way over to Sixteenth Street and the Dominican Embassy.'"

"So I got in his car, and all the way over he kept asking me about you. How long had I known you? What did you do? Were you some sort of secret agent? Funny stuff like that. The odd thing was, of course, that he knew I knew you."

"What did you tell him?"

"I told him you were a special assistant to Nelson Rockefeller and that you were sufficiently important so that you got White House box seats to the Philadelphia Orchestra. After all, Paul," she commented, "you never talk about your work, and what else do I know about you?"

"Well," I laughed, "you know what I'm like in bed. But seriously, do you really think he's moved into your building, or was that just a come-on?"

"I just don't know. I could ask. But I have a curious feeling that he doesn't, and I also think he may have tampered with my car so it wouldn't start because when I came back home that evening it started perfectly."

When subsequent events caused me to reflect on Gloriella's original story about Remington, its only effect originally was to bind the two of us together. My response to it at the time was totally sexual. There was too much involved for me to let it go beyond that. Although I was a total devotee of Talleyrand's maxim that "No man could equal a woman in serving the interests of a friend or lover," and while Gloriella would undoubtedly, if asked, go to work on Remington and find out exactly what he was up to, I felt I could not risk it. She would find out, but she would also report the incident to Generalissimo Trujillo, the dictator and benefactor of the fatherland. It was a pity in a way. For Remington's curiosity about me, done in the early stages of his work for the Soviet Union, if it had been squashed hard by Gloriella, might have made him wise to the dangerous path he was following and might ultimately have saved his life.

It was at this juncture that the FBI called to say that Lanas was about to be drafted and that I should get him an occupational deferment. "Once in the army, he will become useless as a lead to any confederates."

This request put me in a quandary. My overt occupation as an information specialist hardly endowed me with enough power to be persuasive to a draft board. If I asked my overt boss, Jamieson, to do it and at the same time withheld the reason, I knew he would refuse. If I asked Rockefeller and explained why, he would probably demand Lanas's instant dismissal. If I discussed my problem frankly with Foxworth, he would go to Nelson and would suffer the same defeat. If I went to the chief of the Translating Office, he would unquestionably wonder why I now sought a draft deferment for someone I had previously instructed him to restrict to unclassified material.

It was thus clear that I had to bluff my way out of this one, skip over the appropriate officials, and go directly to the chief of personnel and permit no questions as to why a deferment for a lowly translator was essential and, if so, why my request was not supported by his superiors. I did this, and in a peremptory and authoritative manner, demanded a deferment. It worked! Lanas got his deferment. But there was some fallout.

Shortly thereafter, I lunched with Lanas. His draft problem was not mentioned. Instead he suggested I move into his large apartment with him, rent-free. Here my inexperience prevailed. No one had ever given me the slightest instruction in intelligence work. I had merely fallen into it as someone might fall into a shell hole in the dark, as indeed happened to me later in Manila shortly after its recapture from the Japanese. I failed to tell the FBI about the invite. It never occurred to me that the FBI would want me to move in with a foreign agent with securing information as the object in view. I had merely supposed that the bureau's demands of my overtime were limited to occasional nighttime sallies in order to nick typewriters and do other similar minor chores, plus an occasional lunch.

I thus declined the invitation as politely as I could and never told the FBI about it. But much to my surprise, a week later Lanas asked me to drive down to North Carolina with him for his wedding. This second invite put me on the alert. If he had invited me to move in with him a week before, he could hardly have expected me to move out two weeks later in order to make room for his bride. Or did he plan a protracted honeymoon? Not likely! He either had in mind my elimination during the proposed motor trip or an information indiscretion while he lubricated me with drugs or liquor or both. Hence, I finally unburdened myself to Foxworth and added that I thought it might be dangerous to accept. He agreed at once, but I found his ready acceptance of my argument ambivalent. If information on Lanas was vital, as I supposed it was, why had Foxworth not said he would go to Nelson Rockefeller to try and get him to persuade me to change my mind? Nelson knew I was a point man in his shop for the BSC-FBI arrangement. But I now realized that neither the FBI nor the British had any intention of filling him in on operational details. He too was on a need-to-know basis. This conclusion was proven correct very shortly thereafter when, under far more ominous circumstances, I was asked to move in with another foreign agent. This time, as I shall explain later, all three top officials who had jurisdiction over my secret work had either been briefed or were present. Perhaps the FBI had wrongly deduced that my earlier refusal to take a motor trip with Lanas was not due to inexperience but because I had no intention of risking my life unless the top officials involved were fully informed and approved of the assignment, or alternatively, they already had in mind this future assignment. I will never know, and at the time, I couldn't have cared less. As things developed, I was too preoccupied to give the matter further thought.

10

I had lunch alone after a talk with Lanas, and when I got back to my office, I found an unsigned note on my desk: "Go home and pack a small bag with fresh linen, razor, toothpaste and toothbrush, and go to room 323 at the State Department." I asked Mary Lou who had left the note. She didn't know since it had been placed on my desk while she was out to lunch. Jamieson wasn't in his office, so there was no asking him.

So, still wondering whether it was some sort of practical joke, I showed up as directed at State. To my relief I found a young Foreign Service officer waiting for me. We shook hands, and the officer asked me why the bag.

"I was told to bring some clothes," I explained.

"Oh, that was because whoever left instructions for you didn't realize what a high-security rating you have. Originally there was some talk of you having to be locked in here at night. But that won't be necessary."

"Do you mind telling me what this is all about?" I asked, slightly irritated.

"Look, why not sit down at that desk, which by the way is yours, just like this office. I'll pull up a chair. Meanwhile, you might care to call your office and give them your extension here. You'll be here nine to five for at least four days."

I did as had been suggested, still mystified.

"Now," said the young man, "here's the scoop, and it's highly confidential. In fact, it's as secret as just about anything can be. The United States is scheduled to land troops in North Africa on November 8. This operation is called Torch and technically involves the invasion of some neutral countries. Under Secretary Welles has thus sent cables to all chiefs of mission in Latin America, instructing them to ask the chiefs of state, to whom they are accredited, to cable President Roosevelt, saying in effect, 'Congratulations! What you are doing is a fine thing for the cause of liberty and freedom.'"

These cables, due to the time difference in Africa, should start arriving at the White House by noon of the eighth. Both Mr. Welles and President Roosevelt want his answers to these cables to go out no later than an hour after the incoming congratulation messages from the Latino chiefs of state arrive. Because of this press of time, you are to draft the president's replies to the incoming cables and have them approved by Mr. Welles no later than 5:00 PM on November 6. There is one exception. Mr. Welles will personally draft the cable to Argentina. You are to do the other nineteen. Each of course must be different. Before they are finalized, you are to send them to Mrs. Halla, Mr. Welles' assistant, for a critique. She is totally familiar with both Mr. Roosevelt's and Mr. Welles' diplomatic style."

"Good God!" I exclaimed, "You mean I'm to write nineteen telegrams in answer to nineteen other telegrams that have not yet been received and each one must be different?"

"Precisely, and if I may say so, I find it totally humiliating and irregular that a complete outsider has been brought in to draft our own dispatches."

"So do I," I groaned. "But what I'd really like to know is whose idea was it that I'd be called in to do this?"

"I have no idea whatsoever." And with that somewhat acid comment, the Foreign Service officer left me and quietly closed the door behind him. I found myself totally alone and completely enveloped in silence. On the desk in front of me were a couple of lined legal pads and a few sharpened pencils, plus a three-by-five-inch card with both Mrs. Halla's and my own phone extension. In a corner of the room was a small table on casters holding a typewriter.

I sat at my new desk with my elbows leaning on it and my chin rested on my folded hands while I tried to pull my thoughts together. First off, I decided I needed a copy of the outgoing instructions from FDR to the chiefs of mission. Just as I was about to phone Mrs. Halla for it, the Foreign Service officer returned with an envelope marked "Top Secret-Eyes Only" and gave it to me.

"I'm to stay here while you read this," he explained, "and then return it to Mr. Welles' office."

I broke the seal and opened the envelope. It was the outgoing cable. I read it, memorized it, and then put it back in the envelope and surrendered it. "Well," I said. "I guess that does it. But before I do anything, I'd better go back to my own shop and close it down for a few days. Will I see you again?"

"I doubt it. It's your baby. Good luck. Sometime after November 8, we might have lunch. I'll call you back at the Rockefeller office."

I wrote nothing for twenty-four hours. First, I went back to my own office, called Foxworth in New York, and told him to sign off the Lanas case until November 8 as I had a job at State that made it impossible to associate with him until then.

"Cool it, Paul, that's impossible. You can work it out. I know you can. But I'm glad to hear they've put a torch in your hand."

"Yeah, and I'd love to know who did it."

"My lips are sealed, my friend. Incidentally, put it down on your calendar now, meet me at the Mayflower on November 9 at 1:45 PM, and don't be late. Also, be sure to wear a decent shirt and tie, and get a haircut. For someone with a British education, you sure can look shaggy at times."

"OK."

Next, I called Lanas and asked if by chance he'd have a complete list of words by nine o'clock in the morning. "You will? Fine! Just put it on my desk . . . No, I can't make lunch tomorrow. Something has come up out of the building for a few days, but I definitely want a rain check."

I then returned to State and buried myself in the library. En route, as I walked by the White House, I couldn't help but reflect on the irony of it all.

When I had first asked Lanas for the list of words to avoid, it was purely a ploy by which to establish a working relationship, which I could guide into a friendship. I hadn't thought in terms of ever using the list. Now, suddenly, it had become of real utility, and to compound the irony, its usefulness was so secret it could not be revealed. If Lanas ever asked if I had found the list useful, I'd have to lie and say, "Not yet, but I'm sure it will be sometime in the future."

At the library I hypnotized myself by reading for several hours State's diplomatic dispatches between the president and the U.S. ambassadors in Latin America; dispatches between U.S. presidents to the chiefs of state of various Latin American republics; plus speeches by FDR on the Good Neighbor Policy. Once I had memorized various phrases that caught my eye, and once I felt sufficiently hypnotized by what I had read, I went home to bed.

The following morning, after picking up Lanas's list of words, I went directly to my office at State, wrote three telegrams, and sent them to Mrs. Halla for approval. She rejected one by saying, "There's nothing wrong with it, but I feel in my bones Mr. Welles would not approve." I tried again and sent it forward with four more for approval. On November 5, I sent three more. All were approved. The next day I sent the remaining nine.

"May I go now, back to my own shop?" I asked.

"You certainly may. And I'll call you there to tell you the fate of all of them at the White House."

She called on November 8 to say that all nineteen were to go out exactly as I had written them. The following day, just before I was to leave for my appointment with Foxworth at the Mayflower, Nelson Rockefeller sent for me to tell me about a trip to Chester for a ship launching. Making chitchat, he then discussed with me the effect of the landings in North Africa on U.S.-Latino relations and asked if I had taken time to read the president's messages to the Latin American chiefs of state about the landings as reported in the press. Then he told me I should be guided by their content in any speeches I might have to draft in the future.

I gulped, and immediately realized that Nelson had not been told for what Welles had needed me. It took an effort at concealment. "Yes," I said, "I read them. Interesting, weren't they, the way the president connected the landings to freedom and democracy?"

"Indeed they were and in the president's inimitable style!" I then raced out of Nelson's office and grabbed a cab to the Mayflower. Unfortunately, I arrived ten minutes late. Much to my surprise, I found not only Foxworth but also Stephenson of the British Security Administration and J. Edgar Hoover himself, all waiting impatiently for me to show up.

"I'm sorry," I blurted out to Foxworth without thinking. "But I got held up at the office. Then I grabbed a cab and—"

"Go ahead, Kramer," Stephenson interrupted. "I'm anxious to hear the entire story of why America's master intelligence operative was late for an important meeting with his superiors. I'm sure there is a very good reason."

"Well, sir," I began. "On November 2 someone, and I don't know to this day who, told me to go to Room 323 at State. I was put to work on a top secret project that lasted until the seventh."

"And then?" Hoover asked, clearly amused by my embarrassment at being late.

"Then Mr. Rockefeller unexpectedly sent for me this morning. But to be honest, that meeting would have happened earlier had I not arrived at work late."

"Why?" Hoover demanded.

"Well," I sputtered, "because I had a heavy date last night."

"Was it this girl?" Hoover asked and passed me a glossy black-and-white photo of me kissing Gloriella under a tree on the Ellipse the night of the symphony concert.

I found myself too amazed to be able to do anything but mumble, "Yes, yes, sir. That's her". Meanwhile, I glanced at both Foxworth and Stephenson. They were grinning from ear to ear and clearly having trouble not roaring with laughter.

"And have you ever seen this man before?" Hoover continued while he passed me another glossy photo. It was of a young man emerging from behind another tree on the Ellipse.

"Yes, sir, and I imagine it's someone named William Remington. Gloriella has described him to me. He claims to live in her building, and he drove her to work the other day when her car wouldn't start. En route, he asked her if I was some sort of secret agent."

"And what did she say?"

"She told him I worked for Nelson Rockefeller and that I was on a White House social list."

"But you yourself do not know him?"

"No, but I've seen him once or twice before in the Commerce Department cafeteria lunching with one of our pressmen."

"That's all I have. All right, Foxworth, you can take over."

"I'd like to interrupt a minute, before you begin," Stephenson interjected. "Kramer," he said, "you came to our attention highly recommended by G. P. Gooch, and I would just like to say that you have more than fulfilled our expectations. The Matheson case was a superb bit of counterintelligence on your part, and the job you've just done for Welles was superb. It was essentially an operational intelligence propaganda project, and that's why you were assigned to do it."

I was totally incredulous. "You knew about that?"

Stephenson smiled. "I instigated it. I was in Nelson's office when the call came from Welles that he was shorthanded. Nelson wanted to send your overt boss, Jamieson, but I pointed out he didn't have a high enough security clearance, so Nelson called him and told him to send you with a suitcase so you could be locked away for the duration of the project. There was no other solution without revealing to Jamieson your high-security clearance. I hope your arrival with the baggage didn't make the State people think you were somewhat odd."

"No, they caught on right away and ignored it. There was only resentment that an outsider had been brought in to draft their own telegrams."

"Well, Paul, you're to be congratulated, and since the three of us have all had a few drinks at lunch, I'm going to suggest that Sam here fix you one."

Foxworth emerged from the tiny kitchen a moment later with the promised drink and motioned to me to sit on the couch next to Stephenson. Hoover gave me a moment to sample my drink and then spoke. This was the first time I ever met him personally, and events were moving so fast I had no time to analyze him except to note he had a mouth like a steel trap. "Kramer," Hoover said, "the bureau has a favor to ask of you, and I want to make it clear at the outset that if you consent to do what I shall ask you to do, it's purely voluntary. You do not have to do it, but the bureau is frankly shorthanded and has no one with the superb overt cover you have, which is necessary for the job. Also, I have asked Mr. Stephenson to be present so that he can assure you that under the circumstances he is happy to release you from any obligations you might have to his organization."

"As you are aware Kramer," Stephenson chimed in at this point, "the Rockefeller office has been downgraded to the extent that its economic warfare activities have been assigned elsewhere with the consequence that the Axis knows this and is now less interested in the coordinator's office."

I found I had nothing to say. I merely looked at Foxworth, who nodded in agreement with what Stephenson had just said. Hoover paused to give me time to swallow another drink.

"All right, Foxworth. You carry on," he said.

"Paul, the job isn't really dangerous. You'll be carefully watched by the bureau at all times. But we want you to move into room 456 at the YMCA near the White House. As you know, that's within walking distance of your office. Next door to your room is a young Nazi, inserted in the United States and sent to Washington with the express purpose of killing President Roosevelt. The young man is registered at the Y as Kurt Schmidt, and that may very well be his real name. We want you to become friends with this man to see if he will lead us to any confederates he might have here in the District. The job should last no more than three to four weeks."

At this point, I smelled a giant rat. The point was that all three men were acting totally out of character. Foxworth's voice had a different timber to it as if he were coding me a signal. Hoover's admission that the FBI was "shorthanded" was ludicrous. That man would never admit to anyone, including himself, that the FBI couldn't do the job it was legally designed to do. He was, I already knew, so careful of the FBI's reputation that he had his minions carefully expunge from the files any item that might reflect unfavorably on the FBI. As for Stephenson, that he was soft-soaping me was abundantly clear.

I had little time to puzzle all this out before accepting the job, but I deduced at the time that my friend-to-be, Kurt Schmidt was something special and totally apart from the Nazis landed by submarine on Long Island; that British Intelligence and not the FBI, had uncovered him and demanded of Hoover the right to name me as the man to cultivate him. Meanwhile, Stephenson had Hoover by the short hair, and he knew it. If he said no to the Paul Kramer assignment, a leak could mysteriously appear in the British press for a friendly American correspondent to pick up about a failure in FBI security arrangements and its rescue by the BSC.

Whether this deduction was true or false, I was never to know. All I did know was that, as I shall describe later, from the moment that Kurt Schmidt, which I'm sure was not his real name, and I strolled blissfully down Fourteenth Street toward my office in the Commerce Department building and was picked up by prearrangement by the FBI, he totally vanished. There was absolutely nothing in the press about his arrest, indictment, or, I assumed, execution after a trial by a military tribunal. Furthermore, years later, when photos and facts were released about the Nazi terrorists and their fate, Schmidt's photo was not among them. After the Public Information Act went into effect, I examined the FBI files. Nothing! But I knew there was a loophole here. I had been told in the beginning that my own White House file would be expunged. Also, because a portion of my work for Rockefeller was secret, if Schmidt's file was in Hoover's Latin American files, it would have totally disappeared. Hoover, in a perfect snit over his loss of Latin America when the CIA was created, had simply "deindexed" his Latin

American files, which meant that, because of their volume, they had became an amorphous mass of nothing.

The reader will simply have to figure out for himself what this little job was all about. I never could. Basically, I've always thought it was a perfect example of the old need-to-know syndrome where lowly agents on the totem pole of intelligence are simply held in the dark about the real nature of their work for "security reasons"; a phrase that can also include ludicrous and totally insane bureaucratic rivalries.

I gulped down the rest of my drink. "But what happens to Lanas?" I asked. After a pause, "Do you think I can cultivate both of them at the same time? I've already started with Lanas, and I can't drop it without fucking up the operation."

"You'll just have to do the best you can. As Mr. Hoover indicated, the bureau is short of men with a viable cover such as yours. And we know it works. Even your boss, Jamieson, hasn't stumbled into what you really do."

"I'm sure you can do both as well as your overt work for Rockefeller," Stephenson assured me.

"I'll do it gladly," I added. "There's no question about that. It's just a question of my capabilities. I hate to get stretched so thin I might make a mistake."

"You won't."

"What time do I check into the Y?"

"Tonight at 9:00 PM."

"I'll have to tell my roommate, Floyd McCaffree, something."

"We've already told him. He's secure, and he's agreed to scan your mail and phone calls to relay anything really important. Luckily he's on the Y's athletic committee so his presence won't arouse any curiosity."

"Well, I guess you've got me hooked. The only thing is, Mr. Stephenson, I wish you'd suggest to Mr. Rockefeller that my work for him might slide off and that, if so, I can't help it."

"I've already told him."

"Then I can consider it done," Hoover said.

"Yes, sir," I said. "Only one more thing. Who's my liaison on this?"

"As of now, I am," said Foxworth. "But if I'm pulled off for one reason or another, it'll be Mr. Hoover himself."

Hoover rose from behind the desk. They all shook hands with me and waited for me to leave the apartment and disappear.

During the meeting, the weather had suddenly turned cold and rainy. Regardless, I decided to walk back to my office. I had a raincoat and hat with me. That would keep me dry. Anyway, I wanted time to think without interruptions.

I found I was depressed and didn't feel any sort of charge as I usually did when I got a new assignment. I knew myself well enough to know it wasn't the weather, and it wasn't the prospect of leaving a comfortable apartment for the Y. After all, there was a war on.

What both bothered and saddened me was Stephenson's brief remark about the diminished role of Rockefeller in the war effort. That meant my overt job, as distinguished from my covert work, would also diminish. Under these circumstances, I should probably start looking for something else to do. I felt sure I could probably get a transfer to either State or the FBI, but that was no good. Every male in the family, for two generations and in three different wars, plus in some Indian fighting, had been in uniform. Dad had been in World War I and the Spanish-American War, and my grandfather had been in the Union Army during the Civil War. It didn't seem right to me to stay a civilian. My dad, along with his uncle and a cousin, was buried in Arlington, and my mom would be. But what to do was at the moment beyond my grasp.

By the time I reached my office I had decided that as soon as the Kraut project was over, I'd consult Foxworth and then make a move, provided Foxworth was still available to me.

I knew that Hoover was jealous of any recognition his employees received outside the FBI, and he was no doubt apprehensive that Rockefeller, or one of the giant companies the family controlled, would hire Foxworth away from the FBI once the war was over.

11

When I got back to my office, much to my amazement, I found an old Cambridge University friend sitting in my chair and flirting with Mary Lou. This scene of the two of them, responding to each other's charms, made me realize for the first time how beautiful she was. And the pity of it was she was leaving to work in the newly created press office in Brazil. Her aunt, with whom she lived, was giving a farewell party for her the following evening, and I had promised to go.

Tito Arias and I gave one another a warm *embrazzo* in the Latin American style. "Well," I said, "I see you made it out of Lisbon! You know, your father came to see me shortly after Paris fell to the Nazis and asked for my help in getting you a ship. There was nothing I could personally do, but knowing how much Secretary Welles admired your dad, I suggested he go and see him. It apparently worked."

"It did. I was on a ship a week later. Now I've come to ask your guidance on another matter. I was in New York last week and saw Basil O'Connor, President Roosevelt's former law partner and head of the Polio Foundation, and discussed my idea with him. He thought it excellent and told me to discuss it with the Rockefeller office. So here I am. Knowing what a big shot you are, I've come to see you."

"Come off it, Tito. I'm not a big shot and you know it."

"Well, you always had a way of slithering around the goal post before anyone knew you were there."

"Tito, out with your idea! Knowing you, it's either brilliant or a load of bullshit."

"My idea is really very simple. I travel around Latin America, causing an eruption of birthday balls, just like the ones held here in the United States, to raise money for the local treatment of polio and in honor of President Roosevelt.

His birthday is on January 30, so there's time if I leave right away. After all, Roosevelt, in Latin America's eyes, is the Good Neighbor Policy, and that's what this office is all about."

"And you have time to do it?"

"Not only time, but as you know, my father, because of our little communications empire, is a very active member of the Inter American Press Association, and they will back such a project 100 percent."

"And O'Connor approves and is supportive of the idea."

"Absolutely."

"Well, why waste time? Come with me, and let's go and see Nelson."

I carefully outlined Tito's idea to Nelson's secretary, who agreed to tell him we were both in the outer office and immediately available to discuss the project. Two minutes later, she emerged from Nelson's office to say, "No, Nelson doesn't like the idea and is too busy to see Arias at this time."

I turned to Tito and laughed. "Now you see what a big shot I am, Tito. But all is not lost yet! You go right over to Secretary Welles' office and see Mrs. Halla. I'll bet you ten bucks she'll shunt you into Welles, even without an appointment."

"But if he does, who puts up the money for my trip around Latin America?"

"You'll see. We do."

From this point on events moved with lightning speed. There were no conferences as there had been over the Quadros/Cespedes affair. Welles simply sent for Rockefeller, instructed him to buy the project, which he described as quite the best operational intelligence action the coordinator's office had yet financed and directed, and introduced him to young Arias. Rockefeller, furious, returned to his office and sent for me. He instructed me to handle the project myself. He wanted no part in it.

"How about Jamieson?" I asked.

"I'm going to tell him not to touch it. It's 100 percent yours. Arthur Jones will be told to validate each item of expenditure."

"OK, I've got it. Come on, Tito," I said as I turned toward Tito who was standing in the background, "let's get busy."

After we were out of Rockefeller's office and before we reached mine, Tito stopped in the corridor. "What was that all about? Why the anger?"

"It'll pass. Nelson is an empire builder. He doesn't like to be told by anyone else what to do."

"But will he ever forgive you? I'd hate to think I got you into any real trouble."

"Look, Tito, you've got your project. Now make it a success. Go and collect big shots in each country to serve on your birthday ball committees. Meanwhile, I can get our press division to support it, and you do what you can to publicize it in the local papers. Now we're off to see Arthur Jones, and I'll leave you with him. He'll explain his receipt system. Then come by in the morning, and I'll take you up to see Harry Frantz in the Press Division."

"Frantz, the United Press Latin American man?"

"That's who it is. He's with us for the duration."

"I know him well. Our paper is a UP subscriber."

"Fine. But remember after you have seen him you are not to set foot in this office. Officially, we have nothing to do with the project, and you can be damn sure that if anyone ever asks Nelson if he's behind it, he'll say emphatically he has nothing to do with it."

"I'm still bothered by what this whole thing may have done to you."

"Don't be. I'm presently working on two other projects that I handle personally. No one else in the shop can have anything to do with them, just like your birthday balls. The people here don't even know about them. But once all three are done, and that should be around January 30, Roosevelt's birthday, I'm getting out of here. See you tomorrow. I've got to clear my "incoming" basket before I head to the gym for a workout."

The next morning at ten o'clock, Tito and I went up to the newsroom to see Harry Frantz. This was after I'd spent the night at the Y and made my first contact with Kurt Schmidt, the German killer, while standing at a washbasin, shaving. In appearance, he turned out to be an ideal specimen of Adolf Hitler's noble Aryan—blonde, with a superb build, physically strong and muscular. But, as I was to discover later, he was not very bright. This latter characteristic was fortunate. It helped me in my work. He proved to be easily led. He was not like Lanas who was intelligent and thus far more difficult to cultivate. Perhaps the German fooled me, but I felt much more comfortable in my dealings with him than I did with Lanas.

It was odd. I was more meticulously dressed than usual. The grubbiness of my new living quarters, plus the essentially sordidness of Schmidt, encouraged me to be more meticulous about my appearance. It was a sort of declaration to myself of my ability to be totally independent of my surroundings, or as a friend of mine later put it, "Paul has the ability to fall into an outhouse and come out smelling like Chanel No. 5."

As I anticipated, Frantz grasped the essentials of the project at once and understood precisely what was required of his office by way of support, and I thus found for the first time that I could relax with the project and said good-bye to Tito in Frantz's office. Tito, in turn, was anxious to get back to New York to see O'Connor and tell him the project was alive and running.

An hour later, and after Tito had gone, I returned at Harry Frantz' request. "Sit down and pull up a chair, Paul," he said. "I'd like to talk to you. This project of yours, if it works, and that kid ought to be able to pull it off with all the contacts his family has in Latin America, is the best propaganda device this office has cooked up. Congratulations. Is Nelson against it?"

"Totally. So is Jamieson."

"No matter. It's a good one, but that isn't what I want to talk to you about. I should tell you that for years I've known the man who is now chief of naval intelligence, Captain Zacharias. I saw him just the other day, and he asked me if I knew someone in the shop named Kramer.

"I told him I did, but not well. 'Do you know what he does,' he asked me. I said that you were some sort of special assistant both to Frank Jamieson, head of the Press Division, and also to Mr. Rockefeller but that there was a lot of gossip in the newsroom that you had something to do with catching a Japanese spy named Matheson."

"'Oh,' he said, 'now I understand. Stephenson told me to keep an eye out for him, that he'd be perfect for ONI, and he should be available soon now that Rockefeller has been folded out of economic warfare into largely propaganda work.' So I told him I'd pass his interest on to you."

"Thanks Harry, thanks a lot. As you can see, this birthday ball project is somewhat out of the loop, which means I'll have to play nursemaid to it until January 30 next year. Also, I've got two other projects, besides my regular work, that will also keep me busy until then. But you can tell the captain I'll call for an appointment definitely after January 30."

Back at my office, I got a call from Lanas, who said that he had a few more words to add to his list.

"Fine," I said. "I'll tell you what. Mary Lou, my secretary, is leaving for Brazil next week, and her aunt is giving her a farewell cocktail party tonight, six to eight. Why don't you come with me? I'm sure no one will mind my bringing an extra man. I'm going to the gym after work, but you could meet me there at six, and we can go together, and you can give me your list of new words."

"You can . . . Fine. See you then."

My next call was to Gloriella to cancel our get-together the following night. I didn't tell her why; in fact, I couldn't very well tell her that I was working on the Kurt Schmidt case. Gloriella didn't take it well. She decided I had found someone else. Thus, I was caught up in the secrecy and duplicity of my work. I did the best I could and promised Gloriella without fail that we would meet the following Thursday. She accepted that, and when I was again forced to cancel that rendezvous, it was the end of the affair with Gloriella. She simply refused to talk to me.

Meanwhile, my two counterintelligence projects rocked along and in shape. Lanas had invited me to his wedding in North Carolina. I begged off due to the press of work. Kurt Schmidt and I palled around, drinking beer in bars at night. The German had clearly become dependent on me for relief from his isolation. Occasionally I asked him to come to the office and go out to lunch with me.

The only thing he had revealed to me was that he carried a dagger in a sheath fastened to his leg below his knee and concealed by his trousers. "This," he explained one night, "is to protect me from all the blacks and thieves and foot pads in Washington."

Meanwhile, Basil O'Connor had called from New York to ask me to breakfast at the Carlton Hotel in Washington the following Monday. He was bringing with him a sheaf of news reports about the progress of plans for the polio balls in Latin America to show the president, and was ecstatic about them. We met as scheduled, and O'Connor told me he was sure the White House would ask me to write a paragraph or two to append to the usual birthday radio address of the president, thanking one and all for their support in the treatment of polio.

The night after this breakfast my relations with Kurt Schmidt reached something of a crisis point. It began harmlessly enough with supper at a disreputable bar along Pennsylvania Avenue.

Afterward we lingered over several beers. It was curious. Schmidt reminisced about his childhood in Detroit. He said that his father had immigrated there to work in the Ford Motor Company's River Rouge plant, and that he had spent carefree childhood years as well as gone to school there. What he didn't reveal was that when he was ten his family had taken him back to Germany. They decided they didn't like America. But I found it worth noting that he could reminisce so happily about a childhood spent in Detroit. Later, after a few more beers, Kurt complained that he needed a woman and asked me if I knew where to go.

"Of course, Kurt. The Hopkins Institute. I use it all the time. It's good but fairly expensive."

"Can you take me there?"

"Look, Kurt," I explained, "I've got a good-paying job, and as you've explained, you are still waiting for your job to come through at the Bureau of Engraving and Printing. I'll take you there on the condition that I pay. Then when you get on the payroll, you can pay. Is it a deal?"

"Deal!"

Kurt's knowledge of English even included slang, which made me suspect that this had been the basis for his selection, and his killer capabilities had been superimposed on this.

Our visit included some more drinking, whiskey this time, so that by the time we left, I was drunk and out of money. We simply had to walk back to the Y. It was over two and a half miles. Kurt came into my room and collapsed on the floor with his head and one arm resting on my bed. The outing had paid off. The long walk back had sobered me up somewhat; meanwhile, ever mindful of work the following day, and in order to avoid a hangover, I took a glass from my bureau and went to the bathroom for a long drink of cold water.

When I returned, I found that Kurt was sobbing his heart out.

"Hey, Kurt, what's the matter?" I asked softly.

"I don't know what I'm going to do. I'm short of money, and my job hasn't come through. My family in Detroit was supposed to send me some more, but I can no longer reach them by phone."

"The family in Detroit" was presumably his fellow conspirators who were to signal him when to carry out his mission. Kurt didn't know they had already been rounded up, which was why his orders from the leader to execute his mission hadn't come through. Meanwhile, the delay had caused him to run out of money.

"Well," I suggested, "if you can't and you're out of money, you can always join the merchant marine. God knows with the war going on they need people. All you have to do is go to Lower Manhattan to the Seamen's Home, and the people there will see you go to the right place to get hired. You might also find a ship in Baltimore, but you'll have a wider choice of ships in New York. If you need the bus fare to New York, I'll lend it to you."

"Do you think maybe I could find a ship to Spain or Portugal? I don't want a ship to Russia. I hate Communists."

"A ship to Spain; that would be good. I just don't know, Kurt, but you can always try."

The next morning I called Foxworth, who turned out to be somewhere in Latin America and hence, unavailable. I then called Hoover and, to my astonishment, got him on the phone almost at once.

"Yes, Kramer."

"My friend here at the Y is beginning to panic. He says he's almost out of money and tried to call his parents in Detroit but couldn't reach them."

"How did you find that out?"

"He told me after we both got drunk and had a night on the town." "Where?"

"At the Hopkins Institute on Connecticut Avenue."

"Did you watch him?" When it came to sex, Hoover's interest picked up considerably.

"No, sir. We had separate rooms, but his girl said he was sensational. Then we had a couple of drinks, and he went at it again."

"Then what?"

"I was out of money, so we stumbled back to the Y together."

"And?"

"I went to get a drink of water. He was in my room with his head on my bed. And when I got back, he was sobbing. It was a real drunken crying jag. That's when he admitted he was broke. The Hopkins was my treat."

"So?"

"He asked me what he should do, and I told him if he was broke to go to New York and sign on as a merchant seaman. I offered to lend him the fare to New York if he needed it. The interesting thing is he asked if I thought he could get a ship to Spain or Portugal as a deckhand. He said he didn't want to go to the Soviet Union. He hated Communists."

"Good work. I'll be back to you in an hour. Stay in your office."

"Yes, sir. But I'm scheduled to lunch with Roberto Lanas at the Willard Coffee Shop and don't wish to cancel. Because of Kurt, I've been neglecting him. There's no problem if you reach me before noon."

True to his word, Hoover himself called back within the hour. "OK, Kramer," he said. "Take your friend to the Willard Coffee Shop for lunch at twelve noon. Then invite him back to your office, and we'll pick him up on the way on the southwest corner of Pennsylvania Avenue and Fourteenth Street. When that happens, just keep walking."

"OK."

While this conversation was going on, Harry Frantz dropped in with a sheaf of newspaper reports from Latin America on the progress of the birthday balls and gave them to me.

"My god, Harry. He's even got two balls scheduled in BA. Both of the committees read like the Social Register."

"Yes," Frantz admitted. "The Argies want to show what good neighbors they are even if they refuse to declare war on the Axis. But anyway, your secret operation sure looks like it's going to be a resounding success."

"Thanks, Harry. I've been sending your press summaries to Basil O'Connor in New York, and he's ecstatic. He tells me the White House plans to ask me to write a paragraph or two on the balls in Latin America to add on to Roosevelt's annual birthday ball speech."

"I'm sure you can do a good job of it."

"Maybe. But the trouble is I feel as if I'm stretched to the breaking point on the rack. You see this rash on my arm. I went to see the doctor about it yesterday. And you know what he told me? 'It's nervous exhaustion,' he said. 'You're working too hard. And since you can't quit, you should make a point of having lunch alone every day for the next month.' I can't do that. So what I'm going to do after January 30 is join the navy."

"In that case, remember what I told you about Zacharias."

"OK, Harry. Meanwhile, what you can do is tell him I'll call for an appointment on February 2 or 3. If he wants to know more about me than what Stephenson has told him, you can tell him to call Percy Foxworth who used to head the New York office of the FBI and is now in charge of the FBI in Latin America."

"So that explains it," Frantz commented, giving me a sharp look while his eyes widened.

"Explains what?"

"Well, it's common talk around the shop that you had something to do with Matheson's arrest. Even Jamieson has admitted that. But as a former reporter, my guess is that your intelligence involvement is far deeper than what even Jamieson suspects."

"It's a strange, clumsy world, Harry," I said. "I don't like to kid myself. In a way, especially for someone as young as I am, I guess I've been sort of a minor star in this office but so remote in space it's been more as if I'm some sort of stellar fragment lost in the firmament."

As soon as Harry Frantz got back to his desk, he wrote down what I had just said and then called his friend Zacharias and repeated it to him.

"Don't tell him," Zacharias said, "but I've already got a job for him." Harry ignored his injunction and told me what he had done and what Zacharias had said.

There was only one fallout from the birthday ball project. I was walking by the White House on my way to the gym one day when I ran into Hutch Robbins, a relative of President Roosevelt and our liaison at the White House. He stopped me to ask if by any chance I knew why the president of Haiti had sent a large check to President Roosevelt and the Haitian ambassador was impatiently waiting for a "thank-you meeting." No one on the White House staff could figure it out.

"My God, Hutch," I said. "That's for the money raised at a polio birthday ball held in Port-au-Prince in honor of President Roosevelt. The money raised was supposed to be spent locally for the treatment of polio, not sent to the White House."

"I don't believe it," Robbins said, clearly annoyed both by the fact that I knew all about it and he hadn't been told.

"Well, if you don't believe it, call Basil O'Connor in New York. He'll tell you."

Hutch went off back to the White House, clearly annoyed, but there was nothing I could have done. The project had been secret in so far as our office support was concerned, so that I couldn't have briefed Robbins about it. This is a perfect example, in a relatively minor way, of the confusion that can arise even within the high levels of government, over operational intelligence projects.

The day before I left my office for the scheduled interview with Captain Zacharias of the navy, I decided I needed some personal advice and consulted Wallace Harrison, the famous architect and a family friend of Nelson as well as an assistant coordinator. Also, I knew he had served in the navy during World War I.

I explained to him that I had been led to believe that a scheduled interview with the navy's chief of intelligence would probably lead to a commission in the navy and the waiving of two physical defects, my height and my eyesight. Furthermore, my draft status was no problem since I was sure I could get a deferment from other agencies with whom I worked secretly and with which I assumed he was familiar. If the navy commission was offered, I asked him, should I resign from the Rockefeller office and accept it?

Harrison's answer was immediate and direct.

"Paul," he said, "take it. If you don't, you'll regret it for the rest of your life."

This reassurance was all I needed to face the interview with Zacharias the following day.

My departure from the Rockefeller office was as graceful as it could be. The navy, at my insistence, gave me sixty days to notify Nelson Rockefeller that I was leaving and close down my shop. I gave the FBI sixty days to find a substitute far me regarding Lanas. As far as I know, they never did, but they arrested him and convicted him of espionage soon after I left. This I learned from the *New York Times*. Frank Jamieson and his wife, Linda, gave me a lavish farewell party at their home. Nelson and a few of the big shots came. But by this time, I had lost interest in the office, and everyone seemed remote, and the farewell, perfunctory. I had to hang around until the last important guest had left, and when I finally did get ready to go, Frank Jamieson came up to me and made a pretty little speech.

"You know, Paul," he said, "you really achieved for yourself a unique position in the office. In the beginning, I thought you were a real shit. But I learned otherwise. Your achievements were special."

Just how many of my real achievements was he aware of? I asked myself as I pecked his wife on the cheek in a farewell kiss and left.

What, I asked later, had I learned? I'd learned a lot—not only some of the basics of the craft of intelligence, but more importantly, how to function while working among men who enjoyed real power in the world outside government. Even the idiotic socializing among diplomats, which at the time I had hated, had paid off. From the diplomats I was picked up by some of the grande dames of Washington who liked to prove with their malicious gossip that they were in the know. From them I learned such intimate tidbits as "dear Franklin's" bizarre relationship with Eleanor and his mother, Sarah Delano Roosevelt. This sort of gossip almost always ended with a quote. In this case, it was Franklin's mother's first remark when she learned her son had been reelected for a second term: "Franklin! Save an embassy for Bertie Pell."

There was also "dear Winston's" biting remark about his daughter-in-law Pamela Digby Churchill, subsequently to become Pamela Harriman. Churchill was angry with Pamela because in wartime London she had gone off with Averell Harriman while his son was fighting in Yugoslavia with Marshal Tito. "Pretty, but squalid" was his description of her. Sometimes the gossip reached farther back in time. Thus, I was told about President Wilson's stroke and how Senator Borah led a group of senators to the White House to see for themselves the state of President Wilson's health. Borah, suspicious that Wilson was no longer able physically to carry on as president and in a rage over this, had ripped the sheets off the bedridden Wilson. "Wiggle your toes, wiggle your toes, Mr. President," the irate senator had cried out. There were those who claimed Alice Roosevelt

Longworth had put him up to it since she loved Borah. At any event, Daisy Harriman had later called Mrs. Longworth on the phone when she learned Mrs. Longworth was about to have a child. "What are you going to call it?" she had asked. "Deborah?"

All this socializing undeniably solidified my cover as an information specialist and provided me with a totally ludicrous and memorable incident. Todd Rockefeller, Nelson's wife at the time, called me one morning to ask if I'd ever heard of a Princess X. I've since forgotten her name. The princess, Todd explained, had invited Nelson and her to dinner, and she didn't know what to do about it. Who was she, and what should she do?

"Todd," I said, "I'm equally in the dark, but what I'll do is call Stanley Woodward, the chief of protocol at State, and see if he's got anything on her." This I did. Woodward asked for five minutes to consult his files and then called me back.

"What we've got is this," he explained. "The Princess is on the White House C list, which means she's invited to larger musicals and teas. Also, you should know that there's a penciled notation on our card file that reads, 'socially acceptable but somewhat pushy.'"

When I tried to relate this information to Todd, I heard strange gurgles and gasps at the other end of the line plus an occasional phrase that sounded like "Will she find out?" Once Todd got her voice under control, I asked her if something was the matter. "Well," she said, "after I called you, I thought I should really ask Nelson. So I called him, and he said the princess is his cousin."

It became so nothing fazed me anymore about the world's great, and later, in Latin America, I could glide through cocktail elegantes and embassy intimate dinners with aplomb. I found I could even introduce Juan Peron, of Argentina, to the woman who became his second wife, Isabelita, with perfect sangfroid despite the surrounding questionable circumstances.

This story is worth repeating since it gives a perfect picture of Argentina's periodic collapses into a total muddle. I was invited to join a former president of Panama and a medical friend of his, who advertised his skills in treating venereal diseases in the public press, at a local disreputable nightclub. Soon after I joined them, the club's manager came out and told me he was sending to the table, for me to meet, a new young girl, fresh out of Spain. He was sure I would like her. She turned out to be pretty, small, with a lovely, clear skin and shiny brown hair. She wore a small cross, which hung daintily just above her cleavage. The only trouble was that she was very superstitious and was always crossing herself when I did the wrong thing, like lighting a cigarette with my left hand. When I insisted on buying her a proper glass of sherry, she claimed that the stem of the glass wasn't right and hence, inauspicious.

A moment later Juan Peron arrived and joined us in a rage. I had never met him. He turned out to be different in real life from what his photo led one to believe. His face was pockmarked, and he had greasy skin and black hair and was somewhat of a grease-ball. Evita died, he had been overthrown, was in exile in Panama, and hated it. He launched into a tirade about how impossible Panama was.

Suddenly there was something of an exhausted silence, and I put in my two cents worth. "General," I said, "we all have reversals of fortune, and yours has been greater than most. But we have to carry on. What you have to do is get over Evita's death and find solace in another. Look at Isabelita here. She's cute and very pretty. You must first mend your personal life."

Isabelita, of course, from the moment Peron entered the scene, had forgotten all about me and was all eyes on Peron. It was like magic. They clicked, and he eventually married her and was restored to power in Argentina. He then died, and Isabelita found herself in charge. And what could poor, superstitious, ignorant Isabelita do but turn to a soothsayer for guidance? Thus was Argentina ruled for a while. When Andrew Lloyd Weber's musical *Evita* came out with the lovely song "Don't Cry for me, Argentina," I couldn't help feeling that the words were all wrong. They should have been "Please Cry for me, Argentina." What came afterward was much worse. Isabelita had no brains at all. Evita at least had some.

At this point, and in the interest of clarity, one must leap forward forty years when something happened that sheds new light on my Rockefeller years and supplies one with a logical explanation of the various things that had happened to me.

In 1980, there arrived on my doorstep in Georgetown a British military and intelligence writer named Ronald Lewin who had come to Washington to do research on his tenth book entitled *American Magic*. Lewin said he had sought me out for two reasons. First of all, he wanted to know all about the Rockefeller office's role in Latin America derived from British Intelligence from August 1940 until Pearl Harbor on December 7, 1941. Here I was in a position to help him, and we worked out a method by which I would write an article for the *Journal of Contemporary History*, vol. 16, no. 1, 1981, which he could cite in his forthcoming book and which would outline for the first time the details of the Rockefeller office's secret relationship with British Intelligence. For a variety of reasons, I didn't mention my own personal role in the matter, but I did have Paul Nitze, who was then a U.S. delegate to the Strategic Arms Limitation Talks Agreement "vet" the article since it had been he who had written the executive order that created the Rockefeller office in 1940, and it had been he who had engaged in preclusive buying based on information supplied by British Intelligence to the Rockefeller office in its pre-Pearl Harbor days. Below is Nitze's letter of approval.

PAUL H. NITZE

1500 Wilson Blvd.
Arlington, Va. 22209

April 28, 1980

Mr. S. Paul Kramer
3023 Dent Place, N.W.
Washington, D.C. 20007

Dear Mr. Kramer:

I read your article with great interest, having
recently been asked on several occasions to search my
memory for facts on the very subject of the Coordinator
of Inter-American Affairs. I found not one thing I would
change in your article. Congratulations on what I
consider to be a very fine piece.

Sincerely,

Paul Nitze

It was also at this point that Lewin revealed to me how all the Rockefeller people, plus J. Edgar Hoover and almost all those up and down the intelligence ladder in the United States, had been hoodwinked by the British into supposing that all the information about pre-Pearl Harbor Axis penetration of Latin America had come from secretly opened mail intercepts. By no means did all of them come from the intercepts, and this was especially true of Axis agents I befriended and helped the FBI to catch. On the contrary, information about these types came from the breaking of the German code by the British. But this was such a deep, dark secret, especially in its early days, that only very few, such as General Marshall, knew about it. Stephenson of BSC knew, and this was why, according to Lewin, I had developed such a reputation in British circles while at the same time Hoover and Foxworth had been kept totally in the dark about the real sources of the information on which my work was based.

While Lewin and I discussed all the ins and outs of these deceptions, he would continually interrupt our talk with "Come on, Paul, you must tell me what you know about Tricycle. After all, Tricycle had a great impact on your work and was most certainly a reason why you were enticed by Zacharias to leave Rockefeller and work for him."

"That may be true, but I certainly never knew about it."

"You must! You have simply forgotten."

"I didn't and I haven't forgotten."

At this point, we must now digress again from my own role as a secret agent and dip into the far murkier milieu of a double secret agent. Tricycle was the British code name for a sophisticated Yugoslav gentleman named Dusko Popov who, as a secret agent, belonged to the BIA section of the British counterintelligence department of MI5, just as I belonged, while on the White House payroll, to Rockefeller. Popov, however, as a businessman in Portugal, contrived to get himself hired by the Abwehr and thus worked for them while at the same time reporting everything he did for them to his British principals.

In August 1941, the Abwehr sent Popov to the United States (note the date-four months before Pearl Harbor and a year after I was hired by the White House) with detailed instructions in microdot from his Nazi "masters" to find out about U.S. lend-lease arrangements with the British, U.S. aircraft production, convoy organization as well as very detailed information on Pearl Harbor installations. In fact, this was the first time that the British discovered that Germany's spy network was willing to do work for its Japanese ally, just as, thanks to me, it was found that Japan's spy network was willing to do work for Nazi Germany.

But the significance of all this for me personally was that although the British, via Stephenson at BSC, had dutifully warned J. Edgar Hoover of Popov's arrival and mission, Hoover totally botched his end of the job and thus missed a possible early warning about Pearl Harbor. Actually, as I explained to Lewin, the only thing I ever got from the FBI about Tricycle/Popov was an incomprehensible casual remark from one of Foxworth's FBI agents whom I worked with that there was British agent floating around D.C. (did I know him?) whom the "director totally distrusts because he likes to have sex with two women at the same time! Ha-ha!"

Nevertheless, via Lewin, it finally became clear to me that Tricycle had in fact impacted on me because the British, as a result, totally lost confidence in Hoover; and Stephenson, from then on, preferred to work with Donovan and the recently created OSS while at the same time insisting that I handle Lanas and the Kraut maneuver plus the Torch project at State and finally continue my work with them via Holmes-Hopkinson in Brisbane and Manila.

Furthermore, it even gave a pattern to my subsequent work with the navy and with the CIA work where Captain McCollom hired me at a very high salary and said he knew all about my navy work in the Pacific, with emphasis on *all*, the details of which the reader will learn about in the succeeding pages of this book.

PART II

The Navy; Boulder, Colorado

12

I timed the interview on my new Concord watch. It lasted exactly seven minutes. In that brief time I had promised Captain Zacharias, then chief of naval intelligence, that I would do a counterintelligence job at the U.S. Navy Japanese/ Oriental Language School in Boulder, Colorado, and had signed a contract to attend the school as a civilian until commissioned a navy officer. The contract had been submitted to me by a rumpled ex-college professor who was immediately dismissed once it was signed. It required me to be in Boulder, Colorado, on March 5, 1943. Zacharias was a slender, dark-complexioned man with a craggy face. He acted as if he was in a great hurry, and my interview thus turned out to be a monologue on his part. It was at once clear to me, as I suspected, that he had decided to make me an intelligence officer before I arrived.

"I'll be out in Boulder to deliver a lecture in July," he said. "At that time you can tell me what you think and whether there is any truth in this newspaper column, which you may keep and destroy after reading."

After handing me the clip, he then resumed his monologue. "I talked with the FBI about you. They told me that Stephenson at BSC has asked that he be informed of your ultimate assignment and that you keep your high-security rating. I've agreed to that. You should understand that this would preclude your ultimate assignment to do combat intelligence work since we cannot run the risk of your being captured and tortured. Also, I'm aware of what a salary cut you will be taking. There is nothing I can do about that until you are overseas. Good luck. I'll see you in July, and thank Harry Frantz for sending you to me."

The whole thing had gone so fast that the by time I hit the sidewalk in front of the Navy Department building, which was then a temporary structure left over from World War I, I was almost dizzy.

I read the newspaper clipping as I walked back to my office. It was cut from the *Times-Herald*, a militantly anti-Roosevelt Republican paper, and suggested that the navy's Japanese-language school on the campus of the University of Colorado at Boulder was a haven for draft dodgers, fellow travellers, and Communists. I tore it into little pieces and dropped the shreds in a trash basket while en route.

Three months later Captain Zacharias arrived at Boulder and sent for me. "Well," he said, "what's your conclusion?"

"I don't think there are any more Communists or fellow travellers here than on the average U.S. campus. As you know, Communism in America is more or less a middle-class disease rather than a workingman's affliction. Since the students here have been recruited because they were either honor students or graduates from U.S. campuses, you have the usual number of people who knowingly or unknowingly joined fellow traveller organizations, plus possibly one or two Communist Party members. So long as the United States and the Soviets are allies, this would not seem to me to be much of a problem except for those ultimately assigned to code-breaking installations."

"Oh," Zacharias interrupted, "you know about those. How come? "Stephenson was in this field in World War I," I said. "For some reason or another it was explained to me by someone probably in connection with a future assignment."

"But you don't know that."

"No, sir."

"Continue."

"Well, in my opinion, these men and women should be given another security examination. During this time, if they lie about not being members of Communist front organizations, get rid of them or assign them to menial duty overseas. As for the draft dodger charge, it's total rubbish. This place, I'm sure, is as much of a grind as any boot camp, if not more so. So much so that the daily hour of intense physical exercise and subsequent field games comes as a welcome relief and is pleasant."

"All right. Now, to change the subject, do you, Kramer, wish to finish the course here? I recommend that you complete it."

"I do, sir."

"In that case, I shall tell Lieutenant Conover, your administrative officer, to have you present when he must dismiss an officer and to assign you to the reception desk so that when the new men arrive so that you can give them the once-over. I especially have in mind the communications officers and Russian-language men who will arrive before you leave. If you come across anything you don't like, report it verbally to Lieutenant Conover. I believe that is all."

I did come across something I didn't like but hesitated to report it. William Remington showed up as a Russian-language student. After mulling over the problem for several days, I decided to tell Conover that I knew the FBI had some sort of file on Remington and let it go at that, making no mention of his curiosity about what I had done before joining the navy. My work in the Rockefeller office was not something I could discuss with Lieutenant Conover.

Subsequently, Remington was convicted of perjury because he denied he had turned over classified information to a Soviet agent and was sentenced to Lewisburg Federal Penitentiary on February 7, 1954, where he was murdered by a fellow prisoner.

The night of the day I had met with Zacharias in Boulder, Sam King, a fellow student and a friend of mine, and I dined together on the train going east to Chicago. Sam and I were on our first leave from the language school. Since we had the same initials, SPK, our laundry was always mixed up, and we had to meet once per week to sort it out. A lifelong friendship evolved out of these meetings. Sam later ran for governor of Hawaii and was defeated; he then was appointed to the U.S. District Court of Hawaii. The headwaiter sat us at a table with an extra seat, and within thirty seconds, Captain Zacharias materialized and occupied it. As apparently was his custom with junior officers, he dominated the conversation and asked us why we were not being given better instruction in deciphering *sosho* (Japanese grass writing). This is a form of shorthand, enormously difficult to decipher and often used by the Japanese for entries in their personal diaries and for intra-family correspondence. Since all Japanese soldiers were given a diary by the emperor on their induction in the army and told to write in it, these diaries often became an important source of information, especially as evidence of war crimes. I was never able to read them.

There were a number of other Boulder students on the same train who saw our protracted dinner and somewhat animated but whispered conversation with Zacharias. Many became thus convinced that I was a naval intelligence agent assigned for duty at the school, sending in confidential reports on the men. To deny it would only have made matters worse. The only thing I could do was ignore it.

The U.S. Navy Japanese/Oriental Language School was originally on the campus of the University of California in Berkeley. Because of the post-Pearl Harbor anti-Japanese hysteria, all U.S. residents of Japanese origin (even those who were American citizens) were forced to vacate areas within two-hundred miles of the Pacific coast. Since this order included the Japanese-American (Nisei) teachers at the Navy's language school, it had to be relocated, and in mid-June 1942, it was moved to the University of Colorado in Boulder. With the exception of a few Caucasian ex-Christian missionaries and activist members of the Women's Christian Temperance Union, all the teachers were Japanese-Americans, most of whom had no previous teaching experience. The directress of the school was an ex-missionary who drank.

These handicaps were overcome by adhering strictly to a set of instruction textbooks that were quite adequate from the standpoint of the written language and in conversation with middle and upper middle-class Japanese. But in the highly stratified pre-war social structure of Japan, I was later to find that it had limitations when dealing with lower class sailors of peasant origins or with the Japanese of Korean slave labor coal miners.

The original students were Americans who had been born in Japan and who, as children, had Japanese nursemaids and who had learned some Japanese in private English schools. But even most of them did not know all 5,000 ideograms necessary to read a Japanese newspaper. Japanese is a difficult language, further complicated by the country's sudden emergence from being an isolated kingdom to a modern state with close contact with the West. The Japanese, for example, had no chairs until they were introduced from the West, just as they had no shirts. On first seeing a chair, they asked what someone did when he sat on one. To them it seemed as if the occupant was "hanging his hips" and the phrase "to sit down" became "hang one's hips." Never having seen a shirt, they asked a Westerner what it was. He said it was a "white shirt." Thus the word for shirt became *white shirt*, and, for example, a blue shirt became a "blue white shirt."

The war created an enormous demand for U.S. Navy officers who spoke and read Japanese, and the language school turned out about 1,000 of them. The first class graduated in February 1943 and consisted of thirty-one. Twenty-seven were immediately assigned to combat intelligence work in the Pacific and four who were sent to the Office of Naval Intelligence in Washington, where they organized the material from the broken Japanese codes. When this organization was complete, many were sent to Hawaii and attached to the staff of the commander-in-chief in the Pacific. Those assigned to do combat intelligence work were commissioned in the Marine Corps.

Oddly enough, the association with my fellow officers at Boulder broadened my horizons. I know it sounds silly today now that we live in a more egalitarian society, but I suddenly found myself immersed in a large class of men I had not previously known existed. At Princeton, and even more so at Trinity, Cambridge, I had been limited to an association with the elite, and at Cambridge with what can only be described as the then ruling classes. From there to the Rockefeller office was an easy step, for Nelson had most certainly surrounded himself with the ruling nongovernmental elite. These men were not only fellow billionaires but also leaders from the charities the Rockefeller family supported, which included top architects, museum directors, ballet company founders, etc.

There was nothing like this at Boulder. By the time I got there, the supply of BIJs or Born in Japan men, as they were called, was pretty well exhausted. We instead had a large supply of Phi Beta Kappa scholarship men and women who regarded a college degree as a ticket to social advancement. These men tended to regard the war as an unwelcome intrusion on their academic achievements and also as an unnecessary separation from "Mom and blueberry pie." I, on the other hand, regarded the war as simply part of the "great game" in which citizens of a world power became inevitably involved. Also, the food at home, with the exception of the fresh fruits and vegetables, was pretty awful simply because the other three members of the family were all on special diets so that my intake was restricted by their dietary habits. My dad had diabetes and bad teeth, so everything was sugarless, and the meat had to be soft and hence overdone. My brother was allergic to wheat, so the pastries were made with rice flour, and my mother hated anything acidic, so no lemonade, only iced tea, and the fruit at meals was usually melons and pears, although I was allowed to have red raspberries and other fruits between meals as compensation for their afflictions. Also, my childhood rural associations and acquired rural skills such as shooting quail and playing mumblety-peg were totally foreign to these fellow officers, so I suppose the difference showed. It could cause blow-ups.

One day, shortly before receiving my commission and pretty much out of civilian clothes, I found in my suitcase an old seersucker suit from my Princeton days and put it on along with a rather snappy Savile Row tie from my Cambridge days. This costume, totally unexpectedly, induced a rage on the part of a fellow student I didn't even know.

"I know you and your type," he snarled as he came up to me. "You snotty easterners wear those silly clothes just to put us down who are trying to dress decently. You think you can get away with it just because you got money? Well, after the war things are going to be different."

The incident was absurd but taught me to be more careful. I didn't stop wearing the seersucker suit, but sometimes I mourned with them the loss of "Mom and blueberry pie."

After Boulder I was sent, subsequent to a brief intelligence course in New York City, to Washington to read Japanese telephone books (the last naval attaché at our embassy in Tokyo before the war had sent a set of them to Washington in order to locate factories in Japanese cities). This work was ultimately used in the selection of targets for the atom bomb. Soon, however, I was suddenly ordered overseas to Hollandia in New Guinea to join an Allied intelligence unit. It took a long time for me to get there. First I had to wait at the Fairmount Hotel in San Francisco for a ship. When I finally got one, it turned out to be a former Dutch passenger liner called the *Tjisdane*, which was leased by the army as a transport vessel. With the exception of three army officers, the crew was made up of either Dutch or lascars. I was made "unloading officer," which meant that when we reached various U.S. bases in the South Pacific, I had to go ashore and find out what navy personnel was needed, return to the ship so that the army officers could decide who was to be off-loaded, and then go ashore with them and lead them to their new "home." Sometimes I had to spend the night ashore until the base officers compiled their list of who was needed. The *Tjisdane* never docked, and all the going back and forth was done by dinghy. At some point or another ashore, I must have picked up either dengue fever or malaria or both so that by the time I reached Hollandia, exactly a month after leaving San Francisco, I was about as ill as I'd ever been. Aside from catching a tropical fever, life aboard the *Tjisdane* was not unpleasant. The army officers saw to it that my cabin was emptied of other occupants at the first opportunity, and I had a superb lascar steward who did my laundry, polished my shoes, and brought me a pot of hot tea when he came to wake me in the morning. He also produced another steward who cut and trimmed my hair on two occasions. It was all pretty cushy for wartime despite the daily lifeboat drills and other precautions. Having little use for money, I tipped my steward handsomely once a week since he was providing me with such unparalleled service. He told me my generosity might make it possible for him to buy a little house after the war, and I often wondered if he did so. When we finally reached Hollandia, and I was landed by lighter, my steward insisted on carrying my gear ashore for me. Oddly enough, I was, at this point, the sole remaining passenger, which was probably why I had been named unloading officer. Unfortunately, my steward forgot to include with my gear an envelope containing my orders and my pay account. After a night in a transient camp in the port of Hollandia, I got a ride in an army truck up the mountain to a base near Lake Sentani. Here the cooler air made me shiver a lot, and after a couple of hours doing nothing and a drink in a tent that served as an officer's club, I went to sickbay.

13

The deal was that if I could make it on my own two feet to a plane early the next morning, the base doctor would see that I got orders out of New Guinea to Brisbane, Australia, where I would recover faster. I gladly nodded assent and then staggered back to my tent in the transient camp. Before daybreak the next morning, two pharmacist mates appeared, got me dressed and had me put my arms across their shoulders, and then walked me to a bucket seat on a transport plane. The doctor knew I couldn't make it on my own. As the plane climbed higher and it became colder, I began to shake uncontrollably and then lurched forward over my seatbelt into a coma.

At the Brisbane airport I vaguely remembered someone sticking a thermometer in my mouth, reading it, and then attaching a casualty tag to my shirt and painting a large X on my forehead. Then they put me on a stretcher and loaded me into an ambulance, along with my gear. What followed was a blissful and total blank.

The next day I woke up and found myself in a hospital ward. A doctor and nurses bustled about, giving me food, which I rejected; then I got the chills and fever and again oblivion. The morning after my third night in the hospital, I became dimly aware of lots of gold braids beside my bed. Then, as if from a distance, I heard a British-accented voice say, "Got to have someone from the Old Col about." Later and more faintly, "I say, when Kramer is better, would you have him phone this number? London has signaled me about him." Then another blank.

The following day I was feeling distinctly better, and Colonel Parker, my doctor, told me that the fever had broken and I was on the road to recovery. I should now go to the bathroom myself, and when I felt like it, walk about the ward and the hospital corridors, but there was no need to rush it. I would be weak.

"What's wrong with me, Doctor?" I asked.

"Oh, some sort of tropical fever. You might even have had two at the same time, but we won't really know until we see if any of them recur periodically. By the way, be sure to call a Commander Hopkinson. He came to see you, and he also called to ask how you are doing. I've put his phone number on your bedside table."

"Thank you, Doctor. Will I see you again?"

"Every day until you are out of here."

The following day, once I had gained a little strength, the ward nurse suggested I go outside and sit under a nearby tree. The fresh air would do me good.

"What I'd really like to do is get out of this hospital robe and into my uniform."

"But you can't do that."

"Why not?"

"You haven't any uniform. We burned everything you had on at arrival. They might have been infested with New Guinea and South Pacific larvae, and you had no gear of any sort. Nothing but what you had on. We emptied your pockets; your watch, money, and dog tags are in the drawer next to your bed."

"But that's all wrong. I distinctly remember my gear being tossed into the ambulance with me."

"I'm sorry, but there was none when you were brought to the ward. Just a very sick navy lieutenant on a stretcher."

"Well, why don't I go look for it instead of sitting under a tree?"

"If you like. But don't overdo it."

The 42nd General Hospital was a series of one-story wards connected by ramps and corridors. I went to Admission, no gear. Then to Departures; no gear. Then to Laundry; nothing. Defeated, and en route back to my ward, I saw an intelligent-looking sergeant coming my way and discussed my plight with him. "Well," the sergeant said, "there's one place you haven't looked."

"Where's that?"

"The effects of the deceased, and you better hurry because they're making a shipment out later this morning."

There was the missing gear, already labeled and ready for shipment to the effects of the deceased depot in Utah. But I was too tired to carry the duffel bag back to the ward myself, and the loading team offered to deliver it later.

I then returned to my ward, sat on the edge of my bed, totally exhausted and feeling no triumph whatsoever over finding the missing gear. Instead, for the first and only time in my adult life, I burst into tears. While weeping, my doctor appeared. "Well," he commented, "I see you've gone into a post-dengue depression. Not unusual, not unusual at all. Just lie back and enjoy it, and once you're strong enough, I'm going to send you to the beach at Southport for three or four days' recreation. You clearly are used to plenty of physical exercise. So once you get there, swim twice a day, and then you'll be able to go to work again. That commander of yours is a character. Be sure and call him this afternoon, and you can tell him you'll be able to report for duty next Monday."

And I did exactly that. Commander Hokinson motioned me to a chair when I walked into his office. "Do sit down, Lieutenant, and I'll try and explain things. That other door leads to what will be your office. There's a desk in it and a file cabinet with a combination lock. Anything you believe important, stow it in there, and then twirl the combination. In front of the building is my jeep. It's yours. I never use it, never learned how to handle a motorcar. Always had a driver, you know. After I retired from the navy and moved to Malaysia and became a rubber planter, I felt it important not to drive. One has to impress the natives, you know. You'll find the jeep a convenience. They've put you in rather sordid quarters at a seaplane base. Without a jeep, you'll have to ride back and forth like a school child in a bus. Not your lifestyle, I'm sure. And you'll not want to eat there. I've put you up for a men's club in downtown Brisbane. The food is passable there, and alternatively, you can always eat at Lennon's Hotel. Any questions?"

On first impression, Commander Lionel Holmes-Hopkinson seemed the totally Poona-Poona-type of Brit who, before the war could be seen at Raffles in Singapore, enjoying a pink gin fizz and proclaiming that the Malay states with their rajahs and Colonial Office resident agents were the most perfectly governed colonies in the British Empire. Furthermore, his slightly flushed face and graying dark hair and exaggerated "out East" use of phrases like "quite, quite" and "I say" and "rather" all tended to confirm that impression.

But all this was camouflage for his intense shyness. He had great difficulty with strangers, and the fact that I had gone to the same college he attended meant to him that we had enough in common to enable him to overcome his shyness. This was the reason why he had originally asked for me. Underneath all the Poona-Poona, Hoppy, as he liked to be called, was a courageous, totally honest, and kindly man who never complained although he had plenty to complain about and who left compliments unspoken but rewarded one instead as he did in my case with a jeep, a case of whiskey, and three British sailors to help me out. He confessed to me once that the only thing he was really afraid of was snakes, and I believed him. He was totally free of personal bravado.

Hopkinson had served in the Royal Navy during World War I and had retired in the early thirties and bought a rubber plantation in Malaysia where he had lived until the outbreak of World War II when he had been called back to active duty.

This was fortunate since he thus escaped being taken prisoner by the Japanese after the fall of Singapore. His unshakable faith in the permanence of the British Empire sustained him. As he said to me once, "When the war is over, I'll be back at the plantation. The house will still be there, but either the Nips or the locals will have made off with the silver. I'll miss that." Fellow planters who, with their families, had managed to escape to Australia and who were too old to work and were thus penniless, he would mention to his great friend Rajah Brooke of Sarawak, who then took care of them.

Initially he tended to assess people by their class origins, but the moment they demonstrated courage or genuine ability, he laid aside all stereotypes of class prejudice and welcomed them. Like his chief, Colonel Mashbir, he had little admiration for our Soviet ally, and since he was aware of my own feelings toward Russia, this may have been a bond between us although we never discussed it in so many words. I have no idea if he was ever asked by Lieutenant Commander Young to fill out a navy fitness report about me. If he did, he never mentioned it.

I couldn't help but like the man and admire him, and his outward "Poona-Poona Empire and all that" manner amused me and in no way was irritating or offensive as it proved to be to many of the Boulder Japanese-language officers at Allied Translator and Interpreter Service (ATIS). This perhaps was fortunate because he didn't like them either. He described them to me as "drones, rather lacking in courage, don't you know."

"To prolong our discussion, can you tell me what I'm supposed to do?" I asked Hopkinson.

"Oh yes, that won't be too difficult. Did you see all those Nips sitting at the desks when you came in here? I believe you people call them Nisei for Japanese-Americans. They spend their days translating captured documents, diaries, and such. Your job will be to scan what they translate, and if you see anything that I should see, simply put it on my desk. Also, when there are prisoners to interrogate, trot along to the pens with them, and if the POWs are willing to talk, which is unlikely, let me know by phone if I should come down and listen. Also, sometimes when a Nip base is captured, we get Jap training manuals and films, material like that. Go through it for me."

"But what, may I ask, do you do with what I'll send you? Unless I know that, I won't know what's important and what isn't."

"I say, clever of you to think of that. I do several things. If there's something I think Mountbatten and the India-Burma people should have, I send it on to them. Anything of general interest to our navy, I send copies to London as well as to the Seventh Fleet. Anything the Australians should have I send to their unit here at ATIS. Anything I think MacArthur and his staff might like goes to the chief here, Colonel Mashbir, an old friend of the general from the Philippines; uses a lilac scent, rather odd."

"I think I've got it now. Is there anything else?"

"There is, and it's rather difficult, you know. But you'll have to work it out if you wish to be comfortable here. The colonel is frightfully anti-Soviet. He hates the Ruskies almost as much as the Nips. And alas, your navy here has a clutch of pro-Soviet types. Curiously, some seem to come from that Japanese-language school in Boulder you attended—"

"I know exactly what you mean," I said, interrupting the commander. "We had a similar clutch where I worked before joining the navy. I used to call them our radical elements. One got me into trouble with our vice president. Stephenson of BSC and the FBI had to come to my rescue. A damn nuisance."

"Well, stay away from them if you want to win Mashbir's confidence. Not too difficult for you since you work here and they're in another building. We have a couple of other problems, but I'll let them go until later, until you've settled in. But I do have a question to ask you."

"Sure, go ahead."

"Did you really catch a Nip spy in Washington single-handed?"

"Sir, that's total exaggeration, total! You don't catch spies single-handed like the French caught Mata Hari. You do it by teamwork, international teamwork. Without the British knowledge of the Abwehr in Spain, without the British mail intercepts, and without the FBI's help in D.C., it would have been impossible. I was simply a cog in a well-oiled machine, just like I assume I will be here."

Hopkinson, I discovered, had a habit of simply ignoring what he didn't wish to hear. He did so over the Matheson case and quickly changed the subject.

"I say, Kramer," he said, "you've simply got to check in with the American officer who is in administrative charge of you—a Lieutenant Commander Young, an ex-lumber salesman from your Northwest; not your type, not your type at all."

"And now I have a question; it's totally personal, don't you know, but didn't you write part of an act in the Cambridge University's Footlights Show in '36 and '37? And didn't they put part of it on a BBC Empire broadcast?"

"They did. Did you hear it?"

"I certainly did. You were a Captain Roy Rightabout, and you'd just rescued the commandant's daughter from the fuzzy wuzzies. You'd found a black footprint in the desert sand, and then, when you'd saved the girl, she said to you, 'Oh, Captain Rightabout, you call me Gertrude. Why not call me Gert and leave out the rude part.' And you said with such perfect hesitation and shyness, 'Thanks Gert.' Frightfully funny, that. I roared with laughter, so did my wife."

*　　*　　*

"Lieutenant Kramer, sir, reporting for duty."

"Um, I understand you've already checked in with Commander Holmes-Hopkinson," commented Commander Young acidly.

"That's right, sir."

"Your orders from the hospital indicated to check in with me, did they not?"

"Not precisely. They said to report for temporary duty to ATIS. Commander Hopkinson came to see me in the hospital. He specifically told me to come and see him directly."

"Well, I'll let that pass, but I want to make something clear to you. You may be assigned to him, but I'm the officer in charge in so far as the U.S. Navy is concerned. Any duty orders you receive come from me, not him. So will your quarters' assignment."

"Yes, sir."

"Now I'd like to discuss a clerical error with you. You have a high-security clearance; it's even higher than mine. Has this ever happened to you at previous stations?"

"It has, sir, but I'm not at all sure it's a clerical error. It was given to me personally by Captain Zacharias, chief of ONI, when I first signed up, and it was a continuation of my civilian classification."

"Your civilian classification?"

"Yes, my work as a civilian before I joined the navy."

"Then you don't think it's a clerical error."

"No, sir, I do not."

"Well, we'll let that pass. I take it you haven't yet been to your quarters."

"That's correct."

"It's essential that you, like all the other language officers here at ATIS, be on board the bus outside the gate at 1710. Otherwise, there's no transportation to the base. In a week you'll be moved to the Wellington Barracks in town, but as of now, you are at the Seaplane Base on the river west of town. That's over twelve miles from here."

"No problem, sir. Commander Hopkinson has given me a jeep."

"What?" Young was clearly angry at this point.

"He said he didn't know how to drive a motor vehicle, so he's giving me his."

"But that's irregular. It means you will have your own transport, and many officers senior to you do not. It will affect morale."

"Commander Hopkinson seemed to think I'd need it for going back and forth to the POW pens and other duties he has in mind for me."

"Remember, Kramer, whatever substantive duties he gives you, I'm your commanding officer. Furthermore, since you are on temporary duty—why it's temporary, I don't know—you can be pulled out of here and sent back up north at a moment's notice."

"I know, sir. The commander has already indicated there may be other duties but decided to wait to discuss them with me until I'm 'settled in,' as he put it."

From the moment I left Young's office and returned to my own, I knew there would be trouble with Young. In a way, it was similar to the Jamieson problem at the Rockefeller office; it was caused by a similar set of dual circumstances, which meant that I had two bosses instead of one. What I didn't realize was how swift, how petty, and how short lasting Young's revenge would be.

There was always an Australian soldier guard at the entrance to the ATIS compound, which was located in a leafy suburb of Brisbane. Since the navy's Japanese-language officers always arrived by bus and in groups, and thus streamed through the gate in clusters, it was impossible for him to salute them, and once they were in, he would often draw back from the gate a few paces for an illicit drag on a cigarette. This is what happened when I arrived by myself. The soldier, seeing me, tossed his cigarette away and gave a smart salute, but I was still concealed by the fence, so I did not see him or his salute. Commander Young, however, did and immediately ordered me to leave the compound and reenter and properly return the soldier's salute, which I did without hesitation.

The guard, horrified by what he had inadvertently caused, muttered "Sorry sir," and I muttered back, "Forget it, soldier, I'll live."

Shortly thereafter, a U.S. Army captain who had something to do with the Nisei and a navy lieutenant I had known at Boulder asked me to join them and their girls for a night of drinking at Gregory Terrace, which was the local watering hole and officers' club in Brisbane. My date was to be the best friend of one of the girls.

The evening, as I had expected it to be, turned into a night of drinking, idle chatter, and ultimately, sex. What I had not anticipated was that my girl would give an intimate description of my conduct to her girl friend, who in turn repeated it to the army captain, who ultimately described it to Commander Young. The result was a happy one. Young, for whom sex was of supreme importance, recast me in his mind as somewhat of a Casanova and, from this point on, held me in high regard and went out of his way to be kind to me and showed me snapshots of his wife, children, and their house in Oregon. This, as it turned out years later, was a disastrous mistake on his part when he suddenly reappeared in my life in Panama while I was working there.

Things jogged along in pretty much of a routine for three months. As I put it to Hoppy, "Nothing but trash crosses my desk. I haven't seen anything worthwhile since I've been here." In fact, so little had been forwarded to Mountbatten's headquarters that they sent a delegation to Brisbane to see what was going on and to inquire if they had been forgotten. Suddenly, however, and totally unexpectedly, the equivalent of a buzz bomb exploded on my desk, which not only tore apart Hopkinson's and my routine, but also totally changed my life in Brisbane.

One morning at about eleven o'clock—I even remember the time—one of the Nisei translators who occupied a desk just outside the door to my office and to whom I often spoke while going in and out of the building, politely knocked on the door.

"Sir," he said, "I have something here that might be of special interest to you." He then gave me a tiny printed booklet about the size of a kitchen matchbox. The first thing I noticed was that the text was printed on particularly fine and highly digestible rice paper, and the printing, although minute, was superbly done and of the finest quality. It was as though the type had never heretofore been used and had been cast especially for the booklet.

I asked the young Japanese-American sergeant to draw up a chair so that we could look at the booklet together. The first page made it abundantly clear that it was a detailed secret set of instructions to the user on exactly how to proceed from Imperial Japanese Army intelligence headquarters in Tokyo to the Soviet-Manchurian border where another secret agent would meet him and guide him across the Amur River and deposit him within the Soviet Union. I immediately went in to see Hopkinson and suggested that he join the sergeant and me to look at something totally amazing.

Just as I knew he would, Hoppy, usually so vague and indifferent, became totally alert. "My word, this is a find! But where did it come from?" he asked.

"It's hard to say, sir," the sergeant explained. "We emptied a sack that came down from up north last night. It had the usual mix of dog tags off dead Japanese soldiers, little boxes containing sachets of nail cuttings for forwarding to dead soldiers' families, diaries, documents on equipment maintenance, this booklet, and a fairly large, bloody fragment of a hydrographic chart which—"

Sergeant," I interrupted, "go out and tell whoever has the HO chart fragment to bring it to me now."

"My buddy—excuse me, Sergeant Watanabe has it. He sits next to me. I'll tell him."

A moment later Sergeant Watanabe joined us with the bloody chart fragment, which I put on my desk. "Now," I said, "let's go back to the booklet. What do you think, Commander? Clearly we have to process it meticulously, and if you agree, in as much of a hush-hush manner as possible."

"Quite, quite."

"Well, Sergeant," I said, "I'll tell you what. From here on I want you and Watanabe to work together on this in my office. Do not discuss it with anyone else; never leave it or your translations on my desk. Put them in my safe and then twirl the combination if you have to leave. I'll reopen it when needed. And no one, and I mean no one, but you two, the commander here, and I are to be allowed in this office. I'll have a sign put up to that effect. Any questions?"

"No, sir, but I think you should know we have mentioned it to some of the men."

"Well, I'm glad you told me. But no one but you two have read it, and you haven't discussed the actual text with any army or navy officers?"

"No, sir, no one."

"I say, Kramer," Commander Hopkinson put in, having just looked at his watch, "why don't you drive me into Lennon's Hotel and join me for lunch with Rajah Brooke of Sarawak? He was to send a car for me, but you could drive me there."

"I'd like to, sir, very much, but there is a problem here. These two men will have to put the document and their work in the safe when they go to lunch, and they'll need me to open it for them when they come back."

"Oh yes, of course. A pity. I told Brooke[1] you've met one of his daughters, Princess Pearl, the one who married Harry Roy, the bandleader, and he wanted to meet you."

"Well, next time. But don't you agree that I should stay here to reopen the safe for them?"

"Quite, quite. Also, you might look at the HO chart and tell me, when I get back, what it is. We should, you know, compare it with Admiralty and your navy charts. Coral is a living thing, you know, and our people haven't been able to chart the South Pacific for some time."

Two days later it happened. Well before the Nisei sergeants had finished their translation, and despite my precautions, I returned from lunch to find the Nisei gone and a navy lieutenant whom I had known vaguely at the language school looking at the booklet and the translations in my office. Something snapped inside me, and although I preserved what I thought was an outward calm, I was boiling with rage inside.

"Hey, you," I ordered, "put that material down on my desk at once!"

"Who says so?"

"I do. Furthermore, do you see that sign on the door, 'Admittance to Authorized Personnel Only,' signed Commander Lionel Holmes-Hopkinson, RN? That's not me, that's my boss. I shall expect you to respect it."

"Why the sweat? It's a captured document. I have as much right to read it as you do."

"Unfortunately you don't. You put that material on the desk at once and clear out of here, or I'll file a complaint with Commander Young. Take it or leave it."

"So help me, God, Kramer, I'll kill you, and it won't be hard. Do you know how much you are hated around here by the other Boulder men? Why is it you get a jeep and a private office? How come you were promoted ahead of us?"

[1.] James Brooke, an Englishman, had helped the sultan of Brunei put down a rebellion in 1839-1840. In appreciation, the sultan gave Brooke part of his land, Sarawak, and Brooke and his heirs ruled it as "the white rajahs" until it was conquered by the Japanese during World War II. In 1946, the ruling rajah (Hopkinson's friend) ceded it to England. Sarawak became part of the Federation of Malaysia in 1962.

"Look, Lieutenant, if you and your friends wish to dislike me, that's their privilege, and I couldn't care less. But when my chief tells me to keep this office secure, it's my job to see that it's done. Now get the hell out of here, and if you and your buddies wish to plan my demise, go ahead. But one hostile move on your part and you'll be shipped out of here so fast you won't know what hit you."

This last threat worked. The officer retreated, muttering more threats; the moment he was gone, to my utter amazement, Hopkinson emerged from the adjoining office.

"Commander," I sputtered, "I thought you were lunching in town."

"Cancelled, Paul, cancelled. By the way, I heard every word of your conversation with that wretch. We can't have people threatening you for carrying out my orders. I shall go to Colonel Mashbir this afternoon and demand that he tell Young to order him up north to the Biak area. There's still shooting going on there and lots of malaria."

"Then you take his threats seriously?"

"I do. It so happens we know a lot about that man. It's clear he wanted that document to give to the Soviets. He's been in touch with a well-known Communist Australian labor union man here in Brisbane. Of course, he hasn't done anything yet except lose his temper with you, so there's nothing we can do to prove his intent. That's why I'll have him sent up to Biak. Now, while I go about things, I suggest you sit down, read carefully what's already been translated, and start editing it. Also, pay attention to the final instructions about eating the booklet rather than letting it get into the hands of the enemies. Because of this incident with that lieutenant, we're going to have to forward the document to Mashbir soon. You and the sergeants might care to work through the night on it. Also, write a one-page summary that Mashbir can forward to General MacArthur if he wishes."

A Japanese military officer was told exactly what civilian clothing to wear—slightly shabby and clearly worn and made in the Soviet Union. He was then told how to proceed: first north toward Hokkaido, then to backtrack south to Kobe, then to Kyoto, and then south to Fukuoka where he was to take the ferry to Manchuria where, by a highly irregular back-and-forth rail route, he was to be met by another agent at the station at Harbin from where he would be guided back and forth by rail to the bank of the Amur River; then, after crossing the river, he would enter the Soviet Union at Khabarovsk. From there he was to proceed to the port city of Vladivostok where he was to carry out his verbal instructions, which had been issued to him by headquarters in Tokyo.

Since the booklet had been especially printed, it could be assumed that these instructions were not just for one Japanese agent to be secreted in the Soviet Union but for a clutch of them. In this connection, it should be borne in mind that the Maritime Province of Russia had once been part of China. There were still many Orientals living there so that a Japanese man's identity, by means of ethnic characteristics, would be difficult. Also, the agents selected had not, as growing children, worn the typical Japanese bifurcated socks, or *tabis*. Separation of the big toe from the others was one of the standard ways of differentiating Japanese from Chinese men, but this was caused by wearing the bifurcated socks.

The booklet had very limited value to the United States or Britain but was of enormous value to the Soviets. However, Hopkinson, who had already verbally briefed Mashbir about it, had been given instructions by him that when the translation was completed and properly edited, it was to be delivered to him personally, and all working papers and copies were to be destroyed. It was in fact this order that I had been trying to carry out and why I had taken such a dim view of the navy lieutenant's intrusion.

I found myself particularly troubled by the incident. It wasn't the first time that friends of the Soviet Union had made difficulties for me. First there had been the Ana Cecilia Ortiz incident with the vice president in Washington; then there was Remington's querying Gloriella Solis of the Dominican Embassy in Washington. Later he had materialized at Boulder as a Russian-language officer. Now there was an incident in Brisbane with a man my chief had claimed was in touch with a Communist labor organizer. I refused to acknowledge I was the victim of any sort of Soviet plot and felt sure it was all no more than a series of coincidences. But I knew that Hoppy had discussed the incident with both Young and Mashbir, and now I had been told that I was not to leave the ATIS compound until a specially selected bodyguard arrived to protect me, which might take two or three days. What, I couldn't help but wonder, was motivating my superiors?

Chief Beals turned out to be a giant of a man, an old-line navy chief petty officer, a former navy boxer who took his job very seriously. In his eyes, I was just as important as any admiral was and needed constant protection and therefore, surveillance. His presence had the effect of curtailing my personal life. Beals' protection was not required within the ATIS compound or the Wellington Barracks; otherwise he was always present. I was not allowed to drive the jeep; Beals did it. I could not use the room I kept at the Bellevue Hotel. It had two beds, but since Beals snored like a lighthouse foghorn, it became totally impractical to use it. Also, I could no longer eat at the club since it was off-limits to Beals. I thus decided to raise the matter with Commander Hopkinson, but he simply refused to discuss it. Instead, he asked me if I was going to the beach at Southport for the weekend. When I said I was, Hoppy asked me to pick him up at the Dutch consul's house nearby at 4 PM on Sunday and drive him back to Brisbane.

"I'm spending, the weekend with Rajah Brooke who has a place near there. We plan to have a late lunch at the consul's," Hoppy explained. "Should be done by four. See you then."

*   *   *

"So kind of you and Chief Beals to pick me up. Kramer, it's all a bit of a ruse, don't you know? Either Brooke or the consul could have driven me back, but I wanted to talk with you outside of ATIS. Old Mashbir is a bit of a snoop. Even the walls may have ears, and what I have to say is on a need-to-know basis. Don't want him to know of your work with BSC and the FBI."

"Well, sir," I commented, "it's your jeep."

"Good Lord, so it is. I'd quite forgotten. I say Beals, do watch out for the wallabies. The thickets alongside the road are full of them, and they come bouncing out of all the greenery into the road. Best to go a bit slower."

"Now Paul, what I have to say is this. You're frightfully exposed out here. When you worked for Rockefeller in Washington, you had people like Stephenson and Hoover and Foxworth at your beck and call if there was trouble. Here all you've got is me. Zacharias has been given command of a cruiser, and as you know, Foxworth was killed setting up the Casablanca Conference."

Totally unexpectedly, Hoppy's mention of Foxworth's death plunged me into a sudden fit of gloom. Part of me heard Hopkinson go on about my "exposure" and why I had Beals and how Young and Mashbir thought I should have a bodyguard only while handling Jap spy documents and other classified material and how Hoppy insisted I should have him as long as I was in Australia. The other half wanted to stop the jeep, get out, and walk alone in the field beside the road and recall my happy working relationship with Foxworth. But I knew neither Beals nor Hoppy would let me. I thus said nothing, and apparently, they both sensed the reason for my silence and were also quiet.

But if they thought my silence was entirely due to recollections of a happy working relationship with Foxworth, they were wrong. Something else had smashed into my mind as a result of the mention of Foxworth's name, and it was decidedly not a happy memory. It occurred to me what a fool I had been about the Lanas case. Foxworth, the expert on enemy subversion, had known but never told me. It was the old need-to-know thing. Lanas, as a highly trained and gifted linguist, had been, among other things like snooping around the office, subverting the news he was called on to translate. By inserting a noun here, an adjective there, he had taken the Rockefeller propaganda material that had come across his desk for translation and transmission to Latin America and neutralized it or humanized it in so far as the Nazis were concerned; and the pressure was so great that those in charge of the pressroom, or Rivera, the head of the translation section, had missed it.

Once a month Lanas, in typical meticulous German fashion, had sent an itemized bill to his Abwehr masters via a secret address in Spain, and once a month his piecework paycheck arrived in Washington in the form of a dividend check from a brewery in neutral Argentina. Foxworth had this information from British Security Coordination in New York, but, despite his outward warm Southern friendly manner, had never trusted me enough to reveal the duplicity involved for fear that I, out of loyalty to Jamieson and Rockefeller, would feel obligated to reveal Lanas' trickery. All I had been told to do was to cultivate Lanas' friendship to see if he would lead us to other enemy agents. I was still doing this when I resigned and went to Boulder. Lanas, soon after, was arrested by the FBI.

"Two years and I'm still not over it," I finally commented in an effort to mislead both Hoppy and Chief Beals into supposing that my silence had been entirely due to sadness about Foxworth's premature death, but which had, in fact, been prolonged by a realization of my own stupidity in not figuring out what Lanas had been up to, plus the total degree of duplicity involved on the part of all three: Foxworth, Lanas, and me to the extent that I had deliberately cultivated Lanas' friendship for counterintelligence purposes while professing an admiration for his linguistic skills which ironically, I had made use of in connection with the Torch project. The contrasting beauty of the countryside through which we were driving and the uniquely luminous Australian light in which it was bathed emphasized in my mind what a sewer the place I had worked in before joining the navy was.

It was Chief Beals who picked up my remark about not being over Foxworth's death. "These things happen in wartime," he put in, much to my surprise. The man might have looked like a brute, but he was apparently capable of tender feelings. "You can lose your best friend on another ship, and who's to know how you feel. It's life, I guess."

"Thanks, Chief," I said with a slight sigh. "You'll never know how much I really needed that."

This was not the first time that Beals had revealed a certain sensibility. A couple of weeks previously, I had casually said to him that the day marked the end of an era. I was out of Yardley's shaving soap, and it was impossible to replace it in Australia. Yardley's was a luxury shaving soap that came in its own wooden bowl and could therefore be easily lathered.

Beals said nothing, but the next morning after he had picked me up at the Wellington Barracks, he mentioned that if I would look under the seat of the jeep I would find something. What I found was a new bowl of Yardley's soap. Beals read my delight over his gift from my face. He was the type of old navy hand who knew exactly what a sailor should do as well as what he could do. "Well, sir," he explained, "after you mentioned you were out of the soap, I went down to the Fleet post office, and, you know, some of the moms back home don't wrap their packages properly so that by the time they get here they are about to fall apart . . . Well, some of the boys at the post office hurry the process along a bit and throw the parcels against the wall. As luck would have it, one of them that burst open contained a bowl of Yardley's soap. I hope you enjoy it."

"I've been giving your situation a lot of thought," Hoppy said once he noticed I was willing to talk again. "You see, Paul, you've never been willing to face up to your situation."

"Meaning?"

"Meaning that somewhere someone in the vast Soviet intelligence apparatus apparently wants you out of the way."

"But why me? I'm not that important."

"But you are! You are! Perhaps not in your work, but in something more sinister. My guess, and it's just a guess, is that you know something, or perhaps I should say someone thinks you know something that could destroy either that person's career or alternatively his work as a high-ranking secret agent for the Soviets. The problem is that you don't know, or I should say can't remember what it is they think you do know—probably something from your Trinity College, Cambridge, years long since forgotten. I feel rather strongly about it, and since you're my man here, I mean to protect you as best I can."

"Chief Beals here," Hoppy continued, "came down from the Seventh Fleet in a great rush. He's asked for a few days to go back to his ship, collect his gear, and bring it down here. I've told him he can go next week since there is a job for you out of Australia. I know you'll want to volunteer for it once you hear what it is. They need someone who speaks Spanish who will go up to a prearranged spot in Mindanao by submarine and pull out of the jungle a Captain Roybal. He's an ex-army corporal who went AWOL during the Bataan Death March, eluded the Japanese guards, got down to Mindanao, joined up with a Muslim guerilla group, and has been given a field commission. He also has been dropped a two-way radio and has signaled that he's terribly ill and asked that he be pulled out. Why don't you do the pulling? Fly up to Hollandia, go aboard the sub there. You're little, a great advantage on a sub, don't you know? Also, apparently, the guerillas speak Spanish; never bothered to learn English when you people took over the Philippines from Spain, and you claim to know the lingo."

"OK, I'll do it."

"Fine. I'll have Young cut your orders. Roybal has radioed a list of pharmaceuticals he'd like for his guerilla friends. Pick them up before you leave, and don't discuss this mission with anyone at ATIS save Young."

By this time we had pulled up in front of Hopkinson's house, and he was about to leave when I held him back with a question.

"By the way, sir, do you have the list of pharmaceuticals for Roybal that you mentioned?"

"Good Lord, it's here in my pocket. I totally forgot. Careless of me. You'll have your orders from Young by 10:00 AM tomorrow and you should be out of here in the afternoon or the following morning."

"I'll see the lieutenant to his plane, sir and then get my own orders from Lieutenant Commander Young."

"Right, Beals. I think you can count on Lieutenant Kramer being gone at least a week, if not more."

"Aye, aye, sir."

I ran into only one complicating factor before my departure. The medicines were no problem, but Roybal had also asked for a dozen diaphragms for the women in his guerilla group who wished to avoid pregnancy. These were impossible to secure via regular military channels, and I bought them with my own money from the pharmacist who had a store at Lennon's Hotel.

Commander Young absolutely refused to cut orders to send me to the Philippines to rescue Roybal. I didn't argue because it seemed to me he was right. Captain Zacharias had warned me before going to Boulder that there could be no combat intelligence work for me because of my BSC-FBI—Rockefeller work. Technically, what Hoppy had proposed was not combat intelligence, but it was near enough to it so that Young had dug in his heels. When this was pointed out to Hoppy, he agreed with Young and apologized to me for suggesting the assignment in the first place.

Young's cancellation of this little excursion was a bitter disappointment for me. I had been looking forward to a break in my routine as well as to an excursion on a submarine, a type of vessel with which I was totally unfamiliar. Little did I know about what was in store for me in the future, in Japan, and even under the waters of Long Island Sound.

As it happened, I got to know Roybal rather well after his rescue. My old doctor at the 42nd General Hospital had gotten in touch with me when Roybal became one of his patients. "This man," he told me, "is going to need a friend after his release. He's totally disoriented, and you might help him come back to the realities of life. Can you imagine," he explained, "the poor guy has first to go through a court-martial for going AWOL during the Bataan Death March and thus violating the surrender orders. It's a technicality, of course, but he doesn't seem to understand it and has no friends here in Brisbane." I enjoyed the friendship that evolved between the two of us and bid him a fond farewell when he was finally sent back to his home in Wagon Mound, New Mexico, for a well-earned leave.

Because of the cancellation of the Roybal rescue mission, Beals had to make a lightning trip up north and back and was only gone forty-eight hours during which I became a "captive" in the ATIS compound and ate there at the Australian officers' mess and also slept in the compound. Meanwhile, and it took far more time than anticipated, I worked on the bloodstained hydrographic chart fragment with the two Nisei who had helped on the spy document. Our first problem was to discover exactly what part of the South Pacific it dealt with since the location explanation was missing, and there was some confusion about the coordinates. This meant we had to examine countless Admiralty and US HO charts and compare them with what we had. Hoppy joined in the search, and it was he who found what it was—a piece of the coastline of the Philippines, and since he knew a landing there was imminent, the two Nisei and I worked on the project twelve hours a day and finished it in time for Hoppy to send our work forward to Admiral Kinkaid of the Seventh Fleet before the landings.

Meanwhile, our success even before we had finished the job inspired Commander Hopkinson to ask for volunteers to go ashore on the second wave of the landing under the protection of marine bodyguards with the express purpose of seeking out the principal Imperial Japanese Navy's naval installation and locating their hydrographic charts to bring back to ATIS in Brisbane. None of the Boulder grads volunteered, and Hoppy thus fell back on Australian Army volunteers. But they did not speak or read Japanese. I gave them a crash course with our bloodstained HO fragment, plus some U.S. and British HO charts but, regardless, they returned from the landing empty-handed.

The logical choice for the job, since I was forbidden to go, were the two Nisei sergeants who had helped on the project and who were now totally familiar with what to secure from a captured Japanese naval installation. But this was out because their racial characteristics were too similar to those of the enemy's. In the heat of battle, they could too easily be mistaken for the enemy and shot to death.

After this, I complained bitterly to Commander Hopkinson that no matter how hard I'd worked I had accomplished nothing. "Add it all up, sir," I said. "My first important job was the Nip spy manual, and that's locked away in Mashbir's safe, of no use to anyone. Now this fiasco."

"Quite the contrary, Kramer, quite the contrary. Mashbir is ecstatic you prevented the spy document from falling into the hands of the Bolshevik, as he calls them. Then the chart fragment, as you call it. You seem to have forgotten that it was you who immediately recognized its importance and had it brought forward out of the translating pool where it would no doubt have been tossed out. Then after you and I and the two Nisei worked on it, I sent it forward to Admiral Kinkaid of your Seventh Fleet. He was in positive raptures about it, wanted to know all about you and what you looked like.

"And what did you tell him?"

"I told him you and I had gone to the same college at Cambridge, that you were a perfect nut about being physically fit, but you had two physical waivers—eyesight and height."

Soon after Manila was recaptured from the Japanese, I was detached from ATIS for a few days. This time it was Young's idea and no doubt stemmed from my high-security rating. I was to go down to the wharf along the river in Brisbane, sign for truckloads of General MacArthur's secret files, and then see to their secure stowage aboard a Liberty ship which was dockside, waiting for them. I was to wear a side arm at all times, and Chief Beals would add additional security support. Australian unionized civilian dockworkers would do the actual physical loading of the boxes of files. There would be a lot of them.

All went well the first day, and I carefully sealed and secured the hold at the end of the working day. Chief Beals and I ate and slept aboard the Liberty ship. The second day no stevedores showed up for work, and I had to order the return of the day's truckload of documents to MacArthur's headquarters. When I asked what was wrong, I was told that the pub nearest the work site had run out of beer. The nearest alternative was a thirty-minute walk away. When the men had asked for compensatory extra lunch hour time, it had been denied. They were now out on strike for it.

I found the whole job so distasteful, as did Chief Beals, that together we sought a solution. Beals discovered that the alternative pub had a surplus of beer. Thus I simply bought two kegs of beer from it and delivered it to the pub nearest the ship. The stevedores went back to work the following day. Chief Beals was positively ecstatic. As he pointed out, the ship was not like a navy ship. It was dirty, the food was terrible, and the bread was full of weevils. The crew was dirty, unshaven, and their working clothes were filthy. The cabin he and I had been given was a mess.

Shortly thereafter, I was ordered up to Manila. Commander Hopkinson would fly up a week later, and a bodyguard was no longer required since Manila was free of Red-dominated labor unions. Beals was rather touching about it. He told me what a privilege it had been to guard me and the duty had been a gratifying break in his routine. He then admonished me to be careful of Filipinos. You never could tell what they were thinking, he claimed. I promised I would.

Manila in the beginning was chaotic. The city smelled of dead bodies since so many had been trapped in collapsed buildings. Because of this, the city was overrun with rats and shrews. ATIS was quartered in tents in a former suburban racetrack called Santa Ana, and the racetrack clubhouse was used for offices. After waking one morning to find a rat in bed with me, I found an extermination crew at the Fleet headquarters and got them to go to work before Hoppy arrived. I also bought from a nun at the Santa Ana Church a caned plantation chair for Hopkinson's tent. Otherwise he would have no place to sit except his bed. Hoppy, who was an older man, was immensely grateful and later presented me with a case of Scotch whiskey, which he had received as a ration from the British Navy. He also turned over to me three English sailors who had been redeployed from the

Atlantic theatre. The only problem was that there was nothing for them to do. I had hoped they could take the jeep daily to the Fleet headquarters in downtown Manila and pick up the ATIS mail. But since all three did not know how to drive and since I had the only jeep, the mail job was mine.

The truth was that there was nothing for either Hoppy or me to do at this juncture except to get ready for what was supposed would be the invasion of Japan and Formosa. We were made to study booklets that described these places' geography and flora and fauna with special emphasis on poisonous serpents. When I finally got to Japan, I was amused to discover how painfully inaccurate much of the material had been.

The evening of Japan's surrender, I went to an officers' club to celebrate. I was alone and standing with a drink in my hand when I heard a voice behind me ask, "Lieutenant, how long have you been overseas?" I turned to find, to my utter confusion and amazement, that it was Admiral Kinkaid himself. Flustered, I stammered out an answer, and the admiral asked where I expected to be ordered next. When I said that I presumed Japan since I knew the language, the admiral commented, "You look run-down to me. My plane is flying back to Guam first thing in the morning empty. I want you aboard it so you can get some rest and recreation there until you are sent to Japan where I know you will be extremely useful. Your orders will be delivered to you at ATIS tonight."

I returned to my quarters soon thereafter to say good-bye to Commander Hopkinson. He would not be going to Japan, he told me, but he would do everything possible to get back to Malaysia to see what was left of his rubber plantation.

Curiously, Hopkinson's parting words to me were an echo of what Foxworth had said years before when I was first hired by the White House and went to work for Rockefeller. "Do be careful when you get to Japan, Paul," Hoppy said. "In the work you're in and what unquestionably you'll be used for, you never can tell who your enemies really are."

When Commander Young discovered that I had received orders to travel alone to Guam on Admiral Kinkaid's plane, he very sensibly decided that this would be ideal transport for seven other Japanese-language officers who were also in Manila, and he cut orders for them too. On arrival in Guam, I was immediately given a jeep so that I could go to Tumon Bay every day to swim and get over what Admiral Kinkaid had described as my "run-down look." Also, much to my surprise, Admiral Nimitz sent for me immediately after his return to Guam from the signing of the surrender agreement with Japan on the battleship *Missouri* then at anchor in Tokyo Bay. He had brought back with him a bundle of Japanese daily newspapers published immediately before the Japanese surrender, and he asked me to go through them and tell him about anything he should know.

I explained to the admiral that since I had not been a regular reader of the Japanese press, I was unfamiliar with the significance of the placement and format of the articles and the relative size of the headlines in relation to previous headline events. I felt that what I should do was go over the newspapers with Japanese prisoners in Guam's prisoner-of-war camp. He immediately okayed my suggestion, and I took the papers to the camp where one can easily imagine the sensation they caused. I left the papers with the prisoners overnight, and the next morning I read them with two captured Japanese Army officers sitting, one on each side of me at an outdoor table in a shady spot within the compound.

The first thing they pointed out to me was the small size of the front-page article on the dropping of the first atom bomb on Hiroshima and in another paper, the second atom bomb on Nagasaki. There was also a small feature article by a technical writer who had deduced (correctly) that the United States had only three bombs, and two had already been dropped. But what I found even more interesting was that the belated declaration of war on Japan and the invasion of Manchuria by the Soviet Union had received, according to the two prisoners, even bigger headlines than the Japanese attack on Pearl Harbor in December 1941.

This led me to the conclusion, at least from a perusal of the Japanese daily press, that the Soviet's entrance into the war against Japan had been a more persuasive factor in Japan's surrender than the atom bombs. This, of course, was totally different from the U.S. official view of the Japanese surrender, and I so informed Admiral Nimitz. Isolated as I was at the time in Guam, I could not examine the total intelligence "take" on the subject. But regardless, I've often thought that the subject merits research and would make a superb subject for a history student's PhD thesis, especially now that wartime thinking has been able to subside into an objective view of the subject. Even if my conclusion was not correct, it would be interesting to know why the Japanese government at the time had so angled its news in its controlled press so as to lead the reader to this conclusion.

From Guam, I was soon ordered to Sasebo, Japan, and got as far as a rather sordid transient camp in Okinawa where I was stuck. "No transport to Japan itself available at this time," I was told. With nothing to do, and recalling my interesting time spent with the prisoners in Guam, I visited a POW camp on Okinawa for some idle chitchat. There I found an obviously very intelligent Japanese Army captain, and I've never forgotten what he told me.

"You Americans," he said, "have never been to Okinawa in September and have no idea what terrible typhoons we can have here. The weather is already blustery. Furthermore, you tell me you are living in a transient camp at Buckner Bay, as you people call it. Not a very good place to be if there is a typhoon. You should leave the island as soon as you can. The destruction will be terrible if there is a typhoon."

This guy, I said to myself, *knows a hell of a lot more about Okinawa than I do. Listen to him!* I did and found that there was a Catalina flying boat scheduled to take off from a Construction Battalion unit on the other side of the island the following morning. I immediately asked for and received a set of orders to travel on the Catalina and then managed to bum a ride on a jeep across the island. The GI who had the jeep asked me for $50 for this non-ordered diversion from his work, and the following morning I left on the Catalina. Thirty-six hours later a terrible hurricane hit Buckner Bay, causing enormous destruction and considerable loss of life. Never in my life was $50 better spent.

From Sasebo, where I spent one day taking inventory of naval stores in a Japanese warehouse, I got orders to go to Fukuoka and from there to Kokura in northern Kyushu. Before I left, I got a haircut at the hotel where the barber not only cut my hair but also gave me a set of fuck pictures to look at while he did so. He also recommended to me a local geisha house that had, he said, superb food and enticing girls. Furthermore, he explained that it had not yet been discovered by the Occupation forces, and he was sure I would enjoy myself. I rounded up three other Japanese-language officers I knew, and we all had a delightful meal there with enchanting company.

14

The moment I stepped off the train at Kokura, an industrial city in northern Kyushu, on the straits of Shimonoseki, I knew something was wrong. The stationmaster, who had seen me leave the train from his little office in the station, had turned visibly pale. He came out on the platform and advanced uncertainly toward me, then bowed at least 120 degrees; and when he straightened, he said hesitantly, "Welcome to Kokura, honorable Admiral."

I immediately explained to him as gently as I could that I was not an admiral but a lowly naval lieutenant. I had orders to join the 126th Infantry Regiment. Where was it and would the stationmaster phone regimental headquarters to tell them of my arrival and to come and pick me up?

"But there is no American army regiment. You, sir, are the first American to arrive in Kokura and to occupy it."

At that moment, totally nonplussed and feeling that it was essential to cover my own confusion over my predicament, I suggested that the stationmaster carry my gear into his office. This would give me a minute or two to decide exactly what to do. It was clear what had happened. Since there was no language problem for me, once I received orders to proceed to Kokura, it never occurred to me to wait for army transport. If this had been done, I would have found out that the 126th had not yet arrived to assume its occupation duties and would then have stayed in Fukuoka to await its arrival. Instead, I had simply gone to the railroad station and boarded the first train going north that stopped at Kokura. It wasn't a long train ride.

Now, here I was, totally alone. In fact, I was the Occupation force. What to do? The one thing that was clear I should not do was catch the next train back to Fukuoka. That would have been the safest thing, but it would involve loss of face not only for me, but also in so far as the citizens of Kokura were concerned, for the Occupation forces.

Eventually, I followed the stationmaster into his office. "This city must have a mayor," I commented. "Does he have an automobile that works?"

"Oh yes, a beautiful limousine and an aide who always accompanies him. He is a very distinguished retired general."

"Send for him!"

The stationmaster, now visibly relieved that he would no longer have to cope alone with the Occupation, grabbed his telephone and called the mayor to explain that the Occupation had arrived in the form of the U.S. Navy.

Ten minutes later an ancient but spotlessly clean limousine with a charcoal gas device attached to the rear arrived. The aide hopped out and deferentially opened the rear door for the mayor who, without a moment's hesitation, descended and advanced toward me. There was no bow. He simply shook hands and introduced himself; I immediately recognized him as an aristocrat. He was slender, tall, and had fine bones. There was nothing of the peasant squatness about him, and despite his age, he was in excellent physical shape. The general had no difficulty whatsoever understanding my predicament and why Tokyo had not warned him of the time of my arrival.

He then turned to the stationmaster and ordered him to phone a Mr. Tanaka to come to the station to "pick up Lieutenant Kramer [he got my rank correct] and drive him to his hotel." Once that was done the stationmaster was to desert his post for five minutes to carry my gear to the curb where Mr. Tanaka could pick it up. "My aide," the mayor explained, "will go with you to your hotel to sign the necessary documents so that your stay there will be at the expense of the Japanese authorities concerned with such matters. Meanwhile, rest assured that any information sent to me from Tokyo relative to your position will be passed on to you immediately."

At this point, the stationmaster left his office with my gear, and the mayor's tone changed. "You must forgive me," he explained, "if I seem preoccupied, but I have just received word that my only son who was military attaché in Berlin and apparently taken prisoner by the Soviets has still not been located. Queries have been sent via Swedish diplomatic channels but to no avail. Perhaps you Americans will be able to be of some assistance since you and the Soviets are allies."

"I, of course, am far too junior to be able to help you," I explained. "But when the colonel of the 126th arrives, you must, by all means, speak to him and ask that he seek the intervention of General McBride in command of the 32nd Division. He is the man who ordered me up here."

"I shall do that. I assume you too, like my son, are an intelligence officer."

"I am." At this point, I decided to drop a few names; it might help. "I did intelligence work as a civilian for Nelson Rockefeller before Pearl Harbor and before joining the navy. I'd studied at Cambridge University in England and was thus put on some sort of joint U.S.-British operation."

"Ah, so." The mayor's face lit up. "You may remember Prince Chichibu, the emperor's brother, and his visit to Oxford before the war. I was honored to be a member of his suite."

"I certainly do. I was at Cambridge then. A pity his Highness visited the wrong university."

The mayor allowed himself to smile faintly at this rather British wit and then discarded all informality upon the return of the stationmaster. He bid me a ceremonious good-bye and his aide, along with Mr. Tanaka, escorted me to my hotel. Somehow, it must have been warned of my arrival for the entire staff was at the entrance to greet me.

Once settled in my Japanese-style room, I was asked when I wished to have my bath and supper. Meanwhile, tea was produced, and I indicated I wished to be alone for a few minutes. Once undressed and in the provided kimono, someone could come in to pick up my clothing.

I laid back on the straw matting and reflected on my conversation with the mayor. I knew that both what had been said as well as what had not been said were the keys to my future in Kokura, and I reached five conclusions, all of which were ultimately to be proven correct.

1. The mayor was in total command of Kokura and the neighboring cities and countryside. As far as the 126th was concerned, he was the Japanese government.
2. His totally unnecessary reference to the royal family was an oblique way of saying that since the emperor had been preserved as nominal ruler of Japan, he, with his royal connections, would also be preserved as nominal ruler of Kokura.
3. The general's weak point was the fate of his son. He would do anything, even beyond what Tokyo might order him to do, if General McBride intervened to rescue his son.
4. MacArthur's headquarters in Tokyo, or SCAP, as it came to be known, was a sieve in so far as decisions of interest to the mayor were concerned. He had his own sources of information in Tokyo, and they were reliable.
5. I could be sure the mayor would pass on to me any decisions that would affect me and my presence in Kokura even before the arrival of my assigned regiment. Furthermore, even though unarmed and alone, I was perfectly safe in Kokura.

With these conclusions off my chest, I went to take a bath where the young and not unattractive female attendant soaped me all over and then sloshed me with buckets of warm water. When she finished, she accused me of being "shy." I took this as a challenge and proved to her otherwise. What followed was a hot soak in the tub, then supper, then the unrolling and preparation of my bed. I asked for the local newspaper but found, once in bed, I was too sleepy to read it.

The following morning I decided to explore Kokura on foot. My progress about town was a source of enormous curiosity. Most everyone had never before seen a U.S. Navy officer, and there was much speculation as to what my rank was and to what Allied nation I belonged. Perhaps I was a Royal Air Force officer, or maybe even from the French Navy. At a street corner, I ran into a group of high school students in their uniforms and overheard their conversation.

"He's U.S. Navy, I'm sure of that."

"Yes, and he's a captain."

"No, I can tell by the color of his uniform, he's French."

"That's impossible. The U.S. Navy doesn't have French officers. He is clearly navy."

"They say all Americans have a huge penis. Do you think he's got one too?"

At this point, I interrupted to say in Japanese, "I am not a captain. I am an American navy lieutenant, junior grade, and I do not have a giant penis. That is idle superstition."

The kids collapsed in total embarrassment. Their eyes widened in horror once they realized that I had understood them. A moment later, recovering their mobility, they scampered away like a flock of startled pigeons.

Around noon, I found myself in front of the local department store and decided to go inside. There was painfully little on the shelves, but as I stood admiring a carved Chinese crystal bowl, a store employee rushed up to me. "Honorable sir, Lieutenant," he hissed, "you must come with me to the fifth floor, to the manager's office. There is great trouble."

I followed him and found five Korean coal miners, just freed from a slave labor mine, demanding the right to help themselves to anything in the store they wished as compensation for their years of slavery. They carried knives, and one stood in a menacing position with a crowbar.

I immediately realized that having decided the previous day to stay in Kokura, there was now no retreat; the only solution was to bluff my way out of this one.

"Korean coal miners," I said in Japanese as I walked calmly behind the store manager's desk so I could face them. "I am an American Navy officer charged with the occupation of this area. You will cease this disturbance at once and follow me on foot to the railroad station. There a car on the next train south will be cleared of Japanese passengers for your sole occupancy for the trip to Fukuoka where General McBride, in charge of the occupation of all of Kyushu, will have you transported home to Korea. At the station you will be issued American, I repeat American, money with which to buy food for your journey. Now follow me at once."

I did not look back. I didn't need to. The bluff had worked. They followed me like meek children to the utter amazement of the Japanese. At the station, I immediately ordered the stationmaster to wire ahead to clear ten seats on the next southbound train to Fukuoka. Then I demanded that the Koreans produce a leader. This caused a lengthy totally incomprehensible debate in Korean. Eventually the man with the crowbar stepped forward.

I pulled out four five-dollar bills from my wallet and gave them to him. "That," I explained, "is sufficient to feed on the way to Korea. When you arrive in Fukuoka, you are to proceed at once to General McBride's headquarters. Now repeat after me, GENERAL MCBRIDE, three times."

This turned out to be a tongue twister for them. Their mood changed as they began to laugh and repeat, "GEN-EE-RALL MOK-BIDE."

A half hour later, the train arrived. They left, and I breathed a sigh of relief. The stationmaster gave me a cup of tea. I drank it and walked back to the hotel where I found waiting for me a Japanese Methodist preacher who gave me a gift and told me he had studied at Pomona College in California. It was an enormous relief to find someone to chatter away with in English. My Japanese was far too limited for me to be able to relax with it. Also, it was at once apparent that the man had an intimate knowledge of events in the community that the mayor might wish to conceal from the Occupation authorities. The man complained how during the war Christians had been forced to have "heathen" funerals. He also complained that many Japanese army officers were living illegally at government expense in still-functioning military hospitals when there was nothing wrong with them.

I listened politely and then dismissed him but asked that he return the following day at 9 AM. The mayor had phoned to say that an Allied Mission was arriving on the express from Tokyo in the morning and no doubt I would wish to be at the station to greet them. A good guide would no doubt be helpful.

The next morning, dressed in a perfectly pressed and brushed blue navy officer's winter uniform, I was on the platform to greet the Allied mission. Much to my utter amazement, the mission consisted of three British padres, or chaplains, who had come to the area to find out if any British subjects had died in the area during the war, and if so, whether they had received a Christian burial.

This, of course, was right up the Methodist minister's alley. He knew exactly where to take the chaplains. A group of gravediggers was retained to exhume the remains of several British prisoners who had died in a camp during the war and rebury them in a Christian cemetery. The padres conducted the appropriate service, Church of England, Catholic, or Methodist.

Three days later the 126th finally arrived, and I was again at the station to meet them. This turned out to be somewhat comical. Battle-hardened, helmeted men with their rifles at the ready, emerged form the train onto the station platform, not really knowing what to expect but fully prepared to defend themselves. I walked up the platform until I found the colonel, gave him a smart salute, and said, "Welcome to Kokura, Colonel."

"Who the Sam Hell are you?"

"I'm Lieutenant Kramer, sir, with orders to report for duty to your regiment. I've been here almost a week, waiting for your arrival."

The colonel, totally nonplussed, sent for his exec and ordered him to interview me while he deployed and saw to the safety of his troops.

The exec's first question was, "Where have you been quartered while waiting for the regiment to arrive?"

"At the local hotel."

"Where is that?"

"Three city blocks south of here."

"Can I find it on my own?"

"Go first to that high-rise building, which is the local department store. Anyone in there can lead you to Lieutenant Kramer. Just tell them my name and they'll guide you to me."

"I'll be there in three hours. Wait for me there."

"Yes sir."

The executive officer didn't arrive until 5 PM. By that time, he was exhausted, having had no sleep on the overnight train trip from Tokyo. I suggested a bath before dinner and told the bath maid to arrange things. Whatever happened in the bath was not discussed, but a relaxed, shaved, and smiling colonel arrived in my room and announced that he would be taking over my quarters at the hotel, and I was to eat and sleep with the other regimental officers at the Japanese officers' club, which the regiment had already appropriated.

As the colonel explained it, "You know this town, we don't I'm sure the officers will find your foreknowledge useful."

I figured at the time that this was so much baloney. It was no more than a cover for the colonel's delight in the hotel's bathing arrangements, but I said nothing, and curiously, whatever the motives behind his conduct, he was proven correct. The only really useful thing I did for the 126th Infantry Regiment resulted from sitting next to the regimental doctor at lunch one day.

The doctor complained that he had four cases of what appeared to be pneumonia, but they were not responding to new wonder drugs. Of the four, one was near death and he was beginning to lose hope for the other three, one of whom was an army nurse who had been taking care of the rest.

"Doctor," I said, "you know, we are in a strange country none of us really know, and I'm sure there must be strange diseases here we don't know anything about. Why don't you call in a local diagnostician for a second opinion?"

"I'd do it in a minute. But I don't know any."

"Suppose I get you one."

"That would be good, real good. Can you get him to my hospital this afternoon?"

"I'll certainly try."

I went to the phone and called the mayor, who agreed to send an outstanding diagnostician to the regiment's hospital immediately. By the time the doctor arrived, the diagnostician was already there. He took one look at the patients and announced they were suffering from pneumonic plague and recommended a different treatment. Three of them recovered; the first and sickest patient died. The regimental doctor later admitted to me, "In medical school in Cincinnati, Ohio, I was never even shown a case of pneumonic plague, let alone taught how to treat one. Whether you realize it or not, you've saved the lives of two soldiers and a nurse."

Although not lifesaving, the other job that came my way while with the 126th was interesting. On orders from Tokyo, all people within the regiment's jurisdiction were ordered to surrender their arms. This order was so broadly interpreted that the locals had even given up their swords, daggers, and collections of medieval pikes used in ancient nautical battles. Rosters of the owners had been compiled. Custody fell into the preview of a West Point lieutenant colonel on the regimental staff who felt that the surrendered arms, which could be classified as "works of art", should be returned to the owners.

"I'd like to do it," he said, "but haven't any idea how to go about it in such a way that the colonel will approve."

"It shouldn't be too difficult," I commented. "Why not let me go to the mayor and ask him to set up a committee of art experts to determine which are works of art that will be returned. I'm sure the mayor will have no difficulty in gathering such a committee. He is a retired general from an old Samurai family. He'll know just how to go about it."

This was done, and for the next four days, the art committee sat with handkerchiefs in their mouths so that their breaths would not moisten and thus rust the tempered steel of the swords. Everyone was grateful: the mayor, the committee members, the owners, the lietenant colonel in charge of the project, and the commanding colonel of the regiment. I was given one of the swords from the art collection, as a way of saying "thanks" for saving them from destruction.

Another gift I received was of a more curious nature. One day I visited the Imari pottery works located in the regiment's occupation area. The pottery was closed, but a managing director appeared, and while carrying a spade, led me out into an adjoining field to the rear of the factory. Here he began to dig and eventually unearthed a large metal box. Inside were hundreds of tiny, perfect replicas of various Imari pieces of pottery, none more than an inch high. "These," he explained, "are precise detailed models of our prewar line of ceramics. We had our artists make them, and we buried them as a precaution against bombs. In this way we preserved the designs and decorations of our production." He then reached into the box, scooped out two handfuls of the miniatures, and gave them to me. I had the regiment ship them to the United States, and I still own seven of them.

There was also another memorable incident. I went one day to visit the Yawata Steel Works located in the neighboring city of Yawata. The mill was totally shut down, but a director appeared, and he took me to the company's boardroom where we had a pleasant chat. I've never forgotten what he said. It was not really a conversation, but more of a gentle murmuring on his part while surrounded with the trappings of the mill's former executive splendors.

"Lieutenant Kramer," he mused, "when you think that since the day the first steel mill here opened, seventy-eight percent of our production has gone into armaments and hence, nonproductive goods, can you imagine the riches and prosperity the future holds for Japan if our factory should it be allowed to reopen and turn out only civilian and wealth-producing goods? Despite our defeat, and it is cruel—as I'm sure you've noticed since you cannot help but see that the population here is subsisting almost entirely on sweet potatoes—but with proper decisions I now foresee a future of unparalleled economic prosperity for Japan."

* * *

Curiously, my childhood on the family farm adjacent to the 10th Infantry post had been a help with the 126th. I had gotten to know army routines as well as a succession of commanding colonels. As a child, I'd watched many a baseball games among the soldiers and was totally familiar with enlisted men's constant chatter about money and sex. Also, a number of the 10th Infantry's enlisted men became prisoners as punishment for violation of army rules and regulations and were made to do menial work while guarded by MPs. Some were punished for having gone AWOL. Occasionally one of them escaped. The fort's cannon would immediately be discharged and a posse of MPs would go in search of them, usually in the woods on the bluff below our house or in the neighboring forest. Since it was well known that I knew every nook and cranny of these lands, if they came across me looking for quail or en route along one of the paths to the river, they would always ask me if I'd seen the escapee and knew where he was hiding. Sometimes I knew; but I never told them. The truth was I felt sorry for these poor country boys who had learned to hate army life.

This sympathy for the lot of the enlisted man stayed with me, and when the new colonel of the 126th, a former headmaster of a boys' military school and a real martinet, grounded my jeep driver for two weeks for exceeding the speed limit within the regiment's compound, I felt sorry for him. This corporal had nursed and cared for the jeep all the way from Australia to Japan via New Guinea and

Okinawa. He had come to me to report his fate in a state of total dejection. I had told him I'd see what could be done and went to see the colonel. He had heard me out patiently, refused to countermand his order, and then rose and shouted at his adjutant. "Why is it," he demanded, "that Lieutenant Kramer here, a navy officer, has been the first and only officer on my staff who has come to me to stick up for one of his men? Call a meeting of all the officers at once,"

At the meeting, I was made to sit and listen to the colonel berate his officers and point out that it took a navy officer to set an example of proper conduct and go to the defense of his men. I've never in my life been so embarrassed.

This was not my only contact with the colonel. Earlier, some of the other regimental officers had invited me to join them in a poker game. When I discovered the stakes, used as I was to Joe Rovensky's penny ante games, I was horrified at how high they were. These men had nothing but their army salaries, but I went along anyway. Several of the men drank during the game, and their play became childishly erratic. I emerged as the only winner with $240. The colonel heard about the game and sent for me the following morning. "There will be no more poker at high stakes in my regiment," he barked.

Subsequent to this, he asked me to find a nice souvenir for him to send home. Since I knew there was a still-functioning vitreous china factory in the area that manufactured Western-style toilet bowls for export, I ordered one in blue for the colonel and asked that they tool his initials at the bottom of the bowl in bold gold lettering. Although I had my doubts about the suitability of the souvenir, the colonel was utterly delighted with it and personally supervised its crating for shipment back to the States.

During my early days with the regiment, soon after the new colonel had arrived, there had been a bad accident. A brigade had been dispatched to a remote area of the regiment's occupational jurisdiction to see to the destruction of a large cache of Japanese munitions that had been found in a spur railway tunnel for use in the anticipated battle over the island of Kyushu. Unfortunately, the burning of the munitions within the tunnel had caused a giant explosion. The top of the mountain under which the tunnel passed had been blown off, and part of it had landed on a village school and killed a number of students. The colonel had ordered me to visit the site of destruction with his exec and report back to him what I learned.

On arrival, a village elder had taken me to a building in which a room was reserved for the bodies of the schoolboys. There were about twelve of them. All had been washed and reclothed in neat new school uniforms, and their bodies were laid out in rows on the straw matting, and the room remained brightly lit by electric light even though it was daytime. I made the appropriate murmurs of condolence to the village elder over this totally tragic scene, and then I was taken by the lieutenant colonel of the regiment to explore the scene of the explosion. A fire was still burning in the tunnel, and the colonel insisted I go with him to the mouth of the tunnel itself. The explosion was clearly due to brigade's inexperience with destroying munitions, but I said nothing; neither did the exec.

The exec and I were put up at the local Japanese-style village inn where we shared a room. Since he hadn't asked for a separate room for himself, I deduced that this was the way he wanted it and said nothing. Having learned the delight of Japanese baths, however, he immediately asked that I tell the management that we wanted one and to make the necessary preparations, which I did. When it was ready, he suggested we bathe together, and I agreed. Later we had a Japanese-style supper together in our room. While eating, I heard voices in the adjoining room, and I held up my hand to ask the lieutenant colonel to stop talking so I could overhear the conversation.

The talk was between two men, newspaper reporters sent down from Tokyo by their newspapers to report on the accident. They were both discussing just how they proposed to "angle" their stories. Neither of them, I learned, proposed blaming the Americans in any way for the accident and the loss of lives. On the contrary, it was the fault of the wartime government of Prime Minister Hideki Tojo, which was responsible for secreting the munitions in the tunnel in the first place. As part of Japan's recovery program it was necessary to restore the railroad's line so that it could function properly, and this was why the accident had happened.

I told this to the exec, and he seemed disinterested. His only preoccupation seemed to be with the regiment itself, not the Japanese. Later when our bed was unrolled and prepared, I discovered we were expected to sleep together in the same bed and asked the lieutenant colonel if I should order another one. "No," he said, "this place will get cold in the night. We're better off together."

On our return to Kokura, I reported to the colonel and told him what I had overheard the journalists discussing in the next room. He said nothing, but he was clearly interested.

In mid-December 1945, the colonel sent for me and told me that despite his best efforts to keep me on his staff, Tokyo had demanded that I be relieved of my duties with his regiment and sent to Tokyo for a new assignment. I was to take the overnight train the following evening, on which a compartment had already been reserved for me. He said he would miss me and wished me good luck. I thanked him for his consideration and left. Two of the regimental junior officers drove me to the station, and thus ended my occupation duties with the 126th Infantry Regiment.

Alone on the train, I reflected on the reasons for my accomplishments with the 126th. I didn't think they were so much, but at least I'd won the respect of my fellow officers, and I wondered why. Here, and as I've mentioned before, my close contact as a child with a neighboring infantry regiment had been of help, but also, in an oblique way, so had the Boulder Japanese-language school. Even more helpful than my study of the language itself, there had been, gained via the language, the ability to penetrate the Japanese mind. Here too my personal contact with the Japanese teachers had been helpful since I had watched how they approached problems, both scholarly and personal ones and learned thereby their different thought processes. Thus, once in Kokura I found I could be at ease with the Japanese with whom I dealt and whom I could, if I felt it necessary, draw out. Furthermore, and unlike many of the other officers in the regiment, I no longer regarded the Japanese as a cruel and evil enemy. The thing to do, within the limits of my job, was to work toward a future alliance. I decided that the Japanese with whom I'd had to deal sensed this. Certainly the mayor did. We had even discussed it, and he had gone out of his way to be helpful whenever I had asked him for assistance.

While still in Kokura, I bought a complete set of Hiroshige's scenic prints from an antique dealer who had a tiny roadside stall. Later I gave these to the Honolulu Academy of Art in memory of former governor and Mrs. Samuel King, the parents of my Japanese-language school friend, Judge Samuel P. King. The governor and his wife had once had me as a house guest at Washington Place, the governor's mansion. The King family was large, and the only available bed was in Hawaii's Queen Liliuokalani's bedroom. The bed was very large and comfortable, but unfortunately the room was open to view by tourists from the adjoining Lana'i. Fearful that sightseers would discover me naked in the queen's bed, I woke up very early each morning. Not wishing to disturb the King family, I would silently slip out of the house and go off to Waikiki for a swim and a private surfing lesson. It was solely because of this that I learned to master this difficult but utterly exhilarating sport.

Whatever else I did for the 126th was of little importance either for me or for the regiment. The three months I spent with the regiment, however, were happy ones. It originally had been a Wisconsin National Guard unit, and many of its soldiers and sergeants were from the farms and rural small towns in Wisconsin. It consisted of an entirely different breed of men than the Phi Beta Kappa students at the Boulder language school.

Upon my arrival in Tokyo, I discovered to my fury that no one had bothered to forward my mail to the 126th at Kokura. There was a large bundle waiting for me, all hopelessly out of date. When I protested this cavalier attitude to the lieutenant commander of the unit to which I had been ordered to report, he totally ignored my protest. Instead, he demanded to know why was it I had maneuvered things so as to delay my recall to the language officers' headquarters in Tokyo of which he was in charge from October 1, 1945, until December 15. I told him that I had no idea there was such a delay. All I knew was that Colonel Woodward of the 126th Infantry Regiment had told me two days previously that he had lost the battle to keep me with the regiment and that I was to leave for Tokyo on the overnight train, which I had done.

"And you knew nothing of our repeated requests for your recall?" the lieutenant commander asked.

"Nothing, sir."

"I've examined your file and have noted that your commanding officer both in Brisbane and in Manila was a Royal Navy officer, not a U.S. Navy officer and in no way connected with the Japanese-language program."

"That is correct. He came to see me when I was still a patient at the 42nd General Hospital and asked that I report to him immediately on my release from the hospital."

"So that you were disassociated from all other Boulder men while under his substantive orders, which I assume was for the duration of the war."

"Not quite. I was detailed from that duty for four days in Brisbane, and along with my bodyguard, was assigned to supervise the loading of General MacArthur's classified files aboard a freighter for transport to Manila."

"Have you any idea why you were assigned to such non-Japanese-language-related duties?"

"I do, sir, for two reasons. One, I had a personal armed bodyguard in the form of Chief Beals, a U.S. Navy petty officer and champion navy boxer; and two, I already had a "top secret" security rating dating from my civilian work before I entered the navy."

"Did Commander Hindmarsh, who, as you know, is in charge of the Japanese-language program, know any of this?"

"I have no idea whatsoever. Captain Zacharias, who was interviewing me at the time, sent for Hindmarsh and ordered him to sign me up for the Boulder program, which he did. Hindmarsh was then dismissed, and I concluded my interview with Captain Zacharias."

"And what was the nature of your interview?"

"That I am not at liberty to say."

"You mean you refuse to answer my question."

"I do, sir. The nature of the interview was top secret. This was continued during my Boulder and navy career. If you have my file, there must be some indication of it in the file."

This clearly rattled the teeth of the interviewing officer, but he said nothing. Instead, he demanded that I turn over to him any Japanese weapons I might have in my possession. Fortunately, I had had the 126th pack and ship back to the United States the samurai sword that the art committee had given me, but unfortunately I had forgotten a Nambu Japanese officer's pistol that Roybal had taken from an officer he had killed in the Philippines and had given to me as a gift in Brisbane. I thus told the lieutenant commander about it and explained it was with my gear in his outer office. He ordered me to get it at once and give it to him, which I did while resolving at the same time to make a stand.

"This pistol," I said, "was not acquired in Japan. It was given to me in Brisbane by an army captain who personally took it from a dead Japanese officer."

"What proof do you have of that?"

"None whatsoever. But I do have the officer's present address in Wagon Mound, New Mexico, if you care to write or telephone him. Meanwhile, as an officer I must tell you that I resent your question."

This clearly surprised him, and he changed the subject. "I take it," he said. "You haven't yet been assigned your quarters since you still have your gear with you."

"That's correct."

"My yeoman in my outer office will take care of that. I want you back here at nine o'clock tomorrow morning to receive your orders for your new assignment."

"Yes sir." The interview had been so hopelessly unpleasant that en route to my quarters, which turned out to be on a large barge at anchor in a Tokyo canal and outfitted like a second-class hotel, I decided I simply had to do something about it. The problem was clear. The man had clearly personalized Colonel Woodward's running battle to keep me with the 126th as an affront to his authority over the Boulder graduates, and there was nothing I could do to depersonalize it. At the same time I was damned if I would report to duty to him the following morning. I had had no proper leave since leaving Boulder over a year and a half earlier, and I would get myself some even if it was a sick leave.

Thus, on arrival at my new quarters, I went at once to sickbay, asked to see the doctor, and showed him a large growth on my right index finger. A previous one had been surgically removed when I was a teenager, but it had grown back even larger. Also, the doctor at the 126th had noticed it and had told me to have it removed. What the hell, I said to myself. I'll be out of the navy in a few months at the latest. I might as well have it cut out now at the navy's expense rather than wait until I'm a civilian again and have to pay for it.

The moment the doctor saw the growth, he ordered its immediate removal and then gave me a choice. I could let him remove it or, alternatively, he could order me to a navy hospital ship at anchor in the Tokyo harbor, and it could be removed there. He said he would very much like to perform the operation himself. I told him to go ahead, and he then said I was to report to his sickbay at 5 PM. The pharmacist's mates would see to it that I had a light supper and no breakfast the next morning since a general anesthetic would be required. Because the necessary surgery was very delicate, the operation would take about an hour.

Immediately after the operation, at around 10:30 AM, while I was still totally unconscious, my detested lieutenant commander arrived in sickbay, demanding to know why I had not reported for duty at 9:00 AM as ordered. Of course, I didn't hear him. Receiving no reply, he then began to poke me and slap me in the face. Meanwhile, a pharmacist mate who had witnessed the scene sent for the doctor who arrived just in time to witness part of the man's outrageous behavior. The doctor immediately ordered him out of sickbay, demanded to know his name, and announced that he intended to inform his commanding officer of his behavior. He was then escorted to the gangway and was told that future admission to the vessel would be denied him. That afternoon my Japanese pistol was delivered to the ship by a yeoman.

I, of course, knew nothing of this until I was awake and all the gory details were related to me not by one, but by two pharmacist mates who then sent for the doctor. The doctor never mentioned the incident to me, but it clearly made him especially solicitous. I would stay in his sickbay for another twenty-four hours, he explained. I could then return to my quarters for another twenty-four hours. My arm would be in a sling for a week, and my bandaged hand, the dressings of which should be changed daily, would make it impossible for me to dress myself. The pharmacist mates would do this, or alternatively, I could find a Japanese resort hotel that would provide a nurse or a maid to change the dressing. He understood that there were several near the base of Mt. Fujiyama and recommended one of these. It was imperative, however, that I return to him in a week so the stitches could be removed. I knew of a deluxe hotel at the hot springs resort of Atami. We called it, and the necessary arrangements were made.

At Atami, I was given a small bungalow in the garden of the deluxe hotel where I stayed for four days. The hotel supplied a maid to dress me in the morning and change the dressing on my hand.[1] Once I recovered, I returned to Tokyo and was ordered back south again to Sasebo, where I had first landed in Japan, to join a ship at anchor in the harbor there. The offensive lieutenant commander was no

---

[1.]   There was one curious incident while I was in Atami. My Japanese-style cottage was set in a little garden with a protective bamboo hedge. On two consecutive mornings, while, because of the balmy sunny weather, breakfasting on an adjoining verandah, I noticed a Japanese man peering through the hedge at me.

On the third morning, I decided to dress in uniform instead of the provided kimono and go and see who the curious neighbor was. To my utter astonishment, I discovered it was Prince Chichibu, the emperor's younger brother. We had several conversations. Because he was known to be pro-British, he had been totally sidetracked during the war; and although never a prisoner, he had been carefully supervised by the Tokyo government. He was also in delicate health. But in his isolation, he clearly enjoyed the visit of a Cambridge graduate while insisting that the visits be limited to conversations through the hedge.

longer in evidence, and his replacement couldn't have been more solicitous. He advised me to go at once to the Army Transport Office to secure comfortable sleeping accommodations for the long train ride to Sasebo. I did this and was given a luxurious drawing room with an adjoining private bath for my sole occupancy. The car I was in must have originally been used for transport of members of the royal family. I say this because at every station, the stationmaster, even if we didn't stop, was on the platform and bowed deeply toward the car as it passed by. I relished it! What a contrast from the treatment I had received from the totally offensive lieutenant commander!

On one occasion we got to the subject of Henry Pu Yi, the former Japanese puppet emperor of Manchuria. Since it was known that Pu Yi was a homosexual and would have no children, his younger brother and heir had thus been married to a cousin of the Japanese empress. In this way, the royal family had assured themselves that a Japanese bloodline would be infused into the Chinese imperial family. At the time of our hedge talks, neither of us knew what had become of Pu Yi and his brother as a result of the Soviet invasion of Manchuria just before the end of the war. However, the talk did awaken my interest in the imperial Manchu family and years later led me to publish *The Last Manchu* in Britain, France, Spain, Brazil, and the U.S. At that time the U.S. did not recognize Red China. However, a Chinese friend got me a copy of Pu Yi's manuscript written during his brainwashing process out of China via Hong Kong. With the help of a Manchu family in the U.S., it was translated, and I edited out of it the more outrageous bits of communist propaganda and introduced it to the public with an historical preface. Originally, it received a mixed reception. But in France and Spain, it at once became a bestseller, and General Franco included it in his list of fifty favorite books. Later, when Bertolucci made his film *The Last Emperor*, which was based on the book, it was reproduced in paperback and became a bestseller. Bertolucci, however, in order to secure the cooperation of the Peking government, altered the story in various parts, especially that part dealing with the Red Guards, which was not in the book and in some contrast as to what had really happened as reported in the Western press at the time. I found the film, however, first-rate entertainment.

Paul Kramer, LTJG. With glasses, standing with 3 chief petty officers
aboard a surrendered Japanese submarine

15

From the moment I saluted the officer of the deck and asked permission to come aboard the *Nereus*, a spanking new submarine tender just out from San Diego, I knew there would be some initial trouble. The officers and warrant officers were almost entirely old career submariner types. Here was Kramer, a reserve officer, and an intelligence officer who spoke the enemy lingo! The war might be over, but for many men aboard the *Nereus*, just out from the United States, the enmities still existed. What a calamity for the wardroom! They would have to be polite to this guy. "Have you seen him? He's a skinny little runt, less than five feet six and wears glasses. How the fuck can he look through a periscope?"

The analysis had been correct. There was immediate talk of making me laundry officer. Also, I was told it would cost $350 to join the officers' mess. "Sorry it's so high, but we're a new ship, and during the shakedown cruises we had a lot of civilian shipyard engineers aboard and were able to run the mess at a profit."

"But I'm not a shipyard worker. Besides, I don't even know what's in my pay account. It was lost en route overseas."

"Too bad. But the mess bill is $350. Of course, you may get some back when you leave."

"But when will that be? It's already long past my rotation date for return to the U.S."

"Who knows?"

All this chivying quietly evaporated within twenty-four hours. That night after supper, Commander Pierce, along with the commander who was to be my working boss, took me to meet the captain. All three were Naval Academy men and old-line submariners. The captain looked prematurely aged to me. Clearly a submariner through and through, he was very soft-spoken. He had an open file on his desk.

"I see," he said, "you had duty with a Royal Navy commander in Brisbane and Manila before coming to Japan, and three and half months here in Japan with the 126th Infantry Regiment."

"My Brisbane boss, sir, was a Commander Lionel Holmes-Hopkinson. He was a fine man; it was a privilege to work for him. There was a little difficulty with some highly classified material, and I had to have a bodyguard, but other than that, all went very smoothly, just as it did with the 126th."

"I assume the commander here has already explained to you your duties."

"He has, sir."

"There is just one thing. You must at all times go aboard the Japanese subs armed. They have kamikaze human-guided torpedo men aboard. They could be dangerous."

It had become habitual ever since Nelson Rockefeller had originally sent for me to do intelligence work to never hesitate to let a boss know when he had made what I felt was a foolish request, and I did so in this instance, and with conviction. "Sir," I said, "I wonder if that would be wise. I know of course what my duties are—to assist in maintaining the discipline and cohesion of the crews of the surrendered Japanese submarine fleet until the Allies decide what to do with them as well as interpret Japanese, but I don't want the Nips to feel there is any fear of them. What I've got to do is develop a natural give-and-take with them if I'm to do the job. Also, and this is my basic point, for all practical purposes, when a man boards a submarine and climbs down through an open hatch, he's stark naked protection-wise. It doesn't make any difference if he's got a .45 or a submachine gun in his arms, he's helpless. The bottom half of him is below deck, the upper half above deck, and all the enemy has to do is yank him down by his feet and hit him over the head with a baseball bat or slice off his legs with a samurai sword. There's not a damn thing he can do."

Pierce looked at me; my new boss said nothing. The captain stood up. "You're right, of course. Absolutely." He then shook my hand in a gesture of dismissal. "I'm sure," he said, "you'll do a fine job."

Both Pierce and my new chief walked me to my cabin. They wanted to make sure everything was in order. "I'm sure," Pierce said, "the captain had only your welfare in mind when he ordered you to go aboard the subs with a .45." My boss grabbed my wrist and looked at my watch. "Don't ever," he explained, "wear that watch aboard a sub. If you do, it will get magnetized. Ship's stores have a few Omegas. For some mysterious reason they don't become magnetized, I'll tell them to issue you one.

From that time on, there was no talk of me being laundry officer or paying $350 to join the mess. Sasebo Harbor was a long deep-water estuary cutting deep into the southern coast of Japan's southernmost island, Kyushu. It had been an important base of the Imperial Japanese Navy. The twenty-four submarines were nested in groups of three and four toward the mouth of the harbor, and the *Nereus* was anchored between them and the western shore. It was thus a short distance by *Nereus* dinghy whaleboat for me and the three chief petty officers who took care of the mechanical aspects of the subs to travel for our daily morning inspections.

That night in my bunk, I felt a sense of elation surge through me. All the little cares and difficulties of the past ten days vanished. The sudden detachment from the 126th, Tokyo's failure to forward my mail, the idiotic behavior of the man who was apparently in charge of assignments in Japan became totally insignificant and of no consequence whatsoever. In their place, I had a new vision derived from the dual nature of the job that had been given me.

Judging from Captain Follmer's reference to my file, he had wanted an experienced intelligence officer. Well, he'd gotten someone whose experience dated from a year and a half before Pearl Harbor. But there was also something else of greater importance to me. Captain Zacharias, the chief of naval intelligence who had recruited me had a goal that he had never been able to achieve: the assignment of an intelligence officer as ship's company to every U.S. Navy capital ship. The *Nereus* could hardly be described as one, but at least by either accident or design, here I was as ship's company, and my fellow officers were, with one or two exceptions, submariners. Furthermore, I knew this was a very rare assignment for a Boulder man. I thus had a challenge ahead of me if I were to prove that there was real merit to Captain Zacharias' unachieved goal. To do this, I realized, I not only had to win the respect of my fellow officers, but also, as an experienced intelligence operative and as a Japanese-language officer, to do a good job. A realization of this challenge exhilarated me and kept me awake in my bunk far at least an hour—a totally novel experience.

The submarines were kept under what appeared to be casual, but was in fact strict surveillance. They were always in sight of the armed bow watch and the officer of the deck of the *Nereus*.

The next morning, before my first visit to the surrendered subs, my boss gave me the promised Omega wristwatch, and it at once became a prized personal possession, worn every day of my life for the next ten years until I left it accidentally in the washroom of a plane flying between Panama and Miami. During all those years I regarded it as a talisman, symbolic not only of the respect I hope I'd won aboard the *Nereus*, but also of the personal success achieved in that operation, which had turned out to be the most difficult task of my working life. As events progressed, and things did go my way, there were even moments when I wondered if the watch was not only a good timepiece but was also in fact a genuine talisman with occult powers. Silly, of course, but life at sea can be a breeding ground for all kinds of superstitions.

The three chief petty officers with whom I visited the subs daily were all old-line submariners, and because I spent several hours a day with them, I had a chance to observe not only their work but also the interplay of relationships among them. Each one had a particular skill. One was an expert on the maintenance of diesel engines, another of electric motors both as propulsion devices and for ancillary purposes. The third was an expert on pumps and pressure systems. They soon developed a totally harmonious relationship with their Japanese counterparts and also became aware of, and frankly admitted this to their counterparts, any superiority of certain Japanese devices over what the U.S. Navy had. This was particularly true of the Japanese optics.

But what fascinated me even more than the chief's response to Japanese mechanics was the interplay of relationships among the three of them. The most senior of the chiefs was tough and was already looking forward to his retirement on Coronado Island off San Diego where he hoped to buy a bar that could cater to submariners. The second oldest was different. Quiet, soft-spoken, he was a source of amusement to the other two in that it was known he couldn't swim and, in fear of falling overboard when traversing a catwalk between the nested subs, always wore a life jacket. But this fear never made him the butt of the others' jokes. On the contrary, it was quietly explained to me that they always let him on a catwalk first so that he would know they were right behind him and, could, if necessary, jump in the water after him and fish him out. The third and youngest of the three was always being instructed by the other two in the various aspects of their own expertise. Seeing these three men work together as quietly as they did, while at the same time respecting one another's individuality, enhanced my respect for the working navy and also served as a demonstration of why the chief petty officers were in fact the backbone of the navy's submarine fleet.

Although their diesel engines and electric motors were kept in operative condition so that, once ordered, the surrendered submarines could proceed anywhere in the world, their actual mobility depended entirely on orders from Captain Follmer of the *Nereus*, not from their own captains. Their crews were maintained at operative levels. It should be explained here that submarine crews are not interchangeable as are those on surface ships. The danger of an operation error and turning the wrong valve or switch can lead to disastrous results on a sub. This was one reason why it was important to retain the Japanese crews and keep them functioning at an efficient level.

Since many of the Japanese officers spoke English, the *Nereus* petty officers had no difficulty and seldom needed my help with translation. There were no more than the usual jams sailors get into, aggravated by Japanese shortages. The increase in gonorrhea required more sulfa than the subs had been issued. I got it for them. There was more drunkenness ashore and minor absences due to missing the last water taxi at night. I overlooked them. There were rats aboard one of the subs. The skipper asked for some DDT. I got it for him. The subs needed certain standard Japanese navy items, which they were told were unavailable. The shortage was actually an administrative mix-up between the Occupation authorities and the remnants of the Japanese navy. I straightened it out for them. Japanese fuel had become so inferior that it continually fouled the diesel engines. The *Nereus* supplied the subs with properly refined American fuel, which the Japanese crews, when they first saw it, found awesome. Meanwhile, I won the esteem of the *Nereus* officers and men by some maneuvering ashore on their behalf. Commander Pierce asked me to find a suitable structure ashore for use as a submariners' officers' club, and I found a house not far from where the *Nereus* was anchored. A few weeks later, Captain Follmer asked if I could find some souvenirs for the men of the *Nereus*. Since there were no retail stores in Sasebo, the men were unable to buy anything while on shore leave.

"Give me a dinghy and two men after my daily inspection, and I'll be back with something. At this point I don't know what, but in no more than four hours you should have something."

I found a former Seventh Fleet officer who I had known in Brisbane and who was now in charge of the Japanese naval warehouses that had already been inventoried by the American authorities. I explained my dilemma to him and was immediately issued a hundred Japanese rifles and a hundred bayonets. It took over two hours to load them, but once back on the *Nereus*, the news about my "loot" spread like wildfire, and as a show of their gratitude, the crew invited me to a happy hour show they were putting on belowdecks the following night.

All went well until late February 1946 when something happened that should have warned me of danger. The Japanese skipper of the most technically advanced of the subs (a sister sub had been sent to Pearl Harbor for detailed examination) went AWOL. I had a long talk with the sub's exec and learned that the missing skipper was an out and out Communist who was outraged that General MacArthur had not executed the emperor and done away with the royal family. He said that when he had instructed the skipper not to anger me by going away without permission, his response was, "Fuck Lieutenant Kramer Nagoya-style. I've got more important things to do when I get home."

The famous sex store in Kobe in prewar Japan had published an illustrated booklet of the various sexual positions, each one named after a city in Japan. Nagoya-style involved anal penetration.

I was furious. Smitty, one of the CPOs, was standing next to me and saw me suck in my guts while my face flashed in anger. He asked quietly if something was wrong. The conversation had been in Japanese. Smitty couldn't understand a word of it.

"You're damn right, something is wrong. The skipper has gone AWOL. We've got to go to the big sub, the one with the airplane hangar and the 5" gun and talk with the captain; he's the senior Japanese officer present. You can either stay here and do your inspection or come with me. I'll need the dinghy."

All three of them went with me. The sub's captain received me in his wardroom. There was a vase of flowers on the table. He was a typical fine-boned upper-class Japanese of the old school and retained much of the old-fashioned politeness about him. He spoke perfect English but always preferred to begin his conversation with me in Japanese. That way he could sprinkle his talk with honorifics, largely lost metaphors, but exceedingly polite nevertheless. When I asked him if he had recovered from an attack of bronchitis, he bowed and said that since my honorable shadow had cast itself upon him, he had fully recovered, thank you. In my anger, I cut the badinage short and asked him about the AWOL skipper.

"Alas," he said, "he has been disobedient. He went AWOL at 1900 yesterday."

"So?" My frustration was apparent.

"Perhaps it is a good thing. He wasn't liked by his crew."

"But what does that do for the morale of the other crews? They have been waiting for months to go home and rebuild their lives as civilians. We have held them here. Now they see him get away with it."

"But do we really know why he has deserted?" the captain questioned.

"No, we don't. But I can tell you one thing: I'm going back to the *Nereus* to request that Captain Follmer send a platoon of Marines to bring him back in chains. Let his crew and the others see his disgrace and loss of face."

Forty-eight hours later, there was another warning of impending trouble, and I ignored it again. A French journalist showed up wanting to look at the subs. He said he wished to do a feature story on me as well as one on the subs, Ever desirous to remain anonymous, I brushed off the idea, but I did consent to escort him to some of the submarines and let him talk to the crews. I offered to translate for him from French to Japanese and vice versa, and while I did so, I speculated on the man's political orientation. There were a few leading questions about his background, but the French journalist proved just as much an artful dodger about his past as I had been about mine. The Frenchman did, however, express surprise that the Soviets had not yet claimed some of the subs as reparations, especially the one that was so highly advanced technologically that its twin had already been sent to Pearl Harbor for detailed scrutiny.

About three weeks later I got word from my boss that a Soviet delegation was expected to arrive within the next two weeks in order to inspect the subs and decide which ones they wished General MacArthur to deliver to Vladivostok. "I presume," he remarked, "we and the Soviets are still allies."

That afternoon, with everything running smoothly, I paid a visit to the local Sasebo whorehouse. On my first visit during the very early days of the occupation, before being sent to Fukuoka and from there to Kokura to join the

126th Infantry Regiment, it was still a classy place. It was expensive and catered mostly to ranking Japanese navy officers. The food was delicious, and the girls, with their mamasan, retained all the trappings of madams Chrysanthemum and Butterfly. Mamasan was impressed that I spoke Japanese and had gone out of her way to see that I was well cared for.

Now, with the influx of American sailors, all that had changed. The sex cycle was vastly hurried. Madam Butterfly no longer fluttered her wings and hid her face behind the sleeve of her kimono in occasional fits of modesty and amusement. Mamasan, however, remembered me and ushered me into one of the few remaining Japanese-style rooms. There was the standard straw matting on the floor and an alcove with a beautiful scroll and flower arrangement.

The girl sent to amuse me wore an exquisite kimono and obi. After serving me some tea, she produced a tangerine and began to peel it in such a way that the entire peel remained in one piece while the delightful scent of the fruit filled the room. Then, as she separated the segments of the fruit and fed them to me piece by piece, she poured me some sake while the fingertips of her free hand, with a touch as light as the wings of a butterfly, stroked my thigh.

Relaxed, and at the same time visibly excited, I flopped back on some cushions that had been placed behind me. The girl then skillfully removed my trousers and carefully and ceremoniously folded them into a neat rectangle, which she placed beside my head. Just after we had finished enjoying ourselves, we both heard the word *itai* repeated several times; the word, meaning "pain, pain, it hurts" was uttered by someone in the next room. My girl crept on her hands and knees to the paper-and-wood partition that separated us from the next room and silently slid it open a crack.

The sight that met our eyes was entirely pornographic. A sailor from the *Nereus* was naked, his uniform scattered about the room in drunken disarray, was having sex with a girl missionary style. It was from her that the cries of pain came, but it was impossible to tell if her cries were caused by the size of the sailor or from the troublemaking Japanese skipper who had gone AWOL and then been forcibly returned to his sub, since he was beating the girl about the head with his extended organ. We did not know if this was simply an act designed to excite the skipper or the American sailor or both.

My girl quietly slid shut the partition and covered her face with her kimono sleeve and giggled while I pushed the incident from my mind. By this time, I had been around sailors, especially submariners, long enough to know that high jinks and drunkenness ashore merited little thought. Confined as they sometimes were for weeks at a time without liquor or women, once ashore they often lapsed into drunken absurdity. Had my mindset been properly focused, I would have asked myself what an enlisted American sailor aboard the *Nereus* was doing, consorting with a Japanese officer, and a troublemaker at that. Instead, in a relaxed mood encompassed by the delightful odor of a tangerine, I curled up into a deep sleep until Mamasan woke me with a highly detailed and itemized bill; so much for the tangerine, so much for peeling it, so much for the tea, so much for the sake, etc., etc. It was all so blissful and conjured up in my mind Puccini's caressing music from *Madame Butterfly*. It was also very expensive.

Life aboard the *Nereus* was by no means dreary. Besides the nearby submariners' officers' club, efforts were also made aboard ship to relieve monotony and stimulate morale.

Belowdecks, besides movies, the enlisted men held happy hours during which shipboard talents were organized to entertain their fellow crew members. Some of the acts and music and vocals were surprisingly good.

Above deck, with the help of his exec, Captain Follmer organized a lengthy acey-deucey contest that went on for days. Acey-deucey is a variation of backgammon and has the advantage for sailors of being playable on deck because there are no playing cards for the wind to blow away as there would be for poker or hearts or rummy. Because I was away from the ship more often than the other officers, it was necessary for me to play more games at one time than the others. Acey-deucey thus had little charm for me, and I've never played it since leaving the *Nereus*.

Another diversion was the weekly dinner at which the captain joined our mess. He was especially partial to curry. The gossip aboard the ship was that he had personally selected the cook on the basis of his skill in preparing a fine curry with a multitude of side dishes from shredded coconut to peanuts to chutney. Because it was impractical for him to eat his curry alone in his cabin, he always joined us on curry night. The conversation at the dinner table was usually taken over by the old-timers who reminisced about wartime and prewar mishaps and adventures. What interested me the most about these talks was the running thread of conversation about the imperfections of the torpedoes. There had been many of them that failed to detonate; others sank or tumbled about on the surface; one had described a perfect circle and had torpedoed the submarine that had fired it. Although most of this talk was old hat to the others, it was often repeated as a form of camaraderie and fellowship. It was, however, totally new to me and I was thoroughly fascinated.

Four days after my visit to the whorehouse, the exec informed all the officers of the *Nereus* at mess that night that orders had just been received to take all twenty-four subs out to very deep water off Nagasaki and blow them up. A cruiser and a destroyer would be sent down to join the operation, and two landing crafts would be commandeered to accommodate the submarine crews who were to be evacuated from the subs immediately prior to the destruction. He turned to me. "You'll note, Kramer," he said with a grin, "that the destruction of the subs is scheduled before the arrival of the Soviet delegation to select which ones are to go to Vladivostok. That should make life easier for you. Otherwise you would probably have had to go to Russia with the subs to assure the discipline of the crews."

"It certainly does, sir, very much," I admitted, "but before any more time elapses, I'd like to explain something to you and my boss about the Japanese crews. Before joining the *Nereus*, I served with the 126th Infantry Regiment in Kokura in northern Kyushu. Because of a variety of factors, I got to know the mayor very well and thus discovered that he knew every move the United States had in mind for his city before we did. My conclusion was that Supreme Command Allied Powers (SCAP) was a sieve in so far as the Japanese were concerned, and you can therefore count on it that the skippers of all our subs already know about the destruction orders, just as their crews do. I'd therefore like to suggest that a careful watch on them be maintained until we can double-check the amount of fuel they have in their tanks, which can be done tomorrow morning. I particularly have in mind the recalcitrant skipper who went AWOL and who might very well have tampered with his fuel gauges to show he has less than he actually has so that he can slip his moorings and make off to Soviet waters in the middle of the night. I think we can be sure that if the Soviets would like to get their hands on one of the subs it would be his. We know he is a Communist and I should never have asked that he be brought back in chains when he went AWOL."

Later that same evening I skipped coffee and desert and went for a walk on the foredeck of the *Nereus*. I was vaguely aware of the bow watch some thirty-five feet in front of me. Otherwise I was alone since this deck was off—limits to enlisted men, and all the officers were still at supper. Turning toward the port side of the ship, I looked down at the Japanese submarines that were nested peacefully. Then I heard the pop and immediately after a ping from the steel deck no more than eight inches ahead of me. Because it was so sharp, I did not feel the steel deck splinter the bullet had kicked up and embedded in my leg.

For me there was an instantaneous awareness of danger and the conduct necessary for survival. The bow watch who had just fired his rifle was the same sailor I'd seen taking part in the three-way at the whorehouse. The kid was now standing at the bow, fiddling with his rifle. But what was it all about? Was he merely fantasizing that he was guarding a stagecoach from an attack by desperados, or was he really trying to kill, or what? Without either stopping or increasing the speed of my stroll, I shouted, "Drop that rifle on the deck!" and then repeated the order a second time as I steadily continued toward the bow.

"Drop it *now*! You've had an accident."

The moment I uttered the word *accident*, the kid visibly relaxed. There was going to be a way out after all. The loneliness of the kid's action, with no one beside him to tell him what to do, had clearly overwhelmed him.

"On your feet, sailor," I ordered. "Go to the officer of the deck on the double! Report the incident, and tell him to send a relief."

Once he had gone and I was alone on the deck, there was time to think. The war had been fought and won, and I had just had the closest shave of my wartime life. Hopkinson's warning of exposure and need for protection, not from the enemy but from an ally, came back to me, along with Foxworth's warning, six years earlier, of how in my kind of work you never knew who your enemies were. But was what had just happened part of a plot, or simply an accident as I had told the kid it was? The sailor was without doubt the one who had been consorting with the recalcitrant Japanese Communist skipper. So what? At this point, a new bow watch arrived and cut short my speculation, and I pointed to the rifle that was still on the deck where the original watch had dropped it. I then turned, intending to go to my cabin, but my right foot felt sticky, and looking down, I saw there was a little blood oozing out around the top of my shoe. There was no pain. I thus changed course and made my way toward sickbay so the medics could see what was wrong. It was peculiar. Part of my mind seized on the blood as proof that once a civilian again, there would be, on the basis of my work since August 1940, opportunities to continue intelligence work far beyond my work for Rockefeller or the navy. What was quietly seeping out around my shoe became for me a sort of symbol that once back in the United States. I could, even though the war was now over, continue in intelligence. Dr. Sarkesian, in total silence, removed the steel deck splinter and slapped a bandage on my leg. I insisted on returning to my cabin unassisted. While I was resting, my boss showed up with the news that the recalcitrant skipper had disappeared again, and he was going to post a special watch on the sub until the demolition officer, Lieutenant Mullet, lit the fuse to blow it up.

"I don't think that will be necessary."

"Why is that?"

"There probably is a better solution, and it's one that the sub's crew will prefer."

"What is it?"

"If you will reach into the bottom drawer of my bureau, you will find a Japanese officer's Nambu pistol with ammunition in a leather case. A friend took it off a dead Jap officer and gave it to me. Why not give it to the exec of the sub and tell him if that son of a bitch skipper of his ever shows up again to tell him to get the hell off his sub, and if he refuses to shoot him dead. This gesture of faith in the exec will bolster morale. From then on, we won't have to worry. Also, beginning tomorrow, I'm going to visit each one of the subs to make sure of my crew rosters. When the final roll is called, just before Lieutenant Mullet blows them up, I don't want any of the officers or men to go down with their subs. We mustn't create heroes for a new militarized Japan, if that ever happens.

Four days later, the *Nereus*, along with the Japanese subs, was in deep water off Nagasaki. The Japanese crews had gone ashore the night before and gathered bows of Japanese cherry blossoms, the symbol of the Japanese navy, which were then in full bloom, and fastened them to the periscopes of the subs. It made for a magical and spectacular sight to see the procession of twenty-four subs festooned with cherry blossoms on a glorious spring morning and on a calm sea as they proceeded in formation out to deep water for their ultimate destruction. My final roll calls had gone without a hitch. The skippers one by one dismissed their men who, often with tears in their eyes, clambered into the *Nereus* whaleboats for transport to waiting landing ship tanks (LSTs). Then, together with the demolition officer who had already lit the fuse, we left each sub and climbed aboard another *Nereus* whaleboat. When we were one—to two-hundred yards away, there was a dull thud, and the subs sank quickly, with the cherry blossoms often the last thing visible before they slid out of sight beneath the sea. The operation had been meticulously planned and was finished without a hitch.

Despite the steady pace of the operation, from time to time there were pauses that gave me an opportunity to reflect. Since I shared a dinghy with Lieutenant Mullet, the demolition officer, there were occasions when, after the Japanese crews had gone, I stood alone on the deck while waiting for Mullett who was below, to make last-minute adjustments to his explosive devices.

One of these momentary delays occurred on the submarine that had sunk the *Indianapolis* just before the end of the war with great loss of American lives. Forty-eight hours prior, Captain Follmer had asked me to secure from this sub a souvenir for him to give Captain McVay of the *Indianapolis* who had survived the loss of his ship. When I asked him for suggestions as to what to secure, he had simply said, "That's up to you."

It should be mentioned here that my life aboard the *Nereus* was such that I was wrapped in a cocoon in so far as outside world events were concerned. Intelligence headquarters in Tokyo was again not forwarding me my mail, just as had been the case when I was in Kokura. I had no Japanese newspapers to keep me informed of world events and no radio. I did not know that Captain Hashimoto of the *I-58* had been sent to Washington in December 1945 to testify at the court-martial of Captain McVay, who was the captain of the *Indianapolis*, where his arrival had horrified the American public. The press had howled. "What we are doing in this case is putting an enemy in the position of determining the justice we mete out among ourselves. It was a perverted sense of values that produced this course of action," said the *Washington Post*. Hashimoto had to be lodged during the trial in the Washington Navy Yard and was given guards to protect him from harm; such had been the extent of the public hostility.

He had returned to his command of the *I-58* about the same time I had arrived aboard the *Nereus* and never referred to his trip in such discussions as we had previously had. Thus, I knew nothing about his trip or the outcome of

Captain McVay's court-martial. All I knew was that Captain Follmer had asked me to get a souvenir from the *I-58* for him to give Captain McVay.

Aboard the submarine *I-58*, I discussed the problem with Hashimoto. He took me to the forward torpedo room and pointed out the tube from which the fatal torpedo had been discharged. There was an oval brass plate affixed to the round door of the tube, designated with a particular number in Japanese. Captain Hashimoto told me he could have the brass plate removed and suggested it would be a suitable souvenir for the ill-fated Captain McVay. Because such a memento seemed to me somewhat ghoulish, I went along with the suggestion hesitantly, but when I gave it to Captain Follmer the following day, he was delighted with it and proclaimed that it was a perfect choice. All this had seemed a bit odd to me, but by then I had become used to submariners' unusual ways—so totally different from what I had become accustomed to when working with the 126th Infantry Regiment.

There was another short pause on the twentieth sub when I was left alone before Mullett came up from below. The Japanese crew had already gone, and there was total quiet save for the throb of the *Nereus* whaleboat, which was alongside, waiting for us to disembark. This particular submarine was a very large one with a 5" gun on the foredeck and an airplane hangar with a launching track and a retractable retrieval crane. It had originally been one of three subs designed to bomb New York City and the Panama Canal, but by the time it was completed, Japan had been pushed too far back toward the home islands for such use, and it had instead been employed as a tanker to refuel bypassed Japanese Pacific bases. Because the deck of a submarine is so near the surface of the sea, one becomes, while it is on the surface, much more conscious of one's natural surroundings than on a regular surface vessel.

It was this proximity to my surroundings that focused my eyes on the exquisite beauty of the scene around me. Nearby was the totally blue-green surface of the sea on which were resting the few remaining subs festooned with cherry blossoms and in the background a graceful U.S. cruiser, a sleek destroyer and the not ungraceful outline of the *Nereus* itself, which, from a distance, resembled a passenger liner more than it did a working naval vessel. There were also the LSTs waiting to receive the Japanese crews. It was a memorable scene, and it became engraved in my mind and remains there to this day.

Entirely unforeseen, these momentary thoughts became transmuted into a historical perspective. The musings of the managing director of the Yawata Steel Works when I had visited him the previous November had inspired me to believe that what I was now witnessing was not only the end of an imperial medieval industrialized Japan but also a new beginning. Furthermore, the aesthetics of the moment—the eerie combination of cherry blossoms, periscopes, the sea, and the tears of the sailors—proved it for they were still resolute, and thus their progeny would rise from the wreckage to build a new Japan of unparalleled wealth and comfort. Their superb discipline, even in their present adversity, was proof of their eventual success.

In an odd sort of way, I felt suddenly proud that good luck had made me part of it. And best of all, because I was in fact no more than a lowly USNR lieutenant j.g. standing alone on the deck of a doomed submarine, it would thus remain entirely personal, limited to me alone. No one could take it from me and turn it into something else. It was my way of thinking, and the mental process by which I had arrived at it could belong to no one else.

The moment I saw Mullett's head begin to emerge from an open hatch, these somewhat artistic speculations dissolved. Instead, there raced through my mind the problem of what to do about the bow watch who had shot me. The dent in the deck of the *Nereus*, five inches ahead of where I had stood to receive the deck splinter the bullet had kicked up, was still there as a reminder. My job was almost over, and my skipper would want my input on the incident. *Cool it,* I said to myself.

You originally said it was an accident. Keep it that way. Even if it wasn't, even if the recalcitrant Japanese skipper had incited the sailor to shoot as revenge for his loss of face, or even if it was another chapter in your experience with Communist harassment, forget it. Irrefutable proof will be impossible to collect. The assembly of evidence for a court of inquiry will take months and thus delay your return home. Your job is done. And so, quietly, Mullett and I descended again into a *Nereus* whaleboat and shoved off for another final roll call and explosion. The important thing was to preserve the rhythm of the operation.

At mess that evening aboard the *Nereus* congratulations on the superb planning and success of the operation, now called Road's End, came through the loudspeaker from the Commander Naval Activities Japan. This included "Great credit to all participants," which I presumed included me.

The moment this announcement came through, several of the officers at the mess table looked at me and grinned. Nothing was said that in any way connected me with the commendation, and I went on eating my meal. The truth was I was exhausted from the day's activities; but even so, there was a silent mental groping. Why look at me in connection with the commendation? Praise for Mullet was understandable and deserved. His twenty-four separate explosions had worked to perfection. But what did they think I did?

At this point, the officer sitting next to me said, "Well, Paul, I guess those daily trips paid off. I mean you sure got the Nips to cooperate faultlessly in the destruction of their own subs."

This remark clarified my involvement, and when I went to my cabin immediately after supper and stretched out on my bunk without even bothering to take of my shoes, I began to review in my own mind what I had accomplished aboard the *Nereus*.

On my arrival, the men were still filled with wartime hostilities toward the Japanese. In their minds they were a sneaky, cruel, and treacherous lot, and all sorts of precautions were necessary. My attitude was different, and it had come out in the initial discussion of my duties with Captain Follmer when he had ordered me to go aboard the subs armed, and I had persuaded him to withdraw the order.

But this had been only the first obstacle in seeking a cooperative attitude with the Japanese crews. The second had been the arrival of a young ensign just out of Annapolis who joined our little group for our daily visits to the subs. Filled with loathing for the Japanese, he began to throw his weight around with peremptory orders that far exceeded the mission of seeing to the mechanical condition of the subs and the coherence of the crews.

"Look, Lieutenant, we got to get rid of this guy," one of the CPOs had whispered to me.

"Chief," I answered, "this man is an Academy grad who is looking forward to a navy career. I'm just a reserve officer who will soon be out of the navy, and I'd hate to do anything that would rook his future. You three are regular navy men, you handle it. Do it your way."

What they had done was never discussed, but forty-eight hours later, the ensign was gone, off the ship, and his name was never mentioned again.

Meanwhile, I continued playing nursemaid to what I had begun to call "my Japanese crews." But this possessive pronoun had not been adopted willy-nilly. The officers in the wardroom had begun to call them that if they ran into them ashore. To me it was gratifying and an indication that I was achieving my goal of eliminating enough hostility toward them so that a cooperative attitude could emerge. At this juncture, the ship surgeon, Dr. Sarkesian, behaved in such an outlandish way that opinion on the *Nereus* became even more supportive of my point of view. Fortunately, the doctor's conduct was not directed at "my crews," but at me personally so that there was no setback in my work, only a cold fury on my part.

There were rats aboard one of the subs. In late February, the inevitable happened; there was an outbreak of typhus aboard, and the skipper had very sensibly asked me if I could procure for him some DDT, which was unavailable via Japanese channels. He explained that he had never seen or used it, only read about its ability to exterminate insects including fleas and lice, which carried the typhus germs from rats to humans. I told Dr. Sarkesian about the problem and asked for some DDT, which he grudgingly gave me, and I then went to the sub and gave it to the skipper and returned to the *Nereus*.

Sarkesian was waiting for me alongside the officer of the deck the moment I stepped aboard. "Remove all your clothes this instant!" he shouted. "All of them! I'll not have any Nip germs on this ship!" His face was contorted with anger and hostility as if I was plotting a kamikaze germ Pearl Harbor-esque attack on the *Nereus*.

At this point, a crowd of off-duty officers and men began to gather at the gangway. Something like this had never happened before—the stripping down buck-naked of an officer before a crew. Nothing was said, and once I was naked, Dr. Sarkesian sprayed me with DDT powder and then walked away, clasping his powder spray against his chest. One of the enlisted men picked up my uniform and underclothing and gave them to me, and I went to my cabin and showered. From this point on the incident was never mentioned in the wardroom or elsewhere, but the horror on my fellow officers' faces at the time of the incident told the story, and my visits to the infested sub continued. Although furious, my attitude was that as long as the doctor took out his hostility on me and not my crews, I'd let it pass. What mattered was the coherence of the crews.

Oddly enough, Sarkesian's conduct came back to haunt him in an unexpected way. About three weeks later the skipper of the infested sub came to me in a state of agitation. His cook had, by mistake, used some of the DDT instead of flour in preparing some ceremonial cookies that several of his men had eaten. "Would they die an agonizing death of DDT poisoning?" he asked. I asked Dr. Sarkesian to come with me aboard the sub and examine them. He refused. I then said that in that case, I would bring the men to the *Nereus* for him to examine, but I would have to insist that he not strip them naked on the deck in front of members of the *Nereus* crew as he had done to me.

It was at once apparent that he must have received some sort of reproof for his conduct for he acceded immediately to my request. His face and gestures, however, during the examination, expressed his loathing for the Japanese people and his fear of contamination by them. After a cursory examination, he announced to me that they would be OK and stalked away. I told them what the doctor had said and sent them back to their sub in a *Nereus* whaleboat, and then I waited for Dr. Sarkesian's revenge. For about a month, he avoided me and never made an appearance in the wardroom when I was there, and I never ran into him on deck.

Then one day, ashore, I saw a man carrying a beautiful bonsai of dwarfed and gnarled plum trees about to blossom in an oval glazed green dish. I bought it from him and took it back to my cabin.

Forty-eight hours later the doctor struck again. He suddenly materialized in the wardroom and announced in front of all present that he had learned that there had been introduced aboard the *Nereus* a local plant the soil of which was no doubt contaminated with harmful bacteria and germs, and he demanded that I get rid of it at once. He refused to allow the *Nereus* to be exposed to further contagion by me. I threw the bonsai overboard.

In my cabin that night, reveries of the idiocy of Sarkesian's behavior were suddenly pushed aside by a startling and heretofore delayed comprehension. At mess that night, one of my fellow officers sitting across from me had interrupted the chitchat about Operation Road's End with a question. "Paul," he'd asked, "didn't you once tell me you'd come overseas on a Dutch merchantman called the *Tjisadane*?"

"Yes," I'd answered. "It was a former Dutch passenger ship, real cushy."

"You know it was sunk off the coast of New Guinea near Hollandia in '43 or '44."

"No," I commented, "I didn't."

Then the talk angled back to Road's End, and I forgot about it until this moment of exhausted reverie of things past. Now, unexpectedly, it erupted. "Of course," I said to myself. "That's why I came back from the dead according to the nurse at the 42nd General Hospital and why my gear ended up in the effects of the deceased. Some eager beaver assumed I had gone down with the *Tjisdane* since this was my last assignment, and I had never reported for duty in Hollandia before being shipped by a medic to Brisbane in a coma."

The gallows humor of it all spread aver me like a warm blanket, and I fell asleep, utterly contented and didn't wake up until the next morning by which time we were already at anchor in Nagasaki where we stayed for twenty-four hours so the men could see the devastation wrought by the atom bomb.

While at Nagasaki, a curious thing happened. Alone, I went for a walk near the epicenter of the atom bomb explosion. My route followed a railroad track, the steel rails of which had been melted like butter and the wooden ties, still perfectly formed, were in fact cinders. The only structures in view that had survived the blast and remained perfectly formed were two sacred stone gateways. Alongside my path, I noticed a glass bottle that had been melted into an unusual and twisted shape but looked as if it could still contain fluid. Totally ignorant of the radioactive effects of an atom bomb, I picked up the bottle and took it back to my cabin with me.

On our return to Sasebo, I paid a visit to the officers' club for a drink and also took back to my cabin a few daffodils in full bloom and put them in the bottle with water. Three hours later the flowers had wilted. The following day the same thing happened. By then, suspicious that there was something odd about the bottle, I tossed it overboard.

Assuming the bottle may have given off radiation sufficient to wilt the flowers, it didn't affect me. I'm now ninety-one years old and still going strong with no more than the usual old-age complaints.

At anchor in Sasebo harbor, I asked for my orders to return to the United States and was summoned to the captain's cabin for a meeting consisting of me; Captain Follmer; his exec, Commander Pierce; and my immediate boss.

Captain Follmer told me the *Nereus* was to return to San Diego, its homeport, via Suez, England, and the Panama Canal. Would I stay aboard to write the history of Road's End for the navy? he asked. He said I would not be given other duties and would be assigned a proper office for my work and a yeoman. I politely and foolishly declined. My boss then said he had just made out my fitness report and had given me the highest rating he had ever given anyone in his navy career. The exec asked me to stay in the navy permanently. When I repeated what I had told the captain that I had been overseas too long and it was time to go home, the exec blew up.

"You're being a damn fool, Kramer. I've gone over your file of orders from the time that Englishman pulled you out of the hospital in Australia. It's the damndest collection I've ever seen in my entire navy career, and you're so dumb you don't get it. You've never been attached to a unit on a permanent basis. That Englishman got you assigned to him on a temporary basis. Then the war ends, and Admiral Kinkaid sends you to Guam aboard his own plane for some R&R. Then Admiral Nimitz sent you to Japan on temporary duty while you were waiting for an assignment. Then you got temporary duty with the army. Finally, you end up on another temporary assignment with us. I don't understand it, but what it means is that besides getting overseas pay and submarine pay while with us, you've been getting per diem for God knows how long. Also, as a single man, you couldn't possibly have been spending your salary since you were ordered overseas. You'll be a rich man when you leave the navy, but I warn you when you get to Great Lakes it will take them at least three months to figure the thing out, especially since you've had no pay account for two years. What are you going to do? Sit on your ass and wait? Why not stay aboard while we do the job and do what the captain has asked, write up Road's End?"

"We're left with another problem," Captain Follmer intervened. "What do we do with the sailor who shot Kramer?"

I remained silent and waited until both my boss and the exec had had their say. When they finished and all three looked at me, I was ready.

"No one on the ship saw the kid shoot the gun except me, did they?" I asked.

"Not so far as we know. No one."

"At the time the shooting occurred, I said it was an accident, and that was what the kid also insisted from the time he reported it to the officer of the deck as ordered. Under the circumstances, it doesn't seem to me the incident merits a court of inquiry or anything like that. Why can't we let the whole thing slide and be forgotten? Or, if you feel you must do something, dock his pay for a few months."

Captain Follmer gave me a sharp look. It was as if he sensed I was holding something back. There had, of course, been no mention of the three-way with the Japanese skipper in the house ashore; nor had I ever told anyone aboard the *Nereus* the details of the incident in Brisbane when Hopkinson had insisted I have a bodyguard and how the officer who had caused all the trouble over the spy document had defected to Red China at the end of the war; nor had I revealed to anyone my pre-Pearl Harbor work and the story of Matheson, Lanas, the Kraut, and the Argentine girl who had denounced me to Vice President Wallace. It was imperative that there be no prying by a court of inquiry into my past, and that also included what I had done for Captain Zacharias at Boulder.

I thus perceptibly smiled with relief when Follmer commented, "Perhaps what you have suggested is the best solution. I know you wish to get rotated back to the States at once, as you have every right to be. If there were any sort of court, I'd have to hold you here."

He then stood up from his desk, a clear sign of dismissal, and the exec and I filed out of his cabin. It was, save for the formalities, the end of my tour of duty on the *Nereus*.

At the time, I couldn't help but compare the warmth of my departure from the Nereus with the rather perfunctory farewell from the Rockefeller office. True, Jamieson and his wife had given me a farewell party, which Nelson had attended. But there had been no real enthusiasm about it. At the time I had put it down to the peculiar nature of my work and forgotten about it. But now it came back. Six and a half years had gone by since a bug-eyed me had been hired by the White House. The work had deprived me of any real collegiality with my contemporaries and had essentially been a long, lonesome, and lonely trail. It hardened me, molded a thick shell around me, and made me totally self—contained, even though underneath I was sure there were still some human values. At the same time, I realized that although no words had yet been coined to describe what was happening to U.S.-Soviet relations, the troubles I'd had while working for Rockefeller, the deliberate sinking of the subs before the Russians could get to them, the bodyguard assigned to me in Brisbane, plus the possible, but by no means proven, motivation behind the shot that had been fired aboard the *Nereus* meant there would be another job when I got home. I was fully aware that my thoughts on the subject were not entirely clear, that they were still in a bit of a muddle, but maybe Commander Hopkinson had been right. Maybe I was a marked man. Once back in Washington I could survey the scene and decide if I really wished to continue in intelligence work.

PART III

The CIA

16

As I had surmised, after the accidental shooting aboard the *Nereus*, the role of intelligence in the United States would not only continue, but would vastly expand. Part of this expansion took the form of the establishment of the Central Intelligence Agency.

The publicity accompanying its establishment described how it would evaluate and distribute intelligence relating to national security. The director was to be appointed by the president. But this was a small fraction of the total story, which can best be explained by the role of Secretary of Defense James Forrestal in its creation.

Forrestal, who was America's first secretary of defense, and before that had been secretary of the navy, had taken a close interest in Italy's first post-war election in which the newly formed Christian Democrats were pitted against the Italian Communist Party for control of the country. With the defeat of the Mussolini regime and the Nazis by the Allies, Italy's Communist Party, which had been underground, suddenly erupted as a powerful political force with a considerable popular following supported by newspapers and radio stations. Fearful of a Communist victory in the forthcoming Italian elections, Forrestal realized that the United States had no government agency that could contribute to a Christian Democrat victory and, in its absence, had turned to friends in New York's financial circles to raise funds with which to support the Christian Democrats. The success of this project further convinced him of the need for such an agency. Furthermore, while a special assistant to Roosevelt in 1940, the executive order creating the Rockefeller office had been drafted in his own office in order to take advantage of the British Security Coordination's information, which was used to erase Nazi commercial activity in Latin America. These two factors, as much as anything else, prompted the creation of the CIA. Secretly, the CIA was designed to not only coordinate and evaluate intelligence information, but also to engage in operational intelligence (just as the Rockefeller office had done) and to send intelligence agents abroad for various purposes.

I went to work for the newly created Central Intelligence Agency on June 9, 1947. During the year that had elapsed between the time I returned to the United States and my hiring, I had learned to fly an airplane and received a civilian pilot's license. Not particularly adept at it, once I received my license, I never flew a plane again. It was just another case of a derring-do goal I'd set for myself, and once I had achieved it, I totally lost interest.

At the CIA, and totally fortuitously, I received a great welcome. At that time, General Hoyt Vandenberg was its head. Our paths had never crossed. However, I was assigned to the Office of Reports and Estimates. The head of it at that time was a navy captain named McCollum, who was the former head of the Far East Division of Navy Intelligence. I also didn't know him, but when he welcomed me aboard, he claimed that he knew all about my navy work. This was somewhat mystifying, especially since he didn't identify the source of his information; but I asked no questions. He did, however, mumble something about the Seventh Fleet, so I decided he had picked up some of the "raves" that Hopkinson had passed to Admiral Kinkaid, plus my commendation for my work on Road's End while aboard the *Nereus*. Maybe he even knew about my bodyguard in Brisbane. He said he was assigning me to the Latin American branch, and that the head of that branch was really looking forward to my joining his staff. He also said I was to be paid one notch higher on the government professional scale than I had received from Rockefeller. I couldn't possibly object to that since a reason for the high salary from Rockefeller had been its inability to reimburse me for out-of-pocket expenses incurred while doing counterintelligence work from information received from BSC and passed on to Rockefeller via the FBI.

Inadvertently, however, he had raised a problem that was to present difficulties for me from the time I went to work for the CIA and which continued until I resigned. If, as I assumed it did, the CIA had gone through my previous government record, they would have found no trace of my work while on the White House payroll from August 19, 1940, until November 16, 1941, at which time I had gone on to work for Rockefeller as an associate information publicist. Furthermore, J. Edgar Hoover, head of the FBI, had been so infuriated when the CIA was established that he had not only failed to get the job, but had also "lost Latin America," that he had deindexed his Latin American files. This meant, as a practical matter, that there was simply no record of my FBI-BSC work or the reason for my being hired by Rockefeller in the first place. Also, with Foxworth dead, there was no one in an official government position to enlighten an employer, even if security restrictions vis-à-vis British Intelligence had made it possible. I was also sure that U.S. Navy files on the subject were minimal. "Oh well," I said to myself, "this is a perfect example of the hocus-pocus and misrepresentations involved in intelligence work, and since you've voluntarily re-involved yourself in it, you've no right to complain."

As it turned out, and to my utter amazement, the head of the Latin American division was a man named Willmore Kendall, whom I had known slightly while working in the Rockefeller office. Kendall was, as he told me, totally aware of the gossip about me in the Press Division among what I had jokingly called our radical elements, which had regarded me as a malign influence on its chief, Jamieson. He also had heard the gossip about the Matheson case, the true story of which I never told him, just as I never mentioned to him, or to anyone else at the CIA, my BSC connection. Anyway, Kendall regarded me as a genuine asset in his shop and treated me with both kindness and respect.

Will Kendall was a curious but very likeable man. He was intense in his hatred of Stalin and the Soviet regime. But this was not derived from an inherent patriotism that sensed in Russia a dangerous rival. Quite the contrary; it was derived from his profound admiration and depth of knowledge of the precepts of the British eighteenth-century philosopher John Locke, who favored freedom of thought and religion and believed that the sole business of government was to protect the lives, liberty, and property of the people. This put him on a collision course with the French philosopher Rousseau, who, although he hated tyranny, believed in the natural goodness of man. Sometimes I think that Will Kendall believed that the worst mistake George III ever made was not Lord Bute and the treatment of the American colonies but the granting of a pension to Rousseau after he fled to England.

I think it was because his knowledge of Latin America was so limited that he gave me such a free hand. He had no Latin American friends, didn't speak their languages, and I cannot recall any but the most superficial discussion on the subject. What he did enjoy discussing with me in depth was the philosophy of freedom and liberty. Here his arguments were all derived from Locke and mine from Lord Acton, the nineteenth-century British historian who regarded Locke as "reasonable and sensible, but limited and pedestrian." These discussions were totally absurd in a way because Kendall knew little of Acton, and I knew little of Locke. But they did prove to me that Will Kendall was totally miscast. He belonged in academia, especially since his friendly enthusiasm and forceful thinking had an almost magical attraction for conservatively-oriented young people. Eventually I was proven correct, as he became a professor of philosophy at Yale where he was one of the founders of the neo-conservative movement that years later made Ronald Regan president.

Unfortunately, Kendall lived a disorderly personal life. He was a heavy drinker and had a stable of admiring women. He showed up at my apartment on two occasions and asked for a bed, which I gave him gladly. But once I gave him something to eat, he was immediately on the phone, inviting one of his girlfriends to spend the night with him. Why he had suddenly needed a bed, I never asked, nor did he confide in me. He simply seemed to regard me as a stabilizing force, and I was glad to help him out.

Kendall's departure from the CIA after about a year and a half became one of the factors that persuaded me to transfer to Operations. But while he was there, I was able to function with a certain amount of efficiency that was not derived from any innate ability, but from my previous intelligence experience, the depth of which surpassed that of my coworkers.

Once I started work, the first thing I noticed was the perceptible decline in the quality of reporting from Latin America as compared to what I had been used to from 1940 to 1943. There were several reasons for this. First of all, the FBI men in Latin America had, almost without exception, resigned or sought other FBI jobs rather than work for the CIA. Second, the dismissal of Sumner Welles as under secretary of state had a deleterious effect. The subsequent assistant secretaries of state for Latin America had never lasted more than a year or two so that the post became something of a revolving door. As long as Welles had either run it or supervised it, he had demanded quality and excellence on the part of Foreign Service men assigned there. His successors for one reason or another were unable to do this.

Before World War II, Latin America was the only part of the world where America had enough power to practice genuine diplomacy. It could, for example, play off Brazil against Argentina or Peru against Chile or Mexico against Guatemala in order to gain its own ends. To do this, the best and brightest Foreign Service officers sought Latin American postings. But after World War II, this changed. With the enormous increase in U.S. world power and the rapid ebbing away of the French and British empires; with the increase in power of the Soviet Union; and with the total defeat of Germany, Italy, and Japan, there were other newer fields to conquer for American diplomats. Overnight, Latin America became a backwater.

As a way around this problem, I asked Kendall if there was any objection to using my phone to call my own sources of information in Latin America and Washington, which dated from my Rockefeller office days. This was fortunate because the first important estimate I was called on to make was whether or not the Base Sites Agreement that had just been negotiated with Panama would be approved by the Panamanian legislature. During World War II, the United States had extended its protection of the Panama Canal beyond the Canal Zone deep into Panamanian territory. With the war over, the military sought to retain a number of these bases, and the State Department had negotiated an agreement to do so with the Panamanian government. This required the approval of the Panamanian legislature.

The information that crossed my desk on the subject indicated no problem, but the reporting seemed to me mediocre at best. There was no indication that our embassy or the military in Panama had any contact whatsoever with the opposition to the government so that they could assess accurately the fate of the agreement once it reached the legislature.

I called my own sources in Panama and discovered that the fate of the Base Sites Agreement was hopeless. It couldn't possibly be approved, and I told my superiors so. As events developed, it was unanimously rejected. The result of all this was that Admiral Hillenkoetter, the new CIA director, was able to warn President Truman of coming events so that he would be ready to take appropriate action. Kendall was delighted. I got a raise, made a section chief and, given the authority to select my own staff, two of whom became lifelong friends.

My next success produced singularly different results and alerted me to the intrigue and internal hostilities within the CIA. Intelligence agents forever engaging in foreign intrigue are often unable to resist practicing it within their own shop, unless the division chiefs are experienced and have accordingly developed a sixth sense of awareness of it and can thus stamp it out before it becomes a problem. Unfortunately, this was not the case while I was at the CIA. My little success was in fact comparable to the Matheson case, but it did not have such happy results for me personally.

My "take" on the Dominican Republic included not only the classified traffic to and from our embassy in Ciudad Trujillo, but also memoranda by the Dominican desk officer in the State Department. A careful perusal of this traffic alerted me in much the same way as Matheson's previous employment record did in 1941. The U.S. ambassador in Ciudad Trujillo was a highly literate and educated man who liked to use unusual nouns and adjectives in his classified dispatches and telegrams to Washington. What alerted me was that the Dominican ambassador in Washington would sometimes use these same unusual words in discussions of current problems with the desk officer in the State Department.

I thus wrote a memo to Kendall, suggesting that the coincidence of words pointed to the need of a security check in our embassy in Ciudad Trujillo. It was inconceivable to me that a relatively uneducated Dominican in Washington, for whom English was a second language, would use such words unless our classified traffic was available to him via a leak in our embassy.

Kendall bypassed CIA security and sent my memo to Admiral Hillenkoetter who in turn ordered security to investigate. The leak turned out to be the CIA man in Ciudad Trujillo, who was married to a Dominican. The dictator, General Trujillo, had put her family under such intolerable pressure that her husband caved and agreed to pass on to Trujillo the ambassador's classified dispatches and telegrams.

The fallout from all this reminded me of the bureaucratic reaction to the Matheson case, save for the fact that it was more sordid. CIA Security was furious my memo had bypassed them and gone directly to the admiral, with the result that ORE, instead of them, got the credit for plugging a leak. Admiral Hillenkoetter was delighted, however, and sent a memo to the head of ORE, a recently appointed ex-professor from Yale who knew nothing whatsoever about intelligence, complimenting me and pointing out that this sort of analytical work was exactly one of the things CIA was meant to do. But the new head of ORE did not forward the memo to me or to Kendall. I found out about it only because I knew personally the new head's secretary who was so furious at his behavior that she told me. When I told Will Kendall the story, he was disgusted and confided that he planned to leave the CIA at the first opportunity.

It was at this point that I decided to use up some accumulated annual leave and vacation in Panama and Central America. I thus booked a passage on a United Fruit Company's combination freighter and passenger ship called the *Cape Ann*, which was scheduled to stop at Puerto Limon, Costa Rica, and then sail on to Colon in Panama where my college friend Modi Arias would meet me and put me up until I would fly to Guatemala and El Salvador.

The preliminary ocean voyage was pleasant, and I spent a good part of the time, after we had rounded Cape Hatteras, on deck, soaking up the tropic sun. The day before we were to land, I deliberately flopped down in a vacant deck chair next to a Costa Rican whom I knew had been told about me by a mutual friend in Washington. Her name was Murray. She was a Panamanian by birth, married to an Englishman. I also knew she had cousins in Salvador, one of whom was married to a Guatemalan. With such a network of family members across the Central American scene, I thought she might have something interesting to say.

Initially her chatter was totally feminine and of no interest to me whatsoever—"Cousin Louisa is hopelessly overweight, and Carmen is a malicious gossip"—so that I decided she was hopeless until she suddenly switched her chatter to her husband's "closest friend," Pepe Figueres, the president of Costa Rica. Here she made a comment that caught my attention. "You know," she explained, "people can be so jealous of another's success. Just because Don Pepe was able to get his hands on a superb coffee plantation that had been seized from Axis citizens after we declared war on Germany and Italy there are a lot of families who don't like him. It's all no more than envy on the part of malcontents simply because they themselves didn't get the plantation. In Salvador, it's the same thing where cousins of mine came into possession of a plantation owned by Italians. In Guatemala, my relative speaks bitterly because her brother got hold of a plantation originally owned by Germans.

But in Guatemala, I understand it's much worse. There the malcontents are trying to incite the Indians not to show up to pick the coffee when it becomes ripe. And, as I'm sure you know, if the Indians don't emerge from their remote mountain villages to pick the coffee when they should, it is ruinous. The whole thing is like the Montagues and the Capulets, only worse," she concluded rather breathlessly as she gathered up her belongings, took her little son by the hand, and toddled off.

After she left, I couldn't help but speculate on what she had just said while I recalled Under Secretary of State Welles' attitude toward Latin America. In his eyes, most of the countries, and this was especially true of Panama and Central America, were not nations but geographic expressions controlled by ruling families. In this light, Mrs. Murray's analysis of jealousies inflamed by who got what and who didn't from the Axis countries made a lot of sense, no matter how absurdly feminine it sounded. *Curious,* I thought to myself, *that a preoccupied mother of a difficult child should see it and understand it, but our own people don't. It's as good an explanation of any for the restlessness in the area.*

The next morning I slept late and awoke to realize that the *Cape Ann* was dead in the water. All motion of the sea and the throbbing of its diesel engine were gone. We must, I decided, have arrived at Puerto Limon. At breakfast, the ship's dining room was deserted. All the passengers had presumably eaten early in order to witness our arrival. Once on deck, I found them all milling about with glum faces as though they were at a badly organized funeral. "None of us can go ashore," they moaned, "until the arms are unloaded!"

I joined Mrs. Murray at the rail and found her and her little boy waving furiously at an impeccably dressed man in a tropical suit and a superbly blocked Panama hat who was obviously her husband.

In a few minutes, he was allowed on board, along with a resplendent-looking man in a military uniform. After the customary *embrazzos* and a whispered conversation between Mrs. Murray and her husband, I was introduced. Immediately thereafter the military man came up to me, addressed me by name, and explained that he was in charge of unloading the arms and transporting them to the appropriate officials in San Jose. He also added that the train drawn up alongside the pier which was to transport the arms had attached to it a private car in which I could make the journey in total comfort, and he asked that I do him the honor of accompanying him on the train.

Before he even finished his elaborate invitation, I felt a tingling in my toes I hadn't felt since the arrest of Matheson and the shooting aboard the *Nereus*.

So, I said to myself, *the guy thinks I'm a big shot spook type from the CIA instead of an intelligence analyst on a busman's holiday. I better finesse this one.*

I turned to Mrs. Murray. "Are you and your son going up to San Jose on the train?" I asked.

Her reply was instantaneous. "Oh no," she insisted as she pointed to a machine gun nest on the roof of one of the train's boxcars. "My husband thinks it would be much too dangerous. The train might be hijacked by Somoza's soldiers while en route."

I turned to the general and explained that because of the arms I would have time to fly up to San Jose in the morning, return the following day, and still be able to catch the *Cape Ann* before it sailed for Colon.

In my mind, I dismissed the general as little more than a piece of military whimsy. The machine gunner had no uniform, and his ammunition had been so hastily unpacked that its crating lay scattered about on the pier. My involvement in the arms shipment was pure happenstance, and I had thought it best to decline the general's invite, but that didn't mean I shouldn't go up to San Jose on my own.

There was nothing to be afraid of. The general was no Lanas who might have been plotting to do away with me while en route to his wedding, nor was he the Japanese submarine skipper who regarded me as an enemy of communism. I thus had no doubt that if a further attempt to keep me under surveillance was made, it would be equally frivolous. Had I foreseen what was in store for me in San Jose, I would have stayed in Puerto Limon.

Around 8 PM the steward came in to strip my roommate's bunk. He had left the ship earlier that evening. "Too bad he was so deaf," the steward commented. "The poor guy went to the States for an operation but was advised it wouldn't do him any good." Then in an amiable way, he commented on what a dump Puerto Limon was and pointed out that it hadn't seen such excitement since a German submarine, had torpedoed a ship tied up at the dock during the war. When it sank, it had carried the pier with it. The present pier was a flimsy temporary one and couldn't hold much. Hence the unloading delay.

As if to emphasize his concern for my comfort, he gave my pillows an energetic fluffing up. "You are flying up to San Jose tomorrow, aren't you," he asked. It was more of a statement than a question.

"Yes, I am. But how did you know?"

"Well," he admitted, "I saw you go in the ticket office, and since San Jose is the only place the airline goes, I figured that was your destination. I was going to wait for you to come out so I could say hello, but then this military type came up and asked if I knew you, and if so, were you Mr. Kramer, so I figured it was none of his business, and I told him I didn't know. But then I decided I better leave in case you came out and recognized me."

After this, he fluffed up my pillows a second time and then inched sideways toward the door between the bunks and me. "That cabin mate of yours left the ship without giving me a tip," he announced sullenly and then left.

His attitude irritated me. Heretofore, he had never entered the cabin when I was there. I thus dismissed his friendliness as no more than a ploy to encourage me to leave him a large tip to make up for what he had failed to receive from my cabin mate and then picked up a copy of Lord Acton's *Lectures on Modern History*. It was one of several books I had brought along on the trip for leisure reading. But concentration was difficult.

> Cortez was not only the most heroic of the Conquistadores, for there was no lack of good soldiers, but he was an educated man, careful to import the plants and quadrupeds needed for civilisation, and a statesman capable of ruling mixed races without help from home. From the moment of his appearance the New World ceased to be a perplexing burden to Spain and began to foreshadow danger and temptation to other nations.

Was that damn steward to be presumed to be merely venal or someone more honorable? Maybe he was really trying to be helpful by mentioning the curious stranger who had asked him to identify me.

> And a man immeasurably inferior to him, a man who could not write his name, whose career, in its glory and its shame, was a servile imitation, almost a parody, of his own, succeeded thereby in establishing a South American empire equal to that of Cortez in the North.

First the colonel or general, or whatever he was, had wanted me to join him on the train carrying the arms up to San Jose. Then someone else clearly wished confirmation that I was flying up to San Jose as I had indicated to the general that I intended to do.

> The third name is Francisco Pizzaro. He stood by and listened while a native described a mighty potentate, many days to the south, who reigned over the mountains and the sea, who was rich in gold, and who possessed a four-footed beast of burden, the only one yet encountered, which was taken at first for a camel.

So what was in store for me in San Jose? Should I cancel the trip and stay in Puerto Limon? An extra day there was not a pleasant prospect. After all, I was on vacation. Why let some banana republic plotting get in my way?

> There were 4,600,000 ducats in the treasury of the Inca, and he filled his prison with gold as high as he could reach for the ransom which

did not save his life. The mines were soon in working order; and, as the expanse of fertile soil was 3000 miles long, it was clear that Peru, added to Mexico, constituted an important factor in European finance.

Too bad I don't have Chief Beals along as a bodyguard! I thought to myself. *But what the hell, the higher altitude and cooler air in San Jose should calm things down. Costa Rica hasn't got a real army. At most, all they wish to do is conceal from you where they are going to hide the arms.*

I spent the day in San Jose by myself, wandering on foot around the city and enjoying totally its benign climate, the fertility of its rich volcanic soil, and the profusion of flowers. There were no earthquakes or rumblings from the nearby volcano to disturb me.

That evening I joined for dinner some fellow passengers from the *Cape Ann* who had with them their lively little boy. They gave me a vivid description of their day. They had visited friends in the country who had a private zoo with a llama, an ocelot, monkeys and parrots, and even a sloth. The boy then went off to his room, and the three of us each had a drink before going into the hotel's rather stately dining room to eat. Suddenly, and totally unexpectedly, I felt myself falling asleep. No matter how hard I tried, I couldn't stay awake. There was then a vague recollection of being supported out of the dining room to my bed. After that, there was nothing at all until 3 AM when there was a loud knock on my door. Still too drowsy to get up, I merely mumbled, "Enter."

There arrived a doctor who explained he had been summoned by my dinner companions who were concerned about my health. He took my temperature and pulse, listened to my heart with his stethoscope, and announced there was nothing wrong with me. I had overexerted myself sightseeing. This was, of course, utter rubbish, but since all I wanted to do was go to sleep again, I smiled in agreement.

In the morning, I decided to take the train back down to Puerto Limon. *That way you can drink lots of water en route and get the drug out of your system while admiring the mountain chasms and the raging torrents during the descent,* I reasoned. When I checked out of the hotel, I noticed there was no charge for the doctor's visit. The hotel manager explained it was a courtesy call by the doctor who was personally concerned about the health of such a distinguished visitor. As he was sure I knew, which I didn't, the doctor was the brother of the minister of foreign affairs. Maybe when I got to Panama, Modi Arias could explain it all.

He didn't. All he said was, "The moment I got your cable about the twenty-four-hour delay due to the arms delivery by the *Cape Ann*, I figured you had maneuvered yourself into some plotting." But just what the "plotting" really was, he either could not or would not explain. Later, his father, a former president, whom I had first met when he visited his sons at Cambridge, asked me to deliver a sealed envelope to his son, Tito, the birthday ball man, who was in exile in Guatemala. En route to the airport, Modi warned me not to get off the plane if it stopped in Nicaragua. If the letter to Tito was found on me, there might be difficulties.

There were none, and I arrived in Guatemala City on schedule. That night, however, before going to bed, the hotel manager called. "Mr. Kramer," he explained," your room overlooks the main plaza and the Capitol building, and we understand there may be trouble during the night, shooting and an attack on the Capitol. If that happens, the night clerk will ring to signal you to take your mattress from your bed and throw it into the bathtub where you should spend the rest of the night. Your bath is an inside room, and you will be perfectly safe there."

There was no trouble, but I couldn't help but be amused by the fact that the Capitol building that faced the plaza over which my room looked was the one for which I had secured the doorknobs and back plates with so much difficulty when I worked for Nelson Rockefeller.

In the morning, I left for Lake Atitlan, a scenic spot some distance from the city, stopping off at Antigua to deliver to Tito the envelope from his father. Tito didn't discuss either the reason for his exile or the contents of the letter, and I asked no questions. In any event, it would have been a waste of time for not too long afterward, in a sudden political bouleversement of which his country was capable, Tito was elevated from his exile to being ambassador to the United Nations. He also received a divorce from his wife and married Margot Fonteyn, the British prima ballerina assoluta, whom we both had known at Cambridge during the early days of her career.

At Lake Atitlan I took a ferryboat to a remote Indian village at the other end of the lake from my hotel and noticed, while en route, a Caucasian engaged in an animated discussion with two Indians in their dialect. On leaving to go ashore, I maneuvered myself next to him and remarked on his ability to speak the Indian language. His knowledge of it was most unusual, I commented.

"It's not unusual," he corrected me in English with a thick German accent. "I lived here for many years before the war. I managed a large coffee plantation, and to be efficient, I felt it imperative to learn the language of the workers."

"And the plantation was seized at the outbreak of war?" I asked.

"Indeed it was! By an associate of the dictator."

"You were imprisoned as an enemy alien?"

"Oh no. They let me return to Germany with the diplomats. I knew our ambassador. He made the necessary arrangements."

"Too bad you couldn't sit out the war here in Guatemala."

"Not at all," he corrected me again. "I bought a dairy farm in Hesse. It's always best to be a farmer in wartime. Then you have plenty to eat, and there are no bombs."

"Very clever," I commented. "Tell me," I asked, veering our talk away from himself to the natives, "are the Indians here content? Will they show up to pick the coffee?"

"No," he answered with emphasis. "The radicals around President Arevalo are stirring things up! And now," he added, "you tell me. In your election yesterday, Mr. Dewey was defeated and Truman reelected. How could such a thing happen? How?" he demanded.

"It happened," I answered, "because the voting majority wished it to happen." Then I left him, annoyed by his arrogance.

Once back in my office in Washington, Will Kendall asked me how my vacation had gone. "Good," I said. "I got a swell rest on the ship on the way down."

"And then," he queried, "did you learn anything worthwhile?"

"Yes," I admitted. "The whole area is as restless as you and I would be if we drank three cups of strong black coffee before going to bed."

"Why limit it to coffee? Why not indigestion from eating too many bananas?"

"Because coffee is all part of it. There has been some shifting in wealth among the ruling families due to who got the seized Axis coffee plantations and who didn't. Remember Shakespeare's Othello: 'O beware, my lord, of jealousy; it is the green-eyed monster.'"

And do you think the Communists are going to move in on the green-eyed ones and exploit them for their own ends?"

"They just might, in Guatemala. When I was there, I went to see our naval attaché. He had checked in with me here before taking up his post and had told me to drop in to see him if I was ever in Guatemala City. He felt they were beginning to exploit the problem. But I must double-check here in Washington with some sources before I make up my mind."

"When you do, let me know."

"How can I? Have you forgotten? You're leaving."

In early April 1948, an important inter-American conference was scheduled to meet in Bogotá, Colombia. The U.S. delegation was to be headed by Secretary of State General Marshall. The Latin American countries were sending equally high-level delegations. Essentially, the United States planned to demonstrate that despite its emergence from World War II as a preeminent world power, it had not forgotten its Latin neighbors and former under secretary of state Welles' Good Neighbor Policy.

Curiously, I noticed that my fellow ORE associates were not concerning themselves with whether or not Bogotá was a suitable and safe venue for such a conference but were assiduously assembling position papers vis-à-vis the agenda for the conference. This troubled me for two reasons. Such position papers did not seem to me to be the job of the CIA, but of the State Department. But more ominously, I was troubled by the intelligence take from Colombia itself. There had been no discussion of Bogotá as a proper venue for the conference. Because of this, I made a couple of phone calls to friends in Colombia about it and received some alarming news. The political situation in Colombia was, I was told, volatile to say the least. The non-Communist radical leader of the masses, a charismatic man named Gaitan, had an enormous and somewhat hysterical following among the masses, and could, if he wished, wreck the conference. Furthermore, if anything should happen to him, all hell would break loose. The handful of Communists in Colombia at that time hated him and would do anything to get rid of him and thus capture the leadership of the masses—a leadership that was presently denied them by Gaitan. I drafted a memo that the U.S. delegation protection should be increased and strengthened by a substantial number of embassy marine guards since the situation in Bogotá was very unstable. This memo was sent forward to the head of ORE, who did not pass it forward. Alas, my intelligence days proved correct. Gaitan was shot. Riots broke out, the delegates to the conference fled for their lives to their respective embassies, or, a worse fate, to the Grenada Hotel, then jokingly called the "Grand Nada" or "Big Nothing Hotel," and the word *bogotazzo* entered the Spanish language, meaning "a complete and total fiasco," and the minimal U.S. embassy protection was scary to say the least.

Shortly after this, I attended the weekly intelligence briefing of the director in his conference room. The moment I entered and took a seat opposite a sleepy-eyed colonel I had never seen before, the needling started.

"Hey, Kramer, where were you?"

"I thought you were supposed to predict such things."

"Could you have been the '*bogotazzo*,' not the conference?"

"Poor General Marshall. What were you trying to do, get rid of him?"

I said nothing. If anything was to be said in reply, it was up to the new head of ORE, but he maintained a stony silence. Suddenly, in the silence, a total stranger rose from the conference table and pointed an accusing finger at the head of ORE. He was in such a rage that I noticed the cords of his neck were constricted to the extent that he was speechless. Meanwhile, I noticed that the sleepy-eyed colonel was now totally awake and grinning from car to ear.

The unknown stranger finally got his voice under control, and at that moment, Admiral Hillenkoetter walked into the room to chair the meeting. But that didn't stop him. Still pointing an accusing finger at the Yale professor, the stranger addressed the assembled senior intelligence experts. "Don't you make fun of Kramer," he shouted. "He warned of impending trouble. It's that nitwit who held up his memo and who never sent it forward. Go ahead! Ridicule him; he deserves it, not Kramer."

With these minatory words, he sat down, and the meeting commenced. Afterward I went to the adjoining washroom and found my protecting stranger there. "I wasn't going to let that idiot sit there with his mouth shut and let you be picked on," he said. I nodded and murmured "Thanks" and left, assuming the brouhaha was now a thing of the past, but nothing could have been farther from the case.

A week later, when I arrived for work, which was then in a temporary building left over from the war on the site of the present Kennedy Center, the Negro guard of the building stopped me with a broad grin and said, "The boss had me put his morning paper on your desk." Totally puzzled, I thanked him but had no idea what he meant. On my desk, however, I found the morning *Washington Post* with question marks in black crayon alongside two front-page articles on Latin America. A moment later Will Kendall sent for me.

"Well," he said, "you're now famous, or infamous, depending on your politics. That paper on your desk is President Truman's. He left it there personally while on his morning walk. You are to write and type up the answers to his questions yourself and hand-deliver them to Admiral Hillenkoetter before he leaves for his morning briefing of the president at ten thirty, and no one else in the shop is to know about it. Absolutely no one!"

"Do you wish to see what I write before I deliver it?" I asked.

"No, I'm out of the loop. The only reason I have these instructions is that you were late for work and the admiral couldn't reach you, so they left the message with me. Good luck, Paul."

It was at once clear to me after looking at the president's questions that what he was concerned about was the Caribbean Legion. At that time, this small band of revolutionaries was drifting about the Caribbean. To me they seemed no more than an idealistic group of young men headed by an attractive young leader, who was determined to overthrow Rafael Trujillo, the dictator of the Dominican Republic. My "take" on it had nothing in-depth to say about its leader, so I checked through a couple of phone calls—one to Harry Frantz who was back at United Press from the no-longer-existent Rockefeller office, and another to a young Panamanian revolutionary.

"Harry," I asked, "have you got a reading on the head of the Caribbean Legion?"

"Yes, Paul. Our man thinks he's an idealistic young man. Absolutely no Communist leanings. Just out to overthrow Trujillo."

"Thanks, Harry, I'll be in touch."

The young revolutionary in Panama gave me the same answer.

President Truman, I knew, liked to vacation in Key West so that it was clear to me that what troubled him was that it might not be safe to vacation so physically near the legion's planned violent activities. The Secret Service, not knowing anything about the legion, might very well have suggested he vacation elsewhere. I thus angled my memo to suggest that in view of the known idealism of the legion's head, I was sure he had nothing against the president of the United States or our country. All that bothered him was General Trujillo and the compelling need to get rid of him.

As it turned out, this proved to be the case. When the legion finally landed in the Dominican Republic and was rounded up by the dictator's soldiers and put in jail, the story was that Trujillo found the legion's leader such a courageous and attractive young man that he decided he would make a suitable husband for one of his unmarried daughters!

I sought to leave my memo with the admiral's secretary, whom I knew. But she would have none of it, and so I personally delivered it to him. This gave me the opportunity to do two things. I asked him who told the president to turn to me. "Oh," he said, "a great friend of his from the World War I days was at that meeting where they were teasing you about the *bogotazzo*. He told him to cut through the red tape and turn to you out of channels."

"This poses a problem," I explained. "I'm scheduled to leave for two weeks of naval reserve duty at the sub base in New London. I hope President Truman won't leave any newspapers on my desk while I'm gone."

"No problem, Kramer. If he does, I'll phone you and you can dictate a memo over the phone. Just leave the dates you'll be away at the sub base with my Secretary. She'll be able to track you down there."

What I didn't tell the admiral was that my decision to take two weeks away at New London was because I needed a change. I wanted to be free of all the backbiting and intra-office hostilities in the CIA, and two weeks at New London with an occasional submersion below the surface of Long Island Sound was the best therapy I could think of.

All this attention from the front office had an unexpected effect. I got a call from the admiral's office, asking that I take over the duty in his office the next Christmas and New Year. If any vital calls came in, I was to alert immediately the admiral. He, in turn, would keep me informed at all times exactly where he could be reached. Oddly enough, I suppose, this was considered a reward since there were hundreds of others who could have been asked to do the job. The double pay and overtime were substantial—not that I needed it. I was still flush with all my navy pay and the unforeseen extras involved; plus there was the substantial gift from my mother on my twenty-first birthday, which Lazard Frères had increased so handsomely while I had been overseas during the war and which I couldn't possibly spend, not even the interest that had accrued.

As it turned out, nothing could have been better designed to restore my spirits than New London. First off, I discovered that my former boss from the *Nereus* was on duty at New London; so were two chief petty officers, who looked forward to greeting me so that they could give me a rundown on what had become of the three CPOs I had worked so closely with on the surrendered Japanese subs. Meanwhile, another CPO came forward and identified himself as a former shipmate of Chief Beals' who had guarded me so zealously in Brisbane. These old-line navy chief petty officers were the backbone of the submarine navy. If, as a junior officer, they approved of you, decided you had both courage and ability, your career as a navy officer was established.

Perhaps it was due to my old *Nereus* boss, I never knew, but I was put to work on a highly secret submarine intelligence project. At this time, the old battery-diesel subs' days were numbered. It was clear that in a few years they would be replaced by jumbo atom-powered nuclear subs. The project I was put to work on was obviously designed for this new era. It also became clear to me that once the nuclear subs were in commission, they would be in a position to gather an enormous amount of information about the Soviet Union—perhaps even more than the CIA. Save for a couple of days at sea aboard a submarine and a rescue vessel, I devoted all my working time to the project. When I finished my duty, I was told that in view of the highly classified nature of the work I had been given and regardless of my work for the CIA, I was subject to recall by the navy should the need arise; and my navy work had precedence over any CIA work. This made me wonder. Should I reconsider the offer made to me aboard the *Nereus* and rejoin the navy? I mulled over this for a week after I returned to the CIA and was encouraged to be serious about it by the fact that Will Kendall resigned to take up intelligence work elsewhere, and also by the fact that I received a letter from the Atlantic Fleet Submarine Force, thanking me for my interest in the fleet's project and expressing the hope that I could "come back." Instead, in a few months I asked for and received a transfer to CIA's Operations, from which I resigned in 1951 for health reasons.[1]

[1.] This brief tour of duty with Rear Admiral James Fife, COMSUBLANT at the Navy Submarine Base New London, Connecticut, resulted in a fitness report, which, if studied carefully, reveals that my intelligence duty for the navy, both ashore and afloat was of "too high a classification to describe in the report" and is one of the only bits of documentary evidence that I possess which refers to the secrecy of my work, which in this particular case is still secret. Since the report does not reveal its nature, it is reproduced on page 171.

17

I glanced at my prized Omega watch, the one I had been issued just after boarding the *Nereus*. The time was 10:48 AM. It was 1949. I remembered the time because it turned out to be the opening bell for a series of events that were to change my life. At that moment, of course, I anticipated nothing. CIA's operations were on a need-to-know basis, and I knew very little. All I did know was that I had nothing to do, and as a relief from the boredom, I planned to go to the movies that afternoon. No one would miss me. The truth was that I had made a mistake to ask for a transfer from CIA's Reports and Estimates (ORE) to Operations. My areas of skill were Japan and Latin America, and at that time, Operations was out of both. General MacArthur brooked no interference in his Japanese satrapy, and the CIA had yet to recover from J. Edgar Hoover's deindexing of his Latin American files.

Thus, I had simply been put on "hold." Occasionally the special assistant to the director of operations tossed me a few crumbs of work. He was a friend of Admiral Hillenkoetter, then head of the CIA, who had told him of my record in R&E. But this was all. I hadn't felt so frustrated since the first few days in August 1940 after I had been hired by the White House and immediately assigned to Nelson Rockefeller who had just come down from New York to head the Office for Coordination of Commercial and Cultural Relations between the American Republics.

Once having noted the time, I went to the window and looked out. The urban landscape to be seen from my office on the ground floor of a temporary building dating from World War II was one of the most beautiful in the world. Maybe that would dissolve the ennui in which I was enveloped. Directly opposite was the reflecting pool. To the left was the Lincoln Memorial. To the right was the Washington Monument. I even recollected the spiel that the tour driver had delivered when I had first seen it during a visit to Washington with my parents as a child. "See the Washington Monument! The greatest monument ever built to man. At 555½ feet tall, it towers over the nation's capital like the pyramids to the pharaohs of ancient Egypt." The final *t* of *Egypt* had been emphasized to make it all sound more foreign, and thus, bizarre.

Then it was back to my desk, with a groan of boredom. At this point, it was exactly 11:00 AM, and suddenly, a very symmetrical and blond WASPy man appeared in my office. As Kim Philby, the notorious British traitor, wrote much later after he had defected to Moscow, "The CIA men flaunted cosmopolitan positions. They would discuss absinthe and serve Burgundy above room temperature." The description was apt. It described perfectly the young stranger who had just entered.

He introduced himself as a coworker who had an office just down the hall from me. "I understand," he explained, "you are something of an expert on Latin America."

"Not really, but I try," I countered.

"Well, we have a problem."

"Tell me what it is, and I'll see if I can help."

"Well, we have a ship we want transferred to a Panamanian flag of convenience. We hired a Panamanian lawyer three months ago to arrange it, and nothing so far has been accomplished. Time is running short. Maybe you can speed things up."

"I'm sure I can," I told him. "But there is a problem. The man I will call for help comes from a highly political family. I don't think I can ask for his intervention unless I'm sure the transfer would not embarrass his family politically. I'll need to know what you plan to do with the ship before I can do anything."

"You really think you can help?"

"I'm sure of it."

"In that case your need-to-know seems legitimate. You see, we're planning to roll back the iron curtain. We have in mind an invasion of Albania. The aim is to get rid of Enver Hoxha and his Communist regime and install a democratic one to bring freedom and liberty and dignity to the Balkans."

"In other words, to leave out all the nouns, you want to restore King Zog and Queen Geraldine's son Leka to the Albanian throne."

"Precisely."

"That seems to be nonpolitical as far as Panama is concerned. Who are you working with on it?"

"The British. It's a joint operation with Kim Philby of British Intelligence. He's been sent over here to liaison and help us with it.

The moment he mentioned the fateful words, *Kim Philby*, it was as if my stomach had suddenly sunk down to my crotch. I tried not to show it, but I must have paled. The symmetrical "Oh So Social" or OSS type must have noticed it, but he was too polite to say anything. He was obviously desperate and needed me.

"My office is just down the hall," he continued. "You can call your friend from there."

I followed him with a combined mixture of pleasure and distaste. While half of me was delighted with the opportunity to show how an old Latin American hand could solve a problem with a five-minute phone call, the other half found the whole thing totally noxious.

The flashback was both vivid and total. It was early 1945. I had driven down to the seashore with Chief Beals to pick up Commander Hopkinson at the Dutch consul's beach house. He was lunching there with his great friend Rajah Brooke of Sarawak, the white rajah. En route back to Brisbane, I recalled exactly what Hopkinson had said: "Somewhere someone in the vast Soviet intelligence establishment apparatus apparently wants you out of the way." This was merely an elaboration of what Foxworth had told me about not knowing who your enemies really were when I first started work.

From this, the recall moved back to 1938. I had just been given an M. Litt. degree in history and had gone to see G. P. Gooch. We were chatting in his study, and I had just taken Acton's famous phrase about power being a corrupting force and rephrased it into "Imperialism corrupts, and rampant imperialism corrupts absolutely." Gooch had been amused by my play with words, so I asked him for a couple of examples. He had given me the Philbys, both father and son. The father, after a career in the Indian Civil Service of pushing around East Indians, had returned to England under the delusion he had something to offer the British ruling classes. He had run for Parliament and had been defeated. Embittered by the rejection, he had gone to Saudi Arabia where he had become a Nazi. The son, when at Cambridge ahead of me, had become an out and out Communist. They had both irrevocably turned against England.

Was Philby, I asked myself, the source of all my troubles as an intelligence officer? While on the White House payroll I had been denounced by the vice president as a "malignant Nazi." Wallace had demanded my dismissal, a demand circumvented by both Joe Rovensky and Stephenson. While in Brisbane my superiors considered me sufficiently "exposed" to the extent that I needed a bodyguard. While aboard the *Nereus*, I had been shot at and slightly wounded by an enlisted man known to consort with a Communist skipper of one of the surrendered Japanese subs. Meanwhile, I suspected that a dim FBI man in London had me put on a British Intelligence source list. If this were so, Philby would have known about it. Also, he certainly knew what my mentor Gooch thought of him. There was, of course, no proof whatsoever that any of these were Philby's doing. Still I'd had not much ground for suspicion when I first got on the trail of Matheson in 1940, and he had turned out to be a Japanese agent whose arrest I'd witnessed.

All this was parallel to the job at hand. Still, it was ironic. Conceivably, Philby could have been behind the three-month delay in securing the Panama flag of convenience for the Albanian operation. If so, I was about to foil him again, and I would win just as I had in the past. The phone call didn't seem quite so ominous after all.

"Hey, Modi, it's Paul. How are you? I hear you're like me, not married yet . . . Yes, I have. I see her from time to time here in DC . . . Look, Modi, I've got a personal favor to ask of you. I've got a friend here who has a ship he wants transferred to the Panama flag. There's some hurry about it. The ship's name is—, and the lawyer he's hired to do the job is—. Nothing has been accomplished during the last three months. Do you think you can speed things up? By four this afternoon? You can do it that fast? I don't believe it! I'll tell you what, Modi. Once it's done could you call me at this number—? It's my office number. Just tell whoever answers that you've done the job. And if there's a bill, send it to me at my house, 4404 Twenty-Ninth Street. And by the way, Modi, I've got a guestroom and a superb Belgian housekeeper, so come and see me, and give my best to your dad and Tito and all the rest. Good-bye."

"Well," I said to my new associate, "you've heard the phone call, and you'll get the word. As you heard, I gave him your number. I'd appreciate it if you would let me know the outcome.

"I sure will," he said with a mixture of amazement and awe.

"And by the way, you might care to look into the antecedents of that dud lawyer you hired. He might conceivably have been part of a delaying action."

"Oh, I doubt that. As you know, we have no Latin American division. So we asked Philby to recommend one. I'm sure he's OK." At that time, Philby was in Washington, working closely with the CIA as a British intelligence officer.

"Perhaps, but you might want to check with the FBI. They had a rather able man in Panama during the war, and presumably he will know about him."

"Oh no. We couldn't do that. We'd never have anything to do with that fairy, Hoover. That would be . . . well, that would be like being a traitor or a queer or both."

I left and went to the movies, stopping for some lunch beforehand at the Willard Hotel coffee shop. I ordered chicken a la king on toast. When the waitress brought it to me, I couldn't eat it. This was the same dish I'd eaten when I'd enticed the damn Kraut who had been sent to Washington to kill President Roosevelt to eat with me and then walk with me back to my office, knowing fully well he'd be picked up by the FBI on the southwest corner of Fourteenth and Pennsylvania Avenue and I would keep on walking as though nothing had happened. Well, at least we hadn't eaten at this particular table, so why worry about it? "If you can't eat the chicken, eat a desert." I did, but that didn't stop me from thinking. The Kraut job had been about the worst period of my life while overtly working for Rockefeller. I'd had to go out at night and drink beer with him. I'd also had a project from the secret fund to manage, which had been wished on to Rockefeller by Under Secretary of State Welles. Then there had been the Torch project. I got a rash on my arm, and the doctor had said it was nerves from overwork. I should make a point of eating lunch alone. As if I could. I also had the Lanas problem and the need to befriend him to see if he would lead us to any Nazi confederate agents. Then too there was my overt work. Thank God I'd joined the navy. I needed the rest.

The movie was a fiasco as far as I was concerned. Into it for a short while, totally unexpectedly, I got an erection, went to the phone in the lobby, and called Ella at her office. I knew she was supposed to eat that night with her sister, but I talked her out of it. When I went back to my seat, I couldn't help but laugh at myself. I remembered how Sam Foxworth, the FBI's expert on enemy subversion had told me soon after I'd gone to work for Rockefeller, "Paul," he'd said," the work you're getting into is as isolating as all hell. Take it from me, you'll want to fuck even more than normal. So do it often, even if you have to pay for it."

While Joan Crawford rolled her eyes and rattled her teeth on the silver screen, I reached the conclusion that there was nothing I could do about Philby. He was too well-entrenched with the Oh So Social crowd for them to pay any attention to me. *Just shut up and go about what comes your way,* I said to myself. *If the Albanian operation flops, then they might listen to you.*

When I was a kid spending my summers on the family farm in northern Kentucky, my father used to wage an unending war against the moles under the front lawn. What he did was take a watering can full of water and pour it into a molehill. When the mole's snout would emerge for a breath of air, he would take a forceps, snag the snout and pull the mole out of the burrow. My trouble was I had no forceps with which to snag the mole. Until I did, my suspicions about Philby were mostly hot air.

Ella and I made love all throughout that night. She had become engaged to a man she had doubts about. This was her last fling.

Later, things picked up, but not significantly. I was included in a little group of Soviet specialists who met regularly but informally for Sunday night dinners. They had all served at one time or another at our embassy in Moscow. Due to the privations and security precautions under Stalin, it was a close-knit group. They had their own adjectives, their own code words, and their own common reminiscence. In a way, they reminded me of the U.S. submariners among whom I had suddenly been plunged when assigned to the *Nereus* shortly after the war. A confined and restricted life in which common danger had been shared had bound them together into a close-knit group from which outsiders had been barred unless they demonstrated ability and composure under stress. The names of these Soviet specialists have gone down in history as the architects and administrators of our policy toward the Soviet Union. They included Carmel Offie and Bob Kelly of the CIA. Offie had been a clerk and then a professional Foreign Service officer under Bullitt in Moscow and Paris. Kelly had been, for many years, the Soviet desk officer in the State Department in Washington. There were also John Wiley, Bob Joyce, and Freddy Reinhardt from the State Department, all professional diplomats who had once served in Moscow. Admiral Hillenkoetter and George Kennan were also part of this group but did not attend the dinners. But they were always in touch, and there were visits from time to time. Everything was casual, and all of them were on a first-name basis. There was often a rubber or two of bridge. Regardless of who was in the White House, it had been these people who administered and formulated our policies toward Russia.

After an acceptance into this little coterie, I was asked to go to the State Department and explain to a select group of juniors exactly what the operations branch of the CIA was up to. It was difficult assignment. The audience was hostile. Instinctively, they resented an outsider from the bureau intruding on their territory. Also, some were idealists. Never having served in Moscow, they were not personally familiar with what life could be like under Stalin's regime. To them the CIA was repugnant—"dirty work for dirty people." Why did America, the pure, need to be dragged down into the sewer with Moscow?

I kept it as low-key as I could and told them to feel free to interrupt if they had any questions as I went along. The one thing that bothered them was the secrecy of it all. How were they as desk officers in Washington to know if, say, an uprising in Czechoslovakia was indigenous or CIA-inspired? They wouldn't, I explained, but their superiors would. There was coordination at the top levels of government. Then one of them asked if there were any peacetime precedents for this sort of thing.

Here, I was on safe ground and told them about the Rockefeller office's pre-Pearl Harbor secret fund and how Under Secretary Welles had used it for the two projects he favored. In their eyes, trained as they had been in the compelling necessity in diplomacy to search the files and look for precedents, they now felt more relaxed.

Word spread about this little meeting, and at the next Sunday night supper, Freddy Reinhardt, at that time the Soviet desk officer, said to me, "Paul, I must warn you about General Bedell Smith, the new chief at the CIA now that Hilly has retired. He's a bully. You've got to stand up to him if he tries to push you around; otherwise, you'll be lost. If he pushes you hard, just push him back, and then he'll respect you. I know this from personal experience."

"Thanks, Freddy," I said. "I don't know him. I knew Hilly from my work at Reports and Estimates, but not the new chief."

"Yes, I know. He admired you. He forced Wisner [the Chief of Operations at the CIA-funded Office of Policy and Coordination] to take you on." So the little group functioned. It was a whispering gallery. They knew everything that was going on, even all the gossip, perhaps even more than they needed to know.

Shortly after this, while I was idly smoking a cigarette in my office, there suddenly materialized Bill Clark, Nelson Rockefeller's brother-in-law and a former coworker at the office. He acted as though I knew he worked for the CIA, which I didn't. I merely assumed he did since he had gotten in the building unannounced. Without any preliminaries, which was characteristic of him, he announced in somewhat minatory tones, "Frank Jamieson is being seriously considered for a top job here in the CIA. You've got to block it."

This announcement, which was news to me, set my mind to work, reviewing the current gossip. General Bedell Smith, the new director of the CIA was reputed to be close to Anna Rosenberg, the woman who had helped get Nelson his job as coordinator of inter-American affairs and who had recommended Jamieson to Rockefeller as an assistant coordinator. Presumably, she was up to a similar maneuver; but was it merely to supply her friend the general with a good public relations man or to open a path for Nelson as a subsequent head of the CIA? It was conceivable. Nelson, I knew, had always cherished his early connection with British Intelligence, and he might, now that the Cold War was on, regard the CIA as a stepping-stone for his political career. But whatever ambitions were afoot, I preferred to keep my thoughts to myself and not discuss them with Bill Clark.

"Look, Bill," I said. "I had problems with Jamieson as you apparently know, but eventually we were able to work them out."

"And you never complained to Nelson. He was aware of them, but he once told me there was nothing he could do unless you complained, and you never did."

"Nelson had other more important things to do than worry about me. Anyway, as I said, I worked them out."

"But surely you will want to block him from coming aboard here."

"Look, Bill, I'm not at all sure I could, even if I wanted to. If anyone cares to come to me about Jamieson, I'll give him the facts as I know them. But keep in mind one important thing: Jamieson didn't staff his press division with several pro-Soviet men because he was a radical himself. He did it because he was totally aware of fellow traveller influence in the U.S. press at the time. His job was to get Nelson a favorable press, and he did just that. His approach to the problem may have been cynical, but he personally was not a fellow traveller."

Bill listened and frowned at the same time. He left as suddenly as he had arrived, and I heard no more about Jamieson as a prospective high-level employee of the CIA. At any event, Bedell Smith soon resigned the directorship, and Alan Dulles took over. At the time, I never mentioned Bill's visit to anyone, nor did I allude to it in the chapter I wrote for a book on World War II intelligence that Bill's sister had liked so much. The truth was that I regarded Clark's demand as no more than an example of the backbiting and intrigue over the staffing of the CIA, which was expanding so rapidly at that time. Just who would make a good cold warrior was a source of endless debate and gossip.

Subsequently, I was taken to New York a few times. Here, I was introduced to Jay Lovestone and his assistant, Irving Brown. Lovestone was the only American ever to serve on the Comintern and had fled to the United States for his life once Stalin had turned against him. Totally disenchanted with the Soviets and with a fund of knowledge about the Comintern's inner workings that surpassed that of most other Americans, George Meany, the head of the American Federation of Labor had hired him to direct the AFL's efforts to rid labor unions of Communist penetration. CIA worked in tandem with him.

Shortly thereafter, the Albanian operation turned out to be a total and tragic flop. The Communist dictator Hoxha's troops were on the beach at the exact spot where their newly registered Panama ship landed them. Prince Leka's court was eradicated. Philby, meanwhile, remained in Washington as liaison man.

Subsequent to this disaster, I went to a cocktail party given by a cousin. She was a rich, beautiful woman who liked to surround herself with the movers and shakers in the Washington scene. As a wartime worker for the Office of Strategic Services, she took a proprietary interest in the CIA and could at times be a bit loose in her talk about it. Her remarks were not motivated by evil or guile; they were simply the indiscretions of a Washington hostess who wished to prove she was "in the know." On my arrival, I saw Averell Harriman, then an official of some importance, on a settee for two. I joined him, and we had a pleasant chat about his niece Betty and some other relations of his. Our work was never mentioned.

There suddenly appeared the wife of the CIA Operations chief. "Paul," she asked as she approached Averell and me, "I'm feeling thirsty. Would you get me a glass of water?" Returning with the requested water, I found her sitting in my seat and engaged in a vigorous conversation with Harriman. I left the party.

A day later, the Operations Chief sent for me. His rather sumptuous office and large executive desk were brightly lit. The sun was streaming in the window opposite him. I got a good look. There had been a perceptible physical deterioration since I had last seen him, which was before the Albanian debacle. He had previously carried his excess weight well. There had been a distinct emphasis of physical power as though he had been a skilled college athlete. Now, however, there was a tendency to flab, and the flesh below his eyes seemed loose. Also, his thin hair seemed to have grown even thinner

He motioned me to a chair opposite him. His voice was controlled and low-key but was not casual. He gave the impression that he was controlling his voice with some effort.

"Paul," he said, "it's about that cousin of yours, Kay. She's been known to be going around town saying things against me."

Somewhat stunned that he would bother with anything so trivial, I immediately thought of the incident with his wife and Harriman at Kay's party and the ploy over the glass of water. Was he so insecure that he thought, via his wife, that I had been downloading him on Harriman? It was too absurd.

"Um," was about all I could think of saying.

At this point the light in his office suddenly dimmed. The sun had gone behind a cloud. It was totally obvious to me, but he suddenly started. His eyes darted sideways, and he glanced behind as though he thought the sudden diminution of light was the prelude to a stab in the back by an enemy.

Recovering his composure, he continued his attack on Kay. By this time, I'd had enough. "Look, Frank," I said. "my experience has taught me, when faced with such a situation, that the best thing to do is simply confront the person involved and work it out together, not beat around the bush via someone else. There's nothing evil about Kay. She's harmless. You know her. Just talk to her about how you feel. She'll be sympathetic."

"You're perfectly right," he answered.

"Since I'm here," I said, "there's something I feel I should discuss with you. It might be important. It's about the Albanian operation and that ship you used."

He stiffened perceptibly at the mention of Albania. "Look, Paul," he said with a note of irritation, "you're new at this game, so perhaps you don't understand. We're on a need-to-know basis. Albania is out of your concern."

"Not quite true," I interposed. I then explained how I'd become involved in the ship registration and how I'd accomplished in four hours what Operations had been unable to do in three months. I also told him that I'd suggested that the reasons for the three-month delay merited investigation, but this had been waived aside.

"I know nothing about that," was his comment.

"Now you do," was on the tip of my tongue, but instead, I continued ignoring his apparent disinterest in what I was determined to tell him about Philby and my mentor at Cambridge, G. P. Gooch. *Goddamn it*, I said to myself. *Why is it so hard to get to him? Why is it that when with him my sense of well-being and enthusiasm seems to be in an odd sort of way an offense when balanced against his job and importance?* But I went on anyway, and when I told him of Gooch's distaste for both the Philbys, father and son, I noticed that his face flushed, and the hand that had been resting on his desk tightened into a fist.

When I'd first gone to Foxworth, as a totally untutored intelligence officer, about my suspicions of Matheson, at least he'd listened and given me the necessary equipment to trap him via Bermuda and British intercepts. He hadn't reacted like this man, as though it was all a crude exercise of an untutored mind with no depth of intelligence exposure, which at the time of the Matheson incident was true, but not so ten years later.

And so I wrapped up my Philby story and told him why Gooch felt they were good examples of how rampant imperialism corrupted. Again the sun went behind a cloud, and the office dimmed. This time, without thinking, he grabbed a paper weight on his desk and then glanced behind him while his eyes darted away from me. *Is this man,* I asked myself *so absorbed in chasing Communists that like the man in Melville's novel who chased whale, his mind has given way?* There was certainly no evidence of this the previous time I had seen him when he had asked for my help on a letter to General Clay about private funding for a government-supported office. At that time, he'd demonstrated what a fine legal mind he had. But since Albania, he had changed. Now he was unnerved and insecure. But even so, I was hardly prepared for what came next. He stood up from his desk, apparently to give emphasis to what he had to say.

"Don't you think," he asked, "it's somewhat arrogant on your part to be so dismissive of one of the most able and talented members of British Intelligence, a man in whom both we and the British government have complete confidence?"

I left. What more was there for me to say? I walked out of the building and went for a walk around the reflecting pool and up the steps of the Lincoln Memorial while finding solace in Pierre L'Enfant's magnificent distances. Ignoring the tourists admiring Father Abraham's biblical cadences, I went around to the back and looked across the Potomac to Arlington Cemetery. I'd had ten anonymous years as an intelligence officer. As a family, we'd done enough for our country. The thing to do was resign and reinvent myself. There was time. I was still young.

Meanwhile, my doctor had told me I needed some physical repairs. It would take a couple of months. These "reasons of health" would give me a perfect excuse to resign without comment,

Recovering my buoyancy and optimism, I thought back to an incident during my Rockefeller days. Nelson's children were young, and there was a long driveway from the street to his house. He had nailed up a sign to a tree at the head of the drive: Careful! Children at play. Beardsley Rumml, the author of the pay-as-you-go income tax plan was a consultant and was the houseguest of Rockefeller. He had arrived at a project meeting with a large paper bag. When asked for his opinion of the project under discussion, he had simply drawn out of the paper bag the sign about "children at play" and tossed it down on the conference table. That had ended the discussion.

I walked back to the office and during the next few weeks quietly wound things up and resigned, not via Wisner but via the director's secretary, whom I had known when she worked for Hillenkoetter. Never in my wildest dreams did I suppose that my resignation was not the end but a new beginning in my intelligence career. There would be recognition of my work from totally unforeseen quarters, both from foreign enemies as well as friends.

Soon before I resigned, however, Howard Hunt of Watergate fame, then a CIA Operations man, came to see me. He said he had been told to check in with me before leaving for Mexico to become station chief there. At that time, Howard, with a stack of salacious paperback novels to his credit (whips in a seduction scene in a room at the Mayflower Hotel and that sort of thing) had a certain charm, but was, however, so far to the right of Barry Goldwater that I questioned his judgment, especially in radical Mexico.

"Howard," I said, "I've got only two bits of advice to give you. The most beloved American now living in Mexico City is former mayor O'Dwyer of New York. He's retired now as our ambassador there and is a very interesting man. A graduate of the University of Salamanca in Spain, he speaks the most perfect Spanish of any American I've ever known. The leaders and the powerful people in Mexico adore him, and he has real influence with the governing party."

When Howard heard I'd recommended a Democrat, even though he knew I was a registered Republican, his face crinkled into a baleful frown.

"The other man you must contrive to cultivate is Tony Bermudez, the head of Mexico's nationalized oil industry, PEMEX. There is a very good reason for this. Bermudez is in fact, if not in name, the domestic intelligence chief of Mexico. He has a bank of phones on the windowsill behind his desk. Through them, he is in total contact with every PEMEX filling station in the country, the managers of which are to report to him of any potential or real Indian or mestizo restlessness or hostility to the ruling PRI party. Also, he has a total facility for tapping into the phones of any embassy in Mexico City, including our own."

Howard's face fell further. Bermudez as head of PRI since Mexico had seized all foreign oil companies, was a dangerous radical, even though he was a very well-to-do distiller.

After Howard had set up shop in Mexico, I got a call from Bill O'Dwyer.

"Paul," he moaned. "How could you? How could you send that wretch to Mexico?"

"What's up, Bill?" I asked.

"He's made off with my wife!"

PART IV

Beyond the CIA

18

Having resigned from the CIA and finding myself without a profession, I decided to reinvent myself. However, before I did this, I attended to the necessary medical repairs. Fortunately, my new house was presided over by a Belgian housekeeper of unparalleled skill. Besides being an excellent cook, she was an accomplished laundress. She even refused to use detergents but preferred to use fresh lemon juice with plain soap both for its scent and for its superior effectiveness. Since she did all the shopping, I was thus totally relieved of the mechanics of living. I had only to tell her how many there would be for dinner. If a waitress was required to handle the service, she hired one. She also introduced me to the healing properties of various spices and herbs. I could relax and devote myself to my recovery.

Despite all this, my recovery was slow. I became bored and found total solace in a liaison with an ex-Chinese nationalist diplomat whose last post had been in Rome. Elegant, sophisticated, supple, and a good bridge player, she devoted herself to me with the same enthusiasm, only on a different level, as my housekeeper. There was only one drawback, and this involved a degree of sophistication that was beyond me. While in Rome, she counted among her friends Porfirio Rubirosa, the famous Dominican lover and polo player, and also Doris Duke, the much-married tobacco heiress. Although my Chinese friend had the greatest admiration for Rubirosa's accomplishments, she had warned Doris Duke not to marry him. "Keep him on the string as a lover," she advised, "but don't marry him. If you do, he'll be unfaithful shortly thereafter. His only interests are the conquest and a devotion to staying fit physically. In order to do this, he feels polo and sex are the essential ingredients." Unfortunately, Doris Duke ignored her advice and married him. They stayed together only briefly.

In my case, she had another use for sex. Having tried me out and found me satisfactory, so much so that she had to beg off from time to time, she decided to put me to a more useful purpose. At that time, the wife of the Chinese ambassador in Washington and the daughter of an enormously rich Malay tin magnate had an insatiable appetite for young American men.

"Can I," my friend asked, not only once but several times, "take you around to the embassy and introduce you to Mme. X? I know she'll like you. I've already discussed you with her."

I wasn't naive. The motive behind this was not generosity but guile. If I were willing to stud for her, Mme. X might see that she got reinstated in the Chinese diplomatic service. I didn't feel up to it. In my convalescent state, I wasn't sure I could manage. Also, and to my surprise, a mote of submerged puritanism bubbled up. The whole thing just didn't seem right. Coolness developed in our relationship, and I decided to visit friends in Panama. With winter on the way, if I went to Panama, I could get some physical exercise and really rebuild myself.

I thus temporized with my girlfriend. "Look," I said, "you yourself have raved about Rubirosa's glowing good health and physical fitness. I'm no Rubirosa, but if I really wish to get my health and original vigor back, I've got to put in at least a month of daily exercise—swimming, scuba diving, water-skiing, and horseback riding. Let me escape, go to Panama, and restore my body to what it used to be."

She accepted this argument, and off I went, hardly realizing that this trip would not only reinvent me as a businessman, but also provide a cover for my original occupation—a secret agent.

I stayed in Panama for roughly a month as a guest of the man who had caused the eruption of birthday balls throughout Latin America in honor of President Roosevelt during my pre-navy Rockefeller years. Meanwhile, with another Panamanian friend, I decided to found a paper bag factory. Also, I commissioned the construction at a local boatyard of two fishing trawlers. All this entailed much traveling back and forth between the United States and Panama, and if this were not enough, I became a partner in a small New York Stock Exchange firm that required regular weekly trips to New York.

Panama, meanwhile, got a new U.S. ambassador. John C. Wiley was an experienced career diplomat who had served in our embassy in Moscow when Hillenkoetter, my former CIA boss, was just starting his intelligence career. Wiley's path and mine crossed before at the weekly Sunday night suppers at the Chatfied Taylors' where senior Foreign Service experts on the Soviet Union gathered. It was because of this that when Wiley and his wife, Irena, discovered I was often in Panama, they began to invite me to dinner. At this point, it was purely social. As a bachelor and a bridge player, I was useful. Occasionally, the ambassador and I discussed Panamanian politics, but never in depth.

Soon something totally coincidental and fortuitous happened that changed everything. Remón, the former head of the Guardia Nacional in Panama was elected president, and his wife, Cecilia, became primera dama. At this time, I hardly knew them, but they knew of me as a frequent guest at our embassy. In the United States, General Eisenhower was elected president, and his wife, Mamie, became first lady. It was 1953, and the Eisenhower's first state visitors were scheduled to be President and Mrs. Remón, who were coming to kick off negotiations between Panama and the United States for a new treaty between the two countries designed to adjust the Canal Zone to postwar realities.

At the same time, my former roommate, Floyd McCaffree, became chief of research at the Republican National Committee. Floyd's wife, Mary Jane, was Mamie Eisenhower's secretary and public relations gal. Meanwhile, Francis Alstock, Jock Whitney's alter ego in my Rockefeller days, was active in Eisenhower's campaign and put me in touch with two RNC men to ask how Eisenhower could capture the Latin American vote, which Alstock claimed was imperative in five states. My formula was very simple. "Just tell Ike," I said, "to act and speak like their friend in need, their *cacique*—their friend in need, their boss and leader. All he needs to do is make a speech in Texas or California in his fumbling style, saying that he would protect them and have their interests at heart and conclude with a simple phrase in stumbling Spanish. They'll get the point. Nothing specific is required." Much to my surprise, Ike did just that and got the Latino vote.

The result of all this was that Mary Jane McCaffree called me one day to ask if I had any ideas about what to serve the Remóns at the scheduled state dinner.

"Only one," I said. "Serve them Panama shrimp for the first course."

At this point, Mamie herself came on the line to ask how she could get some.

"Don't worry. I'll get them for you. Simply have Mary Jane call me to say how much you need and how to deliver it."

In due time the Remóns arrived in Washington. Unfortunately, Mrs. Remón had failed to label her luggage properly so that some of the clothes she needed for the state dinner had gone to Blair House, across the street from the White House to which they were to move after a night in the White House. In a panic, she called me to ask what to do. Half of her evening dress was in her suitcase at Blair House.

"Don't panic," I said. "There's still time. I'll see if I can get your luggage for you. If not, I'll call and you'll have to ask the head usher for help. Meanwhile, tell someone I'll be driving to the White House via the Pennsylvania Avenue entrance." I found her bags sitting in a passageway beside Blair House and simply tossed them into the backseat of my car and drove across the street and left them at the front door of the White House. It seems incredible today that this sort of thing was possible, but in 1953, things were more relaxed and lethargic.

The net result of all this was that a good part of the chitchat during the state dinner among the ranking guests was how a character named Paul Kramer had not only supplied the first course at dinner but had rescued Mrs. Remón from the embarrassment of finding herself only half-dressed for dinner.

The Remóns were thus so impressed with my personal influence at the highest levels of American government that they invited me to fly back to Panama with them on President Eisenhower's plane. It was arranged that on the morning of their departure from New York, I was to have breakfast with them in their tower suite at the Waldorf and then join them in the escorted motorcade to the airport. Were I to try and meet them at the plane itself there might be a security problem. I did as instructed, and while waiting to board the plane, I found Ambassador and Mrs. Wiley in line just ahead of me.

"Oh Paul," Mrs. Wiley said, turning toward me and smiling graciously. "How kind of you to come and see us off."

"I'm not seeing you off," I said. "The Remóns have asked me to fly down to Panama with them."

All this had an effect. Intelligence is, after all, a "con" game, and the Panamanians were convinced that I enjoyed a special secret relationship with the White House. At this time, a Panamanian was an assistant secretary general of the United Nations. As he told Senator Pell, "There are two levels of intelligence officers in the United States. There are those who work for the CIA and then there are those very high-level secret agents who work directly for the White House. Paul Kramer is one of these."

What our ambassador to Panama, John Wiley, knew or felt was never discussed between us. Alan Dulles, meanwhile, had become head of the CIA, and Wiley knew him well. I presumed he had discussed with him what I had done while working for the CIA. In any event, Wiley sought my assistance from time to time.

But before going into any detail about the various things I did for Wiley during the next few years, I must go back to the farewells of the Eisenhowers and the Remóns in the front hall of the White House. When the Remóns checked into the White House from the Blair House to say good-bye, they found standing with President and Mrs. Eisenhower, Mrs. Eisenhower's sister and brother-in-law, Colonel and Mrs. Moore.

"The colonel," President Eisenhower said, "will soon be going to Panama on a business trip. He has in mind the setting up of a fishing company. I hope you will take care of him."

"But of course," said President Remón. The formal farewells followed.

Not on the plane itself, but shortly thereafter, the Panamanian lawyer who was in charge of the new treaty negotiations, sought me out and told me about Colonel Moore and the farewell. Being a Latin American, he had thought, along with Remón, in terms of a payoff. "Is taking care of Colonel Moore and his proposed fishing company the price Panama must pay for the proposed concessions in the new treaty I am to negotiate?" he asked me. Somewhat shocked by the story and the interpretation the Panamanians were putting on it, I told him not to worry as I would take it up as soon as I got back to Washington, and if I was unable to forestall Colonel Moore's arrival, they could send him to Ecuador where I was working from time to time, and I would help him to get a fishing concession there.

Upon my return to Washington, I discussed the incident with Floyd McCaffree and pointed out to him the danger involved. The Panamanian treaty negotiator was a law partner of the owner of one of Panama's leading daily newspapers, which in turn was a subscriber to Drew Pearson's widely read gossip column. If the incident got into Pearson's column, it would only do unnecessary harm to President Eisenhower's reputation.

I've always had the most profound admiration for the Eisenhowers because of what happened next. Mamie sent word to me via the McCaffrees that the whole incident should never have happened. Her sister had put enormous pressure on her on behalf of her husband, Colonel Moore, by saying, "You have so much and we have nothing." She should never have persuaded her husband to include the Moores in the farewell. "Please ignore the whole thing." I so instructed the chief treaty negotiator, and this confirmed what he knew all along—I was a White House secret agent.

It was at this point that I realized I had a choice of two jobs if I wished to continue intelligence work. The navy one was a standing offer to return to the sub base at New London and do submarine intelligence work. The alternative was more tempting. One of the Soviet experts had told me, "As a businessman in Latin America let us set you up as an 'illegal.'" The word *illegal* requires explanation. Because the offer came from a member of a coterie of Soviet experts who had all served in our embassy in Moscow and knew of my previous CIA work, he thought in terms of Soviet intelligence where the word *illegal* was used to describe a Soviet secret agent type. This type always had independent means of support in the form of a local business, operated totally outside the established intelligence channels, and reported directly to a high official in Moscow. Thus, in my case, I was to report to Under Secretary of State Henderson, and via an associate of his, Ambassador Wiley. Both the designated associate and Henderson had served together in our embassy in Moscow. Meanwhile, the entire U.S. intelligence apparatus was to be ordered to stay away from me.

I chose the Latin American offer because I wanted to get married, and I deduced that the navy offer would involve protracted cruises abroad, which I didn't think suitable for a newly married man in peacetime.

Here, I should mention that whenever I discovered that the U.S. intelligence apparatus was violating orders not to pry, I hit back mercilessly and without compunction. This was a matter of self-preservation. The CIA often sought the assistance of the local secret police and sometimes rewarded them financially. The trouble here was that the CIA at the time was only interested in chasing Communists and totally ignored the drug traffic and remained blissfully ignorant of the danger of a union of Stalinists and Maoist terrorists joining forces with the drug lords for their mutual benefit. Since I was going back and forth to Colombia a lot on private business, I simply couldn't tolerate the risks of local secret police "friends" of the CIA ever finding out what I was up to and telling the drug people.

There were several problems with which the ambassador asked me to help. One of these, in the light of more recent events, proved both significant and ominous. Colombian cocaine was beginning to flow into Panama, even in the 1950s, and what preoccupied our embassy at that time was that it was getting to U.S. troops stationed in the Canal Zone. General McBride, the commanding general complained about it to Ambassador Wiley, and he in turn asked me to go and see Harry Anslinger, the commissioner of the Federal Bureau of Narcotics to see if together we could work out a plan to put a stop to the drug traffic in both Panama and the Canal Zone.

As a preliminary to this request, I learned that a large patch of marijuana had been discovered growing in the Canal Zone, and General McBride had ordered its destruction. I decided to witness the event personally.

At the site, I found an army detachment busy spraying the patch with some sort of inflammable material. When the fire was lit, I foolishly stood downwind from the blaze. A lot of smoke was produced, the marijuana was green, and I thus got a high, as did my soldier companions. It did not, however, in the words of Harry Anslinger, who was an implacable foe of marijuana, "destroy my willpower and break down moral barricades" so that "debauchery and sexuality were the results." On the contrary, I went thereafter to the Chase Bank and deposited a check from the profits from my two fishing trawlers, plus a dividend from the bag factory, and then I made a reservation to fly to Washington and see Anslinger.

I found Anslinger to be totally bald, dressed in an elegant tweed suit, and more of a polished gentleman than I had anticipated based on his occupation. He was totally receptive to my approach, having, I presumed, been warned of my forthcoming visit. Together, after about an hour of work, we devised a plan that I thought might be viable. As step 1, the Bureau of Narcotics would send a team to Panama to buy cocaine from local dealers, who would then be persuaded to reveal their principals. On this basis, we worked out an agreement between the United States and Panama that would give the commissioner of narcotics the right to engage in this proposed antinarcotics action in Panama. As a token of sincerity, the Panamanian government would reimburse the Commission on Narcotic Drugs a token sum that amounted to less than $1,000.

I then took the agreement to Panama and gave it to a young member of the president's Cabinet, who was not only enthusiastic about the agreement but also promised to present it to the president at the next Cabinet meeting. It went down like a lead balloon. The president, with his eyes fixed on the head of the Guardia Nacional, turned it down flat. As my friend reported the meeting to me, the direction of the president's eyes was significant. He knew that if he were to approve the plan, he would be ousted by the Guardia within forty-eight hours. The second in command of the Guardia at that time was Omar Torrijos, later to become dictator of Panama, and he, in turn, had an assistant to whom he later introduced me as "my little gangster" and whose name was Noriega. He succeeded Torrijos as dictator. President Bush had to arrest him by means of an invasion, cart him off to Miami in chains, and jail him there for his role in developing Panama as an entrepot for the drug traffic.

Another one of my efforts as a secret agent was more successful. It involved the American tuna industry. Tuna are caught by means of chumming; in other words, little fish are tossed off a trawler in order to attract the larger tuna fish. Unfortunately, the little fish were only to be found within the territorial waters of Panama, Ecuador, and Peru. For the American tuna fleet operating out of San Diego, to net these little fish without the permission of the Panama government was illegal, and it was up to the Guardia Nacional of Panama to enforce this violation of Panama's territorial waters. But rather than do this, it preferred to accept an under-the-table payment from a shipping agency in the Panama Canal Zone on U.S. territory and thus overlook the American tuna fleet's invasion of Panama's territorial waters.

Ambassador Wiley, acting on valid information from me, asked the governor of the Canal Zone to shut down the shipping agency engaged in this operation, which he did promptly. Not long afterward, the President of Panama was shot, to be succeeded by the first vice president, who was soon overthrown, to be succeeded by the second vice president. After his overthrow, the ex first vp sent word via a mutual friend that he would like to see me. He complained bitterly about the elimination of the tuna graft for the Guardia and suggested that this had been a factor in his overthrow. It was impossible for me to tell whether or not this was true. At the time, I doubted it. But one thing was certain. The Guardia Nacional clearly didn't like losing the graft and soon worked out another method by which to secure it, which was enmeshed in a similar graft in Ecuador and Peru.

Another job that came my way involved Panama's only normal school in Santiago, a provincial city. This school was where all Panama's schoolteachers were trained. Wiley, who was especially concerned about Communist penetration in Panama, claimed that this school was a focal point of Communism, and that its director was a key member of the Communist conspiracy.

"Can you get rid of him for me?" he asked.

"Let me think about it, and if I come up with something, I'll let you know, and I'll give it to you before going ahead with anything."

Wiley had worked out a system of rendezvous for us so that we never met in sight of any of the embassy staff, save his personal secretary. Thus I never set foot in the embassy offices, which were in a separate building from the ambassador's residence, except once to get a new passport, which, to my surprise, was numbered 37, a great convenience in travel in Latin America since most custom and immigration officials assumed the low number meant I enjoyed some sort of official status. I was, however, often invited to the ambassadorial residence for dinner with the ambassador, the governor of the Canal Zone, and the commanding general of U.S. forces in the Caribbean and their wives, plus, from time to time, a few of the European ambassadors accredited to Panama. Except for the British minister and his first secretary, I never accepted any invitations from the diplomatic corps in Panama, and in their case, I only did it because it was indicated from inquiries in London that I had some sort of secret agent status. Indeed, years later at a garden party at the British Embassy in Washington, Prince Phillip came up to me and asked, "Have you retired yet?"

Meanwhile, Wiley had contrived another method of accidentally running into me. We both liked to swim. At that time, there was a small beach in the Canal Zone, complete with shark net and raft restricted to high-ranking U.S. officials and army and navy officers. I would go there in the morning at high tide, sit on the raft, and wait for the ambassador to arrive in his limousine with his wife and his maid. The maid's job was to carry towels to the water's edge for them when they emerged from the water and also to support them when they took off their slippers before entering the water. In this stately way, they avoided having to use the changing rooms in the rather sordid wooden shower house. While his wife paddled about in shallow water, the ambassador headed out for the raft. On seeing him, I would slip into the water and casually meet him in fairly deep water where we would float about for a few minutes, exchanging information. I would then swim ashore, go into the shower house, take a long shower, dress slowly, and allow enough time to pass for the ambassador and his retinue to depart before I did. These athletic and totally "accidental" meetings were perfect for both our needs. If, for one reason or another, we failed to meet, I knew I could always see him alone at the embassy residence by arriving a few minutes early for dinner.

In response to the request about the normal school in Santiago, I discovered that the minister of education was not on the embassy social list and suggested to the ambassador that he have him to lunch or dinner while I discussed the matter with his son, whom I knew well. Besides teaching economics at the university, the son worked at the Chase Bank branch in Panama and handled my banking. "What does your father think about the goings-on at the normal school?" I asked him casually one day.

"He doesn't like it a bit. He's dissatisfied with the quality of the teaching there as well as with the political orientation of some of the teachers."

"Well," I said, "as you know better than I, President Remón is anti-Communist as is, of course, the U.S. ambassador. If Ambassador Wiley were to invite your dad to the embassy for lunch to discuss the matter and make some suggestions on how to resolve it, do you think he would be receptive?"

"Of course. I don't think my father has ever been to the American Embassy. I'll tell him you've told the ambassador to invite him."

"Fine, just perfect."

And so it was started, and with the personal support from President Remón, the housecleaning occurred once the ice was broken. I was never told what information the embassy had in support of the housecleaning.

The meetings at the beach in the Canal Zone were not my only method of exercise in Panama. I also went water-skiing almost daily on Madden Lake, just off the Trans-Isthmian Highway in the middle of the Isthmus in the Canal Zone. It was here I got the idea of water-skiing from the Pacific to the Atlantic Ocean via the Canal and sought permission to do it from the governor of the Canal, who turned me down flat. Most weekends, I spent my time on a ranch in the country where I did a lot of horseback riding. As a result of all the exercise and relatively clean living, I got my health back.

The embassy dinners I attended so frequently were not entirely stuffy. There were the usual one or two tables of bridge both before and after dinner, which was served late, and sometimes, to liven things up, the embassy's natural surroundings intruded to create an unusual atmosphere. Once, while eating and facing the adjoining screened piazza where we usually played bridge, I noticed a strange object that resembled nothing so much as a dust mop very slowly making its way toward the dining room. The guest on my right, the Condesa de Rabago, the Spanish ambassador's wife, who also saw the object, let out a screech and dropped her soup spoon into her bowl of soup, thus splattering a few drops of soup on her dress. "It's nothing," I said in the most soothing tones I could muster. "Just a sloth. It moves so slowly that it won't get to the table until we're finished eating and have gone back to play bridge."

Mrs. Wiley, who didn't hear my soothing tones but who had also noticed the sloth after the Condesa's screech, maintained total aplomb; so did her husband at the other end of the long table. She simply summoned the butler, a retired batman from the British army in India, and told him to summon the kitchen staff and instruct them to bring a large bucket and with which to remove the intruder. All became calm again, save for the Condesa who bemoaned the soup spot on her original Balenciaga creation.

This intrusion resulted from the fact that the embassy residence was perched on top of a steep hill, the sides of which remained jungles. At a subsequent dinner there was a more ominous intrusion. This time it was a green mamba, Panama's most deadly poisonous snake, which had curled itself under the bridge table while we were eating. This one I missed, but the butler saw it, and with imperturbable self-possession, quietly stopped serving the carved joint of meat and slipped back into the pantry and returned with the entire kitchen staff armed with everything from brooms to a cricket bat. The serpent was killed and removed, and the butler resumed serving the meat while apologizing for the interruption in service.

To me this man was such a perfect servant that I was outraged a few years later when he was summarily discharged by the wife of a subsequent ambassador. He came to see me, totally desperate, and in conversation, I suddenly realized he might be entitled to a British pension for his British army service. I took him to see the British minister, who promised to look into his case. As events developed, he was entitled to such a pension, and he decided to return to his original homeland, Jamaica, where he would, as a result of his pension, be able to live with relatives who had promised to take care of him. The only thing he asked of me was to see that he could take his bed with him on the British-registered ship we got to transport him gratis back to Jamaica.

Two other memorable incidents occurred in quick succession that didn't involve the ambassador but were indicative of the kind of thing I had become involved in. They started innocuously enough. I got a call from an American woman married to the man who managed Panama's racetrack. His brother was the head of the Banco Nacional, which was one of the banks I used.

"Paul," she said, "I'm giving a buffet dinner on Wednesday at eight thirty, and I especially want you to come."

"Sure, I'd be delighted."

"Fine, and don't be late."

Since I had never before been to her house, and since Panamanians were always late, I knew something was up. Someone she knew had asked her to invite me. The moment I walked into her house on the dot at eight thirty, I knew who it was. My friend, Panama's treaty negotiator and soon to become foreign minister was there.

The two of us made the customary round of chitchat with the other guests until dinner was served. He then suggested that we get our plates of food and eat together on the patio, which was deserted.

He began somewhat hesitantly. "Paul," he said, "Cecilia Remón has a personal close friend named X. She's a fine woman, has her own business with a little factory, and sells her products locally—"

At this point, we were interrupted by a servant who told the minister that he was wanted on the phone, an urgent call. Left alone, I had no alternative but to wait for him as well as to stop eating. He came back in about ten minutes.

"Paul," he explained, "that was a call from the Guardia. They have just arrested and jailed an American citizen named Irving Brown, a Communist labor organizer seeking to unionize the banana workers in Chiriquí Province."

"My God, Tato!" I exploded. "I know that man. He and his boss, Jay Lovestone, work for George Meany at the American Federation of Labor. They're both even more anti-Communist than you and me. Their job is to get rid of the Communist influence in labor unions. There's obviously been a terrible mistake. You've got to spring him at once. I doubt he can be very comfortable in a jail in Chiriquí. Does our embassy know about it yet?"

"No, not yet. He's being held incommunicado for the time being."

"Please, Tato," I urged. "Spring him at once as a personal favor for me."

"*Bueno*. But that means the personal favor I was going to ask of you will have to be put off until tomorrow. Come to my house at five for a drink. I'll have to leave now to see that what you want is done."

"I'll be there."

Thus, we parted until the next day. On the way home, I debated whether to stop at the embassy and tell Wiley about the Irving Brown arrest and how I had presumably sprung him from jail. There was work here for the embassy staff, the point being to discover who had denounced Brown to the Guardia. It was, I felt sure, either the United Fruit Company, which didn't want any labor organizers on its territory or a Communist in Chiriquí who wished to neutralize Brown's anti-Communist work, or alternatively, an uninformed employee of the United Fruit Company who didn't understand labor politics and had unwittingly become the dupe of a Communist labor type. In any case, this was an embassy staff problem, not mine. My role in the affair had been purely fortuitous. I merely happened to be in the right place at the right time. But it was now too late to tell Wiley what had happened. Anyway, I'd probably run into him "accidentally" the next day while swimming.

As it happened, I never got around to discussing Irving Brown's rescue and simply forgot about it. It really didn't matter. Brown and his bosses, Lovestone and Meany, were experts on the Communist conspiracy, and if the Communists had been secretly behind his arrest, he didn't need the CIA man to figure the thing out. Besides, the personal favor that the Panamanians had in mind for me turned out to be such an amazing coincidence, dating from navy intelligence past that it focused my mind on the past rather than on the present.

"You see, Paul," the foreign minister explained over a drink at his house, "I've turned to you on this because I simply don't know of anyone else here in Panama who can handle the problem. Besides, whether you care to admit it or not, who else outside of official American government circles can I turn to for help in such a delicate and, at the same time, personal matter? The alternative is to turn to official circles, and Mrs. Remón wishes to avoid that. In fact, it was she who suggested I turn to you."

"For Pete's sake, Tato, tell me what it is. You know perfectly well I'll do anything to help."

"The problem," he continued, "involves a close personal friend of Mrs. Remón. She has been having a love affair with a high-ranking U.S. Navy officer stationed in the Canal Zone. He has repeatedly promised to marry her but never has. She's in love with him but feels she must break the relationship off if the promised marriage is out of the question."

"Who is it?"

"You might know him. His name is Bill Young."

"My God, Tato. I used to know a Bill Young when I was in the navy in Brisbane. If it's the one I know, he's married, or perhaps I should say, was married in 1944. At that time, he once showed me a picture of his house and family in Oregon."

"Could you go and see him? He's stationed here on the Pacific side and is a ranking navy intelligence officer."

"Say no more. I'll call him. I'm sure he'll want to see me if only for old time's sake."

Young gave me a great welcome on the phone and invited me to his quarters the following afternoon at 5:15. Bill's navy quarters bowled me over. Since I had last seen him in Brisbane in '45, although he was still in excellent shape and was physically unchanged, he had gone completely Japanese. There was no straw matting on the floor, but there was an alcove with a flower arrangement, plus a small hanging on the wall. Also, he had me sit on the floor and placed our drinks on a low lacquered Japanese table. Bill was wearing a black silk man's kimono as an off-duty costume, the kind Japanese men put on upon returning from work at the office and before their devoted wives pull down one shoulder of the garment so that they can burn a spot of back shoulder flesh with a piece of punk in order to relieve back pain or fatigue.

Instinctively, I sniffed the air for the scent of burnt flesh, but there was none, and Bill immediately launched into a happy reminiscence of our time together in Brisbane. At one point, I interrupted him to ask why he and Hopkinson had insisted on a bodyguard for me, and complained just as I had in January 1945 how it had ruined my personal life even though Beals had been a prince of a man.

Bill ran his hand through his reddish hair before answering. It was as though his mind was still groping with the need-to-know concepts of intelligence and he was deciding just how much he could tell me. "Paul," he said finally, "all I can tell you is you were handling as highly classified material at the time as ATIS had. You deserved protection, and if you want proof of the merit of that decision, you should know that soon after the end of the war, two Boulder graduate officers defected to Red China."

I let the subject drop. It was clear to me that even if he knew of any specific moves against me that had been frustrated, he would never tell me. Instead, I launched into why I had looked him up.

"I assume you know why I'm here, Bill," I pointed out. "Previously I've avoided all contact with the U.S. intelligence apparatus here, just as I assume you have had orders to avoid me, which is why you've never looked me up."

He didn't answer. Instead, he wandered on about Brisbane, so I cut him short. It was curious. He acted relieved I was forcing the issue.

"Paul," he admitted, "the only reason I allowed myself to become involved with the girl was because she was so close to Cecilia Remón. I thought I might get some useful information from her."

This, of course, was pure rubbish, but I pretended to accept it. "Look, Bill," I explained, "I had to tell the foreign minister that I knew you were married as late as 1945, but that's not the point. What is important is that the whole thing be kept out of official channels. Remón has a mistress, as you probably know. That means that as compensation for his wife, he'll move against you if she asks him to. It's none of my business really, but since you are an old comrade in arms and someone who took steps during the war to protect me personally even if I didn't like it at the time, I'd hate to see you get burned."

"Don't worry, Paul. I'll do what needs to be done. Since I was told yesterday you were coming to see me, I've already taken the first step."

"In that case, I'm going to forget the whole thing. And Bill, I'd like to see you again, but you know what's up. Also, I'd like to tell you why I was such a shit when I first saw you in Brisbane and couldn't explain to you frankly why Hoppy pulled me out of the language pool to work with him. But it's the old goddamned need-to-know business, and my lips are still sealed on that one and probably will be for another twenty years. But honestly, if there is anything I can do for you, I hope you'll feel free to call on me."

"Thanks, Paul, I will. As I'm sure you are aware, there's a lot of talk down here about you. No other intelligence officer has been able to accomplish in so short a time what you have been able to do."

"I'm not an intelligence officer any longer. I'm a businessman down here to make some money."

"If you say so, Paul, but my girl, or I should say my ex-girl, has told me what Cecilia told her about the White House dinner."

With that, he walked me to my car. *Funny*, I said to myself, *the role reversal. In Brisbane he'd made it clear to me that he had the power to send me back up to New Guinea if I didn't toe his line. Now here in Panama I've made it clear, but at least in a more elliptical way, that I can have him shipped out of here if he doesn't toe the line. And he's been just as meek about it as I was about failing to return the salute of an Aussie soldier. And to add to the irony of it all, we're both going to pretend from here on that it never happened.*

This meeting with Bill Young had an effect on me. Not immediately, but it simply grew and developed. It was as though I had held a mirror to my face in the dark. Very gradually, the light came on, and when I looked at my face in the mirror, I didn't see myself. I saw Bill Young.

The point was clear to me. We were both intelligence officers. In the official scheme of things, Bill not only outranked me, but he had always been on the administrative side of things, where as I could only be described as a secret agent. But the important thing was that my personal life, just as much as his, was a mess. I had first met Bill after I left Boulder and was attending the Advanced Naval Intelligence School in New York City where he was the administrative officer. I didn't know him well enough then to know about his personal life, but I knew what mine had been, and it certainly was messy and had been that way ever since. The only difference between Bill and me was that I had been a bit more circumspect in my partners, had remained unmarried, and had never used a promise of matrimony as an instrument of seduction. But Bill was older than I was, and if I continued on my present path, that maneuver might come about. There was no sense in deluding myself. A part of the reason for my success as a working intelligence agent had been because of the fact that I was totally free of family obligations. I could thus, at the drop of a hat, cultivate the friendship of Axis agents or travel back and forth to Latin America, have a bodyguard if my superiors insisted on it, visit a brothel with or without an enemy agent, or get shot at, and there was no loving wife to lie to about it or explain things to. As I have mentioned before, I might be the type who could fall into an outhouse and come out smelling like Chanel No. 5, but this couldn't go on forever. If it did, I'd turn into another Bill Young, and this wasn't for me.

There were also practical considerations. Ambassador Wiley would soon be retiring, and I would thus be relieved of any obligations I felt toward him. Also, my business ventures in Panama had been consolidated. The bag factory was well-managed and needed no input from me. I'd taken stock in a large fishing company in exchange for my two trawlers, and this company needed none of my time. Also, I'd been in intelligence for years in one form or another. That was enough for someone at the working level who was not interested in being an executive and pushing a staff around. I was thirty-seven, time to cut it, go back to Washington, enjoy my house, find a wife, and start raising a family; and if I found myself bored with a routine life, I'd find a job in Washington. I did just this and took a job with the National Academy of Sciences. The International Geophysical Year was just getting organized and planned, as a measuring instrument, to launch the first satellite. I worked on that and got married and my wife Mary Lou gave birth to a daughter, our first and only child.

19

Inevitably, there was a certain amount of spillover from my past. During the last months of the Eisenhower administration, Wiley, who was living in retirement in Washington, had asked me to come to his house for a meeting with some high Pentagon brass. Upon arrival, I was introduced to about eight men whose names I have since forgotten. What was wanted of me was my opinion of a proposed invasion of Cuba. I knew all about this from the pre-Castro prominent politicians who had suddenly moved to Washington, some of whom had asked to borrow household items from me such as baby cribs and other infant paraphernalia, which Mary Lou and I had acquired when our daughter Theresa was born.

I didn't mince words. "Look," I said, "the first thing you must realize is that the proposed invasion is definitely *not* a secret. As I'm sure you have been told, I'm not an employee of the CIA and now have nothing to do with it, but if I know all about it—Cubans are by nature leaky—you can be damn sure Castro knows about it too. Also, you must realize that in so far as the Cuban people are concerned, while Castro exudes enormous charisma, the leaders the CIA has selected to lead the invasion have none at all. Do you realize that at the end of World War II, Cuba had the highest per capital gold reserves of any country in the world? Today it's practically gone because of the corruption and foolishness of its pre-Castro leaders. Sure, there were honest hardworking middle-class people who have been exiled or have fled, and some of them are among those working on the invasion. But in the eyes of the majority of people in Cuba today, Castro is their man.

"More than this, the CIA wishes to be sure that, especially because of former corruption and governmental inefficiency, it can retain control of the Cuban government if the invasion succeeds. Thus, it has not provided the proposed invaders with up-to-date armament. What you've really got is an armed group equipped with World War I weaponry to confront a Castro government with

Word War II weapons. Furthermore, I believe Castro has some fighter aircraft he's recently bought, and in so far as I know, the proposed invaders have no air cover at all."

With that blast, I lapsed into silence. But while talking, I noticed that several of those men present had nodded their heads in agreement. Soon thereafter, I left. But before I did so, one of the Pentagon brass, whom I didn't know, got up from the dining room table around which we had been sitting and walked me to the Wileys' front door. I've never forgotten his farewell remark. "Don't worry, Paul," he said. "As long as Eisenhower is president, there will be no invasion of Cuba. Thanks for coming."

There were also two other reasons for my total opposition to the proposed invasion, which I didn't enumerate because they didn't seem appropriate at that particular time.

First of all, I knew that Howard Hunt had been pulled out of Mexico and was helping to organize the Bay of Pigs project. Howard was simply too far to the Right to understand the compelling need to include working-class people from the non-Communist Left in the effort.

But worse than this, the invasion plans were entirely dominated by middle— and upper-class Cubans who had fled to Miami, and there was no real in-depth understanding as to whom these people were. When I worked for Rockefeller, several commercial representatives of U.S. firms in Cuba had been, before Pearl Harbor, out and out Nazis whom we had failed to have dismissed with our voluntary blacklist effort, which was secretly based on British intelligence. We weren't at war then, and their employers pointed out how good they were at selling U.S. products in Cuba and argued that what was good for their companies was good for the United States. Some of these people and their lawyers showed up as part of the Bay of Pigs effort, and of course, the CIA people had no in-depth knowledge of their background.

There was also something else. Soon after Pearl Harbor, Cuba declared war on the Axis. This action, also conducted by all Latin American countries save Argentina, wasn't of course totally altruistic since it gave the ruling families in Latino land the opportunity to absorb into their own pockets German, Italian, and Japanese assets in Latin America such as, for example, the coffee plantations in Central America.

However, Cuba was a special case even though its pre-Castro governments had been incredibly corrupt. For example, there used to be a large diamond embedded into the floor of the Cuban capitol building, directly below the apex of its dome, which served as the beginning mile marker for all highways leading out of Havana. One night the wife of the then president of Cuba arrived at the capitol building with some workmen equipped with hammers and chisels. The workmen extracted the diamond under her supervision, and she pocketed it.

Also, I felt it necessary to keep in mind that Castro's father had been an independent cane grower. These people had simply to accept the price that the U.S. mill owners offered them for their cane on a take-it-or-leave-it basis. As a result, many hated America, and I was fairly sure that this was one of the reasons Castro had become a Communist. Thus it seemed to me imperative that a group seeking to overthrow Castro had to include representatives of not just the middle-class and the very rich, who had fled to Miami a la aristocratic French refugees from the 1789 Revolution, but also Cubans who had fought in the U.S. Army during World War II and then settled in the United States.

Here, it is necessary to go back and explain Cuba's special role during World War II, about which the CIA knew nothing. After Cuba declared war on the Axis, it was decided that Cuba should not send its own army units to fight. Instead, it had encouraged Cubans to enlist in the U.S. armed forces. Many Cubans did so, and because they tended to be short, many ended up as tail gunners on U.S. Army air force bombers. The casualties were great since there was no escape for tail gunners by parachute once their plane was hit by the enemy. Thus our wartime embassy in Havana had an extra military attaché whose duty it was to personally notify Cuban families that their sons had been "lost in action."

Many surviving tail gunners as well as other Cuban World War II veterans had immigrated to the United States. They had all had military training. Yet there was no organized and systematic attempt by the CIA to recruit them for the invasion. To me this was total folly since many of them represented just the same class of people that was missing in the invasion effort.

The second piece of fallout involved Vice President Nixon. In 1958, Nixon made a goodwill tour of several countries in Latin America. The CIA warned him that he might encounter anti-American demonstrations in two or three of the capitals on his route, but there were no intimations of violence. At San Marcos University in Lima, Peru, spit, stones, and rocks started to fly during Nixon's speech, and one stone broke Secret Service agent Jack Sherwood's front tooth. It was clear that the students and faculty to whom Nixon was speaking had been organized to demonstrate with violence. Worse was to come in Venezuela.

Arriving in Caracas on May 13, a crowd erupted into a frenzy of booing and later, in the airport itself, a jeering crowd on the balcony above began spitting down on Nixon and his wife. Word of these hostilities reached Washington where President Eisenhower ordered two companies of marines and two companies of the 101st Airborne Division to move to bases two hours flying time from Caracas.

Meanwhile, I received an unexpected "hurry up" call to go at once to Wiley's house to meet there with Under Secretary of State Henderson. What the secretary wanted was my opinion of the reaction in Latin America: Should the president order troops to Venezuela to pluck out the Nixons? Henderson said that Mr. Eisenhower felt an obligation as president to rescue Nixon. He was not an appointee, but he had been elected by the American people as a standby should anything ever happen to the president. He felt there was a compelling obligation involved. I told Under Secretary Henderson that I thought there would be a great outcry from Latin American Communists and radical pro-Castro groups, in which super nationalists might join at the outset of such a proposed U.S. invasion of Venezuela's territory. But the moment it was realized that the invasion was totally temporary and designed for a specific emergency, it would subside. After all, the propertied elements in Latin America who were in control of all countries save Cuba could hardly be expected to support terrorism with assassination as the obvious end in view. If the president at the time the action was taken would make a short, simple speech in easily and rapidly translatable Spanish and Portuguese, I was sure reason would prevail despite an initial hysterical howl. But it must be coordinated with appropriate murmurs before the United Nations and the Organization of American States. Henderson left immediately for the White House, and I went home. I got a call a few minutes after reaching my house, informing me that the crisis had resolved itself. The motorcade carrying the Nixons, which had been halted by an angry mob spitting and throwing rocks and stones and rocking the cars, had been rescued by a news truck, which had pulled ahead of the motorcade and bulldozed a path through the mob. The accompanying Venezuelan motorcycle escort of the Nixon motorcade had simply vanished. The Nixons were now safe at the American embassy. They had remained calm.

My final excursion into intelligence occurred after my marriage. Mary Lou; Theresa, still a preschooler; and I were living in Panama when I was offered the managing directorship of a large fishing company in Ecuador. The salary and the perks involved were too tempting to refuse. Besides a station wagon and a yacht, I would be given a furnished house in Guayaquil. There was even a rose garden in front of the house, and since roses will only flourish at sea level in the tropics provided they receive constant attention in order to repel insect predators and pre-sunrise watering during the dry season, a retired sailor was hired to do the job. He lived in what can only be described as a shed adjoining the chicken coop in the backyard.

The house was pleasantly furnished, and I thought Mary Lou would be comfortable there. It was one of three houses that took up an entire city block, all of which were owned by three sisters. The owner of our house had died, and her husband decided to take the children abroad for a year. The sister on our right was married to Ashton-Illingworth, the vice president of Ecuador.

Mary Lou and I went to the movies one night and came home late, tired and sleepy. The policeman who guarded all three houses opened our gate. Once inside, Mary Lou went directly to our bedroom while I went to the rear of the house where I had a two-way radio for long-distance communication.

I had no sooner started to operate the device when I heard a shriek from Mary Lou. Rushing to the front bedroom, I found her already in her nightdress, pointing to the mosquito netting over our bed. Under the netting there was a fully dressed man, sound asleep, snoring blissfully. It was Ashton-Illingworth, our neighbor.

What to do? There was a certain amount of etiquette involved. As a foreigner living and working in Ecuador, I was reluctant to disturb the vice president. Even if, instead of a "Get the hell out of our bed" I had politely suggested that he was in the wrong house, it still seemed tactless. By morning I was sure everything would be sorted out with appropriate apologies. "Let it go," I said to myself and persuaded Mary Lau to sleep in a guestroom.

The next morning Illingworth was gone, and I went to my office. Before noon, his wife, bearing fresh fruit, vegetables, and a freshly killed and plucked chicken, came to call on Mary Lou. Her husband drank, she explained, and, knowing how much she detested his return intoxicated, had the habit of sleeping it off next door at his in-laws. Alas, he had forgotten the house had been rented to strangers.

This incident, combined with several others soured Mary Lou on Guayaquil. First was the total collapse of the dining room table due to termites when our large and heavy Thanksgiving turkey was placed on it; second was the accidental death of an employee in Quito, whom Mary Lou liked; and the final straw was when Theresa developed a serious illness after drinking her bathwater (the water and sewage pipelines in Guayaquil ran parallel, and due to frequent earthquakes, often opened so that there was a certain amount of interchange of fluids). She preferred to go back to Panama with Theresa. I could commute.

I agreed to accompany her and arranged what I thought would be a luxurious departure. The three of us, plus Theresa's Ecuadorian nursemaid, would fly on a chartered plane to Esmeraldas in northern Ecuador where we would board a large Belgian ship for a relaxing ocean voyage to Panama. At the airstrip in Esmeraldas, located on the opposite side of the river from the town, we were greeted by a group of porters. One hoisted Theresa on his shoulders so she wouldn't get her feet wet on the jungle path to the riverbank. The others carried our luggage to the river where we boarded a large dugout log canoe equipped with an outboard motor. These canoes were the equivalent of airport limousines in Esmeraldas. Once aboard a company mother ship where we were to wait for the departure of the ocean liner, its skipper told us how lucky we were to have made the canoe trip that day instead of the previous one. There had been a cave-in of about 150 feet beneath the water of the harbor. The harbor was in fact over the crater of a long-extinct volcano that had collapsed. This had created an overwhelming rush of water into the cavity and had swallowed up two canoes loaded with passengers who had just arrived by plane. This horror only confirmed for Mary Lou the wisdom of her return to Panama. The sea voyage was also a disappointment. At the ship's dining room, the fellow passengers who joined us spoke only French and Flemish, neither of which Mary Lou could understand.

Once back in Guayaquil from the trip to Panama, I got a call from the minister of fisheries in Quito who suggested I fly up to see him. There were problems. In his office the following morning, he told me that an American tuna combine was bribing the legislature right and left in order to secure the passage of a bill that would permit them to fish in Ecuadorian waters. "Since the existing laws allow such fishing only with Ecuadorian-built vessels, as is the case with your company, I assume you will wish to oppose such legislation. Furthermore," he added, "the American Embassy is supportive of this new legislation."

"Look," I said to him with some irritation, "I moved against these people's corruption in Panama, and I can do it again in Ecuador. Let me use your phone."

The American ambassador agreed to see me immediately. Once in his office, he insisted that he had have never supported such legislation. Then he picked up his phone and called the minister of fisheries and emphatically told him the same thing. This brief phone call promptly put a stop to the proposed legislation, and the minister, to whom I returned before going to lunch with the ambassador and his wife, was delighted.[1]

[1.] That phone call caused lot of trouble for the ambassador, al-though I'm happy to say he may never have known about it. The U.S. tuna companies were all based in California, and President Nixon was then a senator from that state. This resulted in a com-plaint about the ambassador from Nixon that ended up on Under Secretary of State Henderson's desk. Loy Henderson was also a Republican, but he asked me about the ambassador who had made the phone call. Because he was a third-generation Foreign Service officer, Henderson explained that he was particularly troubled about the complaint. I then gave Henderson the details of what the tuna people had done in Panama and were doing in Ecuador, and thus the ambassador was "saved."

But this is not the end of the story. The tuna people went ahead anyway, despite their failure to get a concession in Ecuador, to fish for bait in Ecuadorian territorial waters. The Ecuadorian government then began seizing tuna trawlers from time to time. But the tuna people soon discovered that the Ecuadorian fines they had to pay to get their trawlers back made their conduct financially unacceptable. They thus developed a new system of paying graft to the armed forces of Panama, Ecuador, and Peru that worked like a charm.

Even though the graft continued, I felt I had won a victory. Under the new system of bribery, it was not committed on U.S. territory, as had originally been the case in the Canal Zone, and it was never committed by an American citizen. This, to me, was the important point, as indeed it was to our government as well.

At lunch, the ambassador suddenly interrupted the social talk, which was all sea mist and haze, to mention that he was totally informed about me and what I had done in Panama.

"I like to be helpful," I said, "but there have been times when what I've done has been a total flop."

"You mean that project you worked on with Anslinger to interdict cocaine in Panama."

"Precisely."

"You ought to take another shot at it. The situation has gotten much worse. Colombia is becoming a giant cocaine factory, and you must have contacts there."

"I do."

"Why not stop off there. Most planes between here and Panama stop at Cali."

"Perhaps I will."

My friend Jorge gave me a great welcome at the airport in Cali, Colombia, as I knew he would. Besides a friendship dating back to our Cambridge days when his father had been ambassador to Britain and his father-in-law-to-be was the Cuban ambassador to France, I had once done a favor for a family connection of his. While in Panama, an associate was approached to ask if he could fly a plane secretly to Colombia to pluck off his cattle ranch a man who had been arrested, tortured, and then ordered to remain sequestered at his ranch by the dictator of Colombia, Rojas Pinilla. This rescue would involve the filing of false flight papers with the Panamanian aeronautics authorities to indicate the plane was to fly to Costa Rica rather than to Colombia. I went to the president of Panama and told him I was totally supportive of the rescue and hoped he would overlook the filing of the false flight pattern when the actual rescuers, who had opposed his election as president, came to see him. The president assured me he would give his instant consent, no questions asked.

I had learned this trick while working for Rockefeller when Under Secretary of State Welles had often done favors for the "outs" of a dictator. In Welles' eyes, Latin republics were not countries like the United States or France or Britain, but simply geographic expressions ruled by prominent families. Their dictators never lasted forever, and the United States should store up goodwill among the outs against the time they would become the "ins." At Welles' suggestion, the Rockefeller office had a number of "outs" on the payroll, even from Somoza, the dictator of Nicaragua who had been created out of nothing by the U.S. Marines when they had occupied the country. My friend Jorge, I was sure, had been told of my role in the rescue.

While we drove from the airport to his sugar plantation near Palmira, a small town forty-five minutes from the airport, he pointed out to me the features of the

Cauca Valley through which we were driving. There was eighteen feet of topsoil, and, unlike Cuba, sugarcane could be harvested all year round, thus making production more efficient. There were also lush pastures for cattle and a benign climate due to the altitude.

His house, I discovered, was set in a five-acre garden of flowers and vegetables adjacent to the mill, all of which were surrounded by a high link fence within the gate of which was a tower for armed guards. In order to diminish the penitentiary aspect, great care had been taken to give the house a Palm Beach look, with awnings and a swimming pool and a two-room guest cottage where I slept and was served breakfast.

Unfortunately, this luxurious domestic aspect was somewhat diminished by the warning that I was not to wander out of the guesthouse during the night when specially trained and ferocious police dogs were allowed freedom should invaders breach the protective arrangements.

Later that morning Jorge led me on horseback on a tour of his cane fields. It was then that I raised the subject of the drug problem. Colombia, he said, did not grow coca as it does now. The leaves were brought in from Ecuador, Peru, and Bolivia. Colombia, in contrast to these other countries in which it did grow, had the know-how in refining it into cocaine. "We have any number of skillful chemists who can do the job, and since a number of them are refugees from the collapse of the Nazi regime in Europe, and hence, poor and not properly integrated into our small middle class, they need the money and are available to the drug lords," he explained.

"Do you know where these factories are located?" I asked.

"Not all of them. But you are the sort of person who could find out."

"Why do you say that?"

"Because I've never known another American who can operate so well among the elite, and this in an elitist country."

"Come on, Jorge, that's plain silly."

"It's not. You've apparently forgotten. At Cambridge, I once ran into you buying an antique silver candlestick. And who was advising you on what to select? Queen Mary! Later that same day I burst into your room, and who did I find there? The wife of a cabinet minister and her son. You always got around."

"Pure coincidence. Anyway, I'm married now, and I promised Mary Lou I'd never do any more intelligence work."

"Then what are you doing here?"

"Well, I shouldn't be. But there are extenuating circumstances. I once did a cocaine job that was a total and humiliating flop. Meanwhile, several years have gone by, and the drug situation has changed for the worse. I thought I might redeem myself with a little inside information on how the drug traffic is now operating. And from what you've just told me, I gather the thing to do is find the location of the factories via the mestizo employees of the ruling classes and blow them up from the air."

"Look, Paul. Let me make myself clear. If you don't do it, your government will send down some middle-class types who don't have the social and political skills and background to find out anything. We don't mix socially with your embassy staff or your CIA people. I don't know a single one of them, nor does anyone from my family."

With that blast, Jorge rode off to talk with one of his foremen, and I passed the time in conversation with a couple of cane cutters working nearby.

"Do you speak Spanish or some Indian language?" I asked. They both looked more Indian than white to me.

"Spanish, señor. I learned it from my mother."

"Where are you from?"

"From Palmira. I live here."

"But you don't look like the people here."

"No, señor, I was born in the south. I came up here to find work."

"Do you ever go back to your native village?"

"Oh no, señor. That would be dangerous."

"Why?"

"The drug people. They don't like to see strangers. If they saw me talking with any of my brothers and sisters, they would kill them."

"Won't the army protect you?"

He laughed, put his machete on the ground, took off his hat, and wiped the sweat off his brow. "This is Colombia," he answered, "not America."

"And your compadre here, where does he come from?"

"I come from the east, señor, but I live in Palmira," his coworker answered. "Why?"

"For the work. Your friend the *cacique* pays us well, and it's safe."

"Then why are you hiding your bicycles here under the sugarcane?"

"Because they would be stolen if we did not hide them. There are many poor people who would like nice bicycles like ours. We sleep with them too."

"And where you come from in the east, there's much trouble too, just like in your friend's village."

"*Si* señor, much trouble."

"Perhaps someday I may send someone from America to talk with you."

"That would be an honor. Will he be a white man and a friend of the *cacique*?"

"It's possible. I must go now with the *cacique* back to his house for lunch. *Pase bien.*"

It seemed to me that this little conversation with the two cane cutters told it all. They would talk with a white gringo provided he was with the *cacique*.

Otherwise they would clam up or, if they felt threatened, would politely and with due deference give their interlocutor totally false or misleading information. Their subservient position, during the past three centuries, to the white man, and before that to their Inca conquerors and masters, had left a negative impression. As Lord Acton had pointed out, the Incas had statistics, and this had made them, among all the primitive people, the most ferocious dictators on earth. It is a curious commentary on world history that Karl Marx got his ideas on how to communize agricultural production from the Incas.

After a family lunch with Jorge and his wife, Marianna, and his Cuban in—laws who were in exile from Castro's Cuba, I took a siesta and then a swim. Jorge sent word to be ready to leave at five thirty to drive to Cali to play bridge and have supper with friends.

En route Jorge opened up again on the drug problem. It was clear to me that he saw it not only as a public nuisance but also as a potential threat to his own power and influence. "Look, Paul," he said, "we have here in Colombia, as you probably know, two separate groups of terrorists—the Maoists and the Stalinists. Both are short of money with which to buy arms to protect themselves, and I doubt they get much money or support from either the Soviet Union or China. The Maoists are the more ideological and ferocious of the two. At present they are relatively harmless; but they are growing. Both are reputed to be ready to start a wave of kidnappings for ransom as a means of raising money. That, I think, is controllable, but is the reason we live under such guarded conditions as you have seen. They are, as of now, as much a threat to the drug lords as they are to us. But that isn't my point. The danger is that the drug people may make an agreement with them: You leave us alone, and we'll pay you enough to buy all the arms you need. If that happens we're in real trouble, and unfortunately, your State Department and the CIA only see the Communist angle and refuse to face up to an alliance between the two. That's why you've got to do something about it."

At this point, we had arrived in front of the house where we were to play bridge. "Our host's name is Walter Eder, by the way," Jorge explained.

"My God, Jorge! I knew a relation of his in the States. She was married to a man named Jamieson in the Rockefeller office. Her parents had a fit over the marriage. Jamieson, though a Pulitzer Prize winner, was a recovering alcoholic and divorced."

Jorge laughed. "Without realizing it," he commented, "you've just proved my point about circulating among the elite. Besides, don't think I don't know a lot about you since our Cambridge days. Tito Arias, who sought refuge here from one of his aborted revolutions, told me how you got him a passage on a ship from Portugal after the Germans took Paris and how you maneuvered Welles into supporting his birthday ball project over Rockefeller's objection."

"Jorge, that's total exaggeration. Tito did the maneuvering, and his father got him on the ship via Welles."

Walter Eder and his wife and Jorge and I played bridge both before supper and afterward. Around ten o'clock our host's brother who was the minister of hacienda and tesoro suddenly entered the room. When he saw we were playing cards, he insisted we continue.

"Don't let me interrupt," he told his brother, "I'm here in Cali from Bogotá unexpectedly. I'll simply go across the street and spend the night at our mother's house and come and have breakfast with you in the morning. We can talk then."

With that, he vanished. We were the last people who saw him alive with his head on. He was picked up by terrorists while crossing the street. Later his severed head and his body were found in a ditch beside the road down which we drove that night back to Jorge's sugar plantation. A book was subsequently written about this incident. His murder was a mistake. He was supposed to have been treated well and held for ransom. His murderers simply got their orders crossed.

The next morning, under the pergola by the pool, I wrote a letter to John Wiley, then living in retirement in Washington, spelling out what I had learned from Jorge and his cane cutters and outlining his fears for the future. Later, Jorge drove me to the airport. We now had, I noticed, an armed guard beside the driver who had a revolver within easy reach on the floor.

"Why the extra armament?" I asked.

"I didn't tell you because I didn't want to upset you and also because I didn't want you to mention it to Marianna who doesn't know yet," he explained. "But our host's brother, the minister, was found beheaded in a ditch beside the road this morning."

Jorge left me at the airport and returned immediately to Palmira. While waiting for the plane, which was late, I bought some stamps and mailed my letter to Ambassador Wiley. While buying the stamps, someone behind me accidentally brushed against me, and the eyes of the girl who was waiting on me suddenly widened, not at me, but at the person behind me. Then, recovering her composure, she took the letter and offered to affix the stamps and mail it for me. Finished, I turned around. But by this time, no one was there.

Back in Panama, Mary Lou and Theresa gave me a great welcome. The twenty-four hour delay in my return was overlooked. Later, I explained to Mary Lou the real purpose of my stopover in Cali. Unfortunately, by this time, Eder's murder was in the Panamanian newspapers.

"Isn't he the man you played bridge with?" she asked.

"No, it was his brother. The one who was killed came to the house, but when he saw we were playing cards, he went across the street to sleep at his mother's house. Apparently he didn't make it."

At that, Mary Lou went into what I can only describe as a hysterical rage, her point being that I had promised to give up all intelligence work and had broken my promise despite the danger. She threatened to leave me if I ever did it again. "How do I know it wasn't you they were after and not the man whose head they cut off?" she demanded.

Two weeks later, I made a quick trip to Washington to see about our house. The tenant, who was a nephew of President Trujillo, the dictator of the Dominican Republic, was paying the exorbitant rent I charged him on the dot even though he and his family had moved to Spain three months after signing the lease. Someone from the Dominican Embassy came to the house twice every twenty-four hours. At night, he turned on the lights and turned down the beds and then returned in the morning to turn them off and make up the beds in case they should return during the night. No one was cutting the grass or tending the garden.

I called the embassy to see if something could be done. It was immediately taken cared of and later I went to see Ambassador Wiley. He had never received my letter. When I started to explain its contents, he asked me to wait until lunch when Under Secretary of State Henderson would join us. I then relayed the contents of my letter, and then I returned to Panama and Mary Lou. In this way, convoluted terrorism had triumphed over intelligence. I never regretted it. I had been at it over fifteen years at the working level. That was enough. There were, however, repercussions, even in my totally civilian existence.

In October 1956, along with General Gavin of the army and Dr. Joseph Kaplan, chairman of the American chapter of the International Geophysical Year, I was asked to fly up to Fort Churchill on Hudson Bay to represent the National Academy of Science at the dedication of a rocket-launching facility. We stopped at Ottawa to attend an elaborate luncheon with Canadian officials at the Chateau Laurier and then flew on to Fort Churchill, arriving there in time for an official dedicatory dinner.

This luncheon had an unforeseen effect on my new non-intelligence life, which confirmed the wisdom of giving up any work as a secret agent. Sitting next to me at the lunch was a Canadian scientist and geologist who had a profound knowledge of the Canadian North. He mentioned to me that at several places along the North Slope he had personally seen petroleum oozing out of the ground. Soon thereafter, my financial people in New York recommended that I buy some stock in a small Calgary oil company that was negotiating for a concession to explore for oil on the North Slope. Because of my coincidental lunch encounter with the Canadian scientist, instead of buying a little stock in this unheard-of company, I bought a lot. The stock went, because of the North Slope and later because of the North Sea oil discovery from $4 to the equivalent, after many splits, of $240 a share. I sold it in dribbles on the way up and made enough money after taxes to buy a commercial building in Georgetown where my daughter, Theresa, who had become a ballet dancer, now runs her highly successful ballet school.

But more significant than this was my visit to the launching site. I retained a mental picture of what the construction and layout of such a facility looked like. A few years later, in 1961, while flying back to Washington from Panama on a Braniff plane, there was an incident. It was a crystal clear day, and we were flying at a relatively low altitude. I was with an associate. Some time after takeoff, I went to the washroom and there I took off my prized submarine Omega wristwatch, which dated from my *Nereus* days, in order to wash my hands. Suddenly there was a pounding on the door, followed by, "Paul, come out at once. You gotta see this!"

I dashed out, leaving my watch on the sink, and looked down out of the plane's window. I saw clearly what was unmistakably a construction going on for a rocket-launching site in the Cuban Cordillera, not dissimilar to the final product I had seen at Fort Churchill in the far Canadian North on Hudson Bay. Later, I went back to the washroom and found that my prized Omega watch was gone! At the time, this seemed totally symbolic and the final termination of an intelligence career that had lasted over fifteen years. Fortunately, the original agony of the loss of the watch soon subsided. There was to be a significant substitution. The construction I had seen was the beginning of the Cuban missile crisis that erupted during Kennedy's presidency in October 1962.

In 1968 there was published in Communist East Germany by a Dr. Julius Mader a little book entitled *Who's Who in CIA*. It was described as a biographical reference work on the intelligence officers of the civil and military branches of the USA in 120 countries. "... the time appeared to have come," the author wrote, "to demask a first representative selection of leading officials and officers, collaborators and agents of the U.S. intelligence services who are operating on five different continents." I was listed as an operator in Washington.

As if this was not enough, there appeared a book published in Argentina in 1970 and republished in 1971 entitled *La Red y La Tijera* (The Net and Scissors) by Jorge Flores McGregor. I was also listed in this one as someone who slithered back and forth between private enterprise and the government.

My reaction to the publication of these two books was not like the agony of losing the watch. There was no chagrin. On the contrary, it was more like, "Hey, Buster, what do you think of this? So you lost the last physical reminder that you were once a reasonably successful intelligence man. Also, you've got no files, no letters, and no documents to prove your former occupation. Forget it! Now you've got something even better. Two Communist publications that describe you as an evil, capitalist, imperialist American secret agent!"

This was my initial reaction, but it was followed by something different: a sort of Wagnerian leitmotif interwoven into the resounding crash of accomplishment.

I couldn't help but think of the various people who had got in my way and who had suffered as a result. First of all, there had been the three Axis agents. One should not be deluded into supposing that all enemy agents are able. Our own intelligence people, as well as fiction writers on the subject, like to portray them in this light as a means of inflating their own accomplishments or creating tension in their novels. But this is not necessarily so. Take Matheson as an example. He was apparently a devotee of Kipling and thus subscribed to the view that the "East is East, the West is West, and never the twain shall meet." Well, it did meet in so far as his employment record in Japan was concerned, and that started him on the downward slope to entrapment.

The Kraut was a total wimp. Enough said. As for Lanas, he seemed to me to be a very able young man, but since I was never told how the FBI got wise on him, I can have no real opinion.

On the other side of the coin, the Leftists who bothered me had, like me, all been young. Several were able. Most, but not all, had not been evil, merely misguided. They had, like I was, been drawn from the educated middle class. There were two exceptions: the Argentine girl who had sought to get me dismissed from the Rockefeller office and the sailor who had consorted with a Japanese navy Communist officer. The girl was of upper-class Argentine origins but apparently had a middle-class lover who dominated her. The sailor's shot may well have been an accident just as I said it was at the time.

What saddened me about all this was that in almost all cases their professional careers had been wrecked. One had been murdered in prison; some others had defected and disappeared. Looking at all the cases dispassionately, I couldn't help but feel that to some extent they had been victimized by the times in which we lived. Furthermore, they did not have my advantages: a well-to-do family whose only economy during the Great Depression of the thirties was the decision on my mother's part not to buy any more new hats, a father who was an implacable foe of both the Nazis and the Communists, a British academic mentor of unassailable reputation steeped in European realpolitik, policies based on power rather than ideals, plus ancestors who had served my country in uniform in every war from the Civil War to my childhood.

In contrast, most of those in my way endured poverty and suffering in the Great Depression and thus became easily subverted by Communist propaganda that told of no unemployment and prosperity in the Soviet Union, which in turn had succeeded a corrupt and utterly outmoded Tsarist regime. Furthermore, a number of their college professors shared similar circumstances and allowed their international views to be guided by sentiment rather than what was best for the country. In truth, they had almost all been innocents abroad and dupes of the times at home. I could deplore them but could not hate them. Also, it should not be forgotten that from Pearl Harbor to the start of the Cold War, the Soviet

Union was our ally, and sentiment was deliberately cultivated for war purposes that Stalin was "good old Uncle Joe" and not a syphilitic monster who shot right and left people whom he imagined might oppose him.

The final and most tragic of all was the suicide of Frank Wisner subsequent to my resignation. In an odd sort of way, I couldn't help but equate his end with the murder of William Remington after his imprisonment for perjury. To me, both had been destroyed by intelligence—Remington, by the Soviet intelligence apparatus, which he probably didn't understand, and Wisner, a totally devoted cold warrior, because he placed too much faith in British Intelligence as a useful foil to Soviet expansionism.

In Wisner's case, he also did not have the advantages of my early working days in the Rockefeller office where Soviet penetration of British Intelligence had been somewhat of an inside joke among those intelligence contacts with whom I worked. Instead, his wartime experience had been limited to the Office of Strategic Services (OSS), which had been, for all practical purposes, a wartime subsidiary of British Intelligence. The same was true of his chief of security. It was thus inconceivable to Wisner that a young subordinate such as me, whose pre- and post-Pearl Harbor work was unknown to him, could conceivably be on the right track. He dismissed my interference as arrogance. This in itself was not a tragedy. These things happen in a bureaucracy. What was tragic was the dragon's tooth I might have sowed in his mind—the precognition that Kim Philby was conceivably a traitor. For it may have been this which drove an otherwise able and fine man to his tragic end. Intelligence has had many victims, and by no means have all been traitors. Many have been but innocent victims of the intelligence apparatus they devoted their lives to serve, but in Wisner's case, there can be no question that seeping doubt did much to destroy him.

POSTSCRIPT

The United States is now engaged in a war on terrorism. In my lifetime, the U.S, has been at war with Germany, Japan, and Italy, and then separately, with North Korea, Vietnam, and Iraq. It has also fought a protracted Cold War with the Soviet Union. This is a new state of affairs for our country. In my father's lifetime, the United States was engaged in only two wars, and in my grandfather's lifetime, in only one. The role of intelligence in these wars has increased in direct proportion to the increase in the number of wars in which we have found ourselves engaged.

The present struggle has certain very unusual characteristics. Having suffered terrorist attacks that resulted in unparalleled loss of life, we feel compelled to engage in a war against a small organization without either a proper army or a territory of its own but which is headquartered in a host country. Something like this has never happened before, unless we recall the raids by Pancho Villa who shot Americans riding on Mexican trains and who in 1916 killed sixteen people during a raid on the U.S. territory. In retaliation, the U.S. invaded Mexico but failed to capture Villa himself.

Is there profit to be gained from studying my experiences as an intelligence agent in relation to the present struggle? I believe the answer is a resounding yes!

As a start, recall my pre- and post-Pearl Harbor work while employed by the coordinator of inter-American affairs. My ability to assist in the entrapment of three foreign agents affords a perfect example of the compelling need for international cooperation in the intelligence field. Without cooperation between Britain and the United States at that time, via the BSC and the FBI, success would have eluded me.

Osama Bin Laden may have started the present war, but now we are in it; it is as an international team that the war must be fought. When venom is hurled

---

215

against a hostile leader like Bin Laden, one must always remember that this is somewhat of a propaganda device to simplify understanding and encourage greater effort. In such a struggle as we are now in, where there will be no "front" and no naval battles but merely al Qaeda cells and cells of successor or related organizations scattered about in any number of host countries and requiring elimination, international intelligence cooperation will be of even greater importance at present than in the past.

There is also an important corollary to this. In its need for assistance from other nations, the United States, as the world's most preeminent power, must be careful not to offend the nationalist sensibilities of possible foreign sources of information. Nationalism, quite apart from the global nature of today's economies, remains the most vital characteristic of the world's political structure. Thus, if the United States allows its leaders to travel to foreign countries and tell them in blunt terms, designed to please the electorates back home, how to conduct their affairs, it will only diminish the effectiveness of international cooperation in intelligence. Take China, Georgia, Uzbekistan, or Tajikistan as examples. All these countries have large Muslim populations. All are proud—China because it is an ancient civilization that essentially regards all foreigners as barbarians and the others because of their recently won independence from Russia.

Meanwhile, intelligence has a habit of bubbling up to the top from the lower echelons of its respective bureaucracies, just as my information and analysis while working for Rockefeller, the navy, the CIA, and as an individual operator, was passed on up the line to my superiors. If that worker's sensibilities are offended by an overbearing attitude toward his country or himself, it is very easy for him to withhold his information and the conclusions he has gained.

If, before Pearl Harbor, Britain or the FBI had been offensive in its conduct toward my country or me, it would have been easy to withhold my suspicions about Matheson, the Japanese agent. No one would have known. Also, recall the incidents that happened while I was working for the CIA when my division chief not only withheld a commendation, but also failed to forward to the director a warning of possible danger about a forthcoming international conference. This dereliction was exposed, and the offending division chief was subsequently bypassed by President Truman himself. But this can hardly be expected to be repeated. Had my office not been located parallel to the president's early morning walk, and had he not had an inherent distrust of the intelligence bureaucracy, I doubt it would have happened, and it is most certainly not likely to be repeated.

Finally, and most importantly, rivalry and hostility among intelligence organizations must not be tolerated. This is the tornado that can twist and destroy the ability of intelligence to do its job. Recall two incidents during my own career as shining examples of the results of such rivalry. No sooner was the COI, the predecessor of the Office of Strategic Services (OSS), set up than a vicious rivalry erupted. Fortunately, in my own case I was warned not only to be aware of it but also to be aware of Communist efforts to exploit it and encourage it for their own ends. Shortly thereafter, I was asked to do a counterintelligence job that would most likely have been disastrous. Later, while working for the CIA, I was able to preserve the utility of a ship for an Albanian operation by effecting its immediate transfer to a flag of convenience. But when I suggested an examination of the factors that had, prior to my intervention, caused the delay of this transfer, this suggestion was clearly waived aside because it would involve cooperation with the hated FBI. One cannot now be sure, but if this delay had been properly examined, it might have opened a trail leading to Philby, the notorious British traitor and Communist agent.

A president and his staff must move immediately to nip in the bud any such rivalry, just as President Roosevelt did when Sumner Welles went to him to complain that Rockefeller was not clearing his Latin American operational projects with the State Department. Unfortunately, neither FDR nor his successors did this with the OSS and later, with the CIA vis-à-vis the FBI.

Translating the foregoing into al Qaeda terms, what can Bin Laden or his successor organizations be expected to do? First of all, they will have plenty of money. Saudi Arabia and the Arab Emirates are awash in petrodollars, and even if they are friendly toward the United States, they will not be unwilling to give al Qaeda money to keep the terrorist cells away from their own countries, just as the drug lords in Colombia pay handsomely to Colombia's brand of terrorists to protect them from government troops. Using petrodollars, the al Qaeda and its allies can be expected, if they have not done it already, to secretly buy American publications, just as the Japanese did, to use as propaganda weapons.

Next, they can be expected to exploit to the full any fissures or cracks that may develop among rival U.S. intelligence organizations while at the same time doing their best to undermine the cooperation among friendly foreign intelligence organizations. Having already lost a host country in the form of Taliban-ruled Afghanistan, they can be expected to settle elsewhere. From new focal points of power they will resume their war of terror, all the while lubricating it with petrodollars secured, if necessary, by outright and secret blackmail.

Contemporaneously, the United States will make mistakes in its military efforts. In wartime, people are always killed by accidental or misdirected friendly fire. In our struggle against al Qaeda and what is presumed will be its successor organizations, some of these mistakes will be the result of deliberate misleading intelligence innocently fed to us by friendly Muslim intelligence organizations. The moment these mistakes occur, the enemy can be expected to exploit them for propaganda purposes designed to diminish our resolve against our perceived enemy. These efforts will afford the United States valuable clues as to al Qaeda penetration, and they must be carefully observed and examined, especially if, as

President Bush has predicted, our war on terrorism will be a long one. Also, one must keep in mind that the enemy, though not perhaps in great numbers, is all around us, and they will not necessarily be of Muslim descent. There are people in the United States today who hate our government and its policies and thus feel alienated. A foreign war can give birth to strange bedfellows. One must be, as we already are, on the watch for them.

That this will be an immensely difficult and complex struggle is already apparent. It will not be, as Bismarck described our Civil War, a case of two armed mobs chasing each other about the countryside from which nothing is to be learned. On the contrary, even while fighting it, we shall have a lot to learn, from both our friends and our enemies. Some of it will be old and hence forgotten, and some of it will be new, if only because of the novel characteristics of the present struggle. This is neither an armed struggle against the Axis nor is it the Cold War nor is it the war against North Korea or North Vietnam. It is new and different from anything seen or known before.

Printed in the United States
71086LV00002BD/1